Pro PowerShell for Microsoft Azure

Sherif Talaat

with contributions from Wagdy Ishac

Apress®

Pro PowerShell for Microsoft Azure

ISBN-13 (pbk): 978-1-4842-0666-9

ISBN-13 (electronic): 978-1-4842-0665-2

Managing Director: Welmoed Spahr
Lead Editor: Gwenan Spearing
Technical Reviewers: David Cobb, Raymond Elias, Ahmed Sabbour
Editorial Board: Steve Anglin, Mark Beckner, Gary Cornell, Louise Corrigan, Jim DeWolf, Jonathan Gennick, Robert Hutchinson, Michelle Lowman, James Markham, Susan McDermott, Matthew Moodie, Jeff Olson, Jeffrey Pepper, Douglas Pundick, Ben Renow-Clarke, Gwenan Spearing, Matt Wade, Steve Weiss
Coordinating Editor: Melissa Maldonado
Copy Editor: Kimberly Burton
Compositor: SPi Global
Indexer: SPi Global
Artist: SPi Global
Cover Designer: Friedhelm Steinen-Broo

Distributed to the book trade worldwide by Springer Science+Business Media New York, 233 Spring Street, 6th Floor, New York, NY 10013. Phone 1-800-SPRINGER, fax (201) 348-4505, e-mail `orders-ny@springer-sbm.com`, or visit `www.springer.com`. Apress Media, LLC is a California LLC is a California LLC and the sole member (owner) is Springer Science + Business Media Finance Inc (SSBM Finance Inc). SSBM Finance Inc is a Delaware corporation.

For information on translations, please e-mail `rights@apress.com`, or visit `www.apress.com`.

Apress and friends of ED books may be purchased in bulk for academic, corporate, or promotional use. eBook versions and licenses are also available for most titles. For more information, reference our Special Bulk Sales–eBook Licensing web page at `www.apress.com/bulk-sales`.

Any source code or other supplementary material referenced by the author in this text is available to readers at `www.apress.com`. For detailed information about how to locate your book's source code, go to `www.apress.com/source-code/`.

To my wife, Israa, for all her love and support

Contents at a Glance

Contents

About the Author

Sherif Talaat is an IT professional with more than 10 years of experience in the IT industry. He has worked on Microsoft's core infrastructure platforms and solutions, focusing on IT process automation and scripting techniques. In 2013, Talaat joined a team of technology specialists and solutions architects responsible for cloud computing and enterprise mobility.

Sherif is a well-known community guru and one of the early adopters of Windows PowerShell in his region, the Middle East, and Africa. He was awarded Microsoft Most Valuable Professional (MVP), PowerShell seven consecutive times since 2009. He speaks about Windows PowerShell at technical events and user group gatherings. He is the founder of the Egypt PowerShell User Group (`http://egpsug.org`) and the author of the first and only Arabic PowerShell blog (`http://arabianpowershell.wordpress.com`). You may catch him at `sheriftalaat.com` and follow him on `Twitter@SherifTalaat`.

About the Author

[illegible]

About the Technical Reviewers

David Cobb is a system architect for CheckAlt Payment Solutions, providers of automated and electronic check transaction processing since 2005. David is a Microsoft Certified Trainer, training people on SQL Server since 2002. He is also the principal consultant for Cobb Information Technologies, Inc., founded in 1996, providing technology consulting with a focus on SQL Server. David's passion for new technologies includes PowerShell, Azure/cloud, and Docker.

David and his wife, Eivina, are raising two wonderful boys in Boca Raton, Florida.

Thomas LaRock is a head geek at SolarWinds and a Microsoft Certified Master, SQL Server MVP, VMware vExpert, and a Microsoft Certified Trainer. He has over 15 years' experience in the IT industry in roles that include programmer, developer, analyst, and database administrator.

LaRock has worked in numerous IT roles, with much of his career focused on database administration, leading to his role as technical evangelist for Confio. While at Confio, his research and experience helped to create the initial versions of the software now known as the SolarWinds Database Performance Analyzer.

LaRock joined the SolarWinds family through the acquisition of Confio in 2013. His many Microsoft accreditations include SQL Server MVP, MCSM, MCM, MCT, MCITP, MCTS, MCDBA, and MCP—whew!

LaRock is also president of the Professional Association for SQL Server (PASS) and is an avid blogger, author, and technical reviewer for numerous books about SQL Server management. He now focuses his time by working with customers to resolve problems and answer questions regarding database performance tuning and virtualization for SQL Server, Oracle, Sybase, and DB2, making it his mission to give IT and data professionals longer weekends.

Ahmed Sabbour started at Microsoft three years ago as an Azure Technical Evangelist. He then moved on to drive the Platform as a Service scenarios as a technical solution professional. He is now a Technical Black Belt for Enabling Application Innovation on Microsoft Azure.

Prior to Microsoft, Ahmed worked at Nokia as a technical manager, enabling partners across India, the Middle East, and Africa in building solutions for the Nokia ecosystem. Ahmed holds a master's of computer science and engineering degree from the German University in Cairo.

Acknowledgments

I still cannot believe that I finished the entire book. It has been a very long journey since I started this writing project, but I have to admit that I have enjoyed every single moment working on it. Although this is not my first time writing a book, this time was absolutely different, especially when writing about a trend like cloud computing and a booming technology like Microsoft Azure. I would never have done it without all the help and support I received from the people around me.

First, I really want to thank my family for everything they have done to me. I thank my mom for her love and prayers. To my wife, Israa, and my dear son, Yahia—thanks for the support and patience during the long days and nights I have spent writing this book.

To Gwenan Spearing, lead editor, thank you for giving me the privilege to work with Apress. It has been a dream that finally came true. Thanks for being supportive, flexible about the frequent changes, open to new ideas, and patient about those deadlines I missed.

To Melissa Maldonado, coordinating editor—thanks for taking care of the chapters, following-up with everyone, and making sure that everything was on the right track.

To Kimberly Burton, copy editor—I really cannot find the right words to describe how I am so grateful for what you have done to this book. I still remember the moment I read the first copyedited chapter and I was surprised to see how my unreadable and boring technical writings became a smooth, flowing, and interesting thing that everyone can enjoy reading it. Thanks for the amazing efforts.

To the technical reviewers, David Cobb, Ahmed Sabbour, and Raymond Elias—your honest feedback and invaluable comments helped a lot in getting the book in great shape.

A special thanks to my dear friend and brother, Wagdy Ishac, for his contribution to this book. Wagdy's experience in Big Data and SQL Server has increased the quality of the content of this book.

Last but not least, a very sincere thanks to the technology role model, to the one who made the life of thousands of IT Pros and developers much easier and more productive, thank you Jeffrey Snover. It wouldn't be possible to take such a step to write a book and stand here today, proud of what I have done if PowerShell wasn't there. Thanks for inventing Windows PowerShell, thanks for positively impacting our technical skills, and thanks for being a god father to the PowerShell MVPs and community.

Introduction

An Overview of this Book

Chapter 1: Azure Architecture Overview

This chapter introduces the Microsoft Azure architecture and the services covered in the upcoming chapters. This chapter is not meant to teach Microsoft Azure for beginners, but to set the base for readers and refresh their memories before they start.

Chapter 2: Getting Started with Azure PowerShell

Microsoft Azure has its own PowerShell module known as Azure PowerShell. This chapter teaches you how to download and install the Azure PowerShell module, and how to configure it and make it ready to connect to your Microsoft Azure subscription.

Chapter 3: Managing and Maintaining Azure Storage

Storage is a constant in any computing or IT formula. Desktops, servers, routers, switches, and smartphones will never work without storage—and this applies to cloud computing as well. Storage is a component that all of these services rely on before digging into the different Azure services and workloads. In this chapter, you get ready for and become aware of Azure storage. You learn about the Azure storage account and the different types and services. Also, you learn how to configure it using PowerShell.

Chapter 4: Virtual Machines Deployment and Management

Let's learn about the deployment and management of the virtual machines portion of Azure Infrastructure as a Service (IaaS). This chapter covers the different operations that can be performed on virtual machines and its different components, including disks, operating systems, security, endpoints, high availability, imaging, and so forth.

Chapter 5: Virtual Networking Configuration

This chapter continues the discussion of Azure IaaS components with Azure Virtual Networks (VN). It covers basic VN operations, such as network deployment and creation, as well as advanced operations like configuring external gateways, site-to-site VPNs, Traffic Manager, Azure DNS, and access control lists (ACLs).

Chapter 6: Deploying Azure Web Apps

As part of Azure's PaaS offerings, Azure Web Apps provides a platform for hosting web sites and web apps, whether they are written using Microsoft technologies such as .NET, or other technologies, such as PHP and Python. Managing a single web app sounds fine, but managing multiple web apps—especially if you are a service provider—could be a nightmare. Therefore, the aim of this chapter is to teach you how to use PowerShell to create, configure, manage, and monitor Azure-hosted web apps.

Chapter 7: Azure SQL Database

Azure SQL Database is another Azure Platform as a Service (PaaS) offering; it is simply the cloud-hosted version of Microsoft SQL Server. This chapter demonstrates how to use PowerShell to manage Azure SQL databases and servers to create, configure, access, and query Azure SQL databases. It also covers backup and recovery, along with the georeplication of the databases.

Chapter 8: Azure Automation

One of the cool things about Azure is having a PowerShell module; but the coolest thing is to have one of the services, Azure Automation, which is built on and relies on the Windows PowerShell and Windows PowerShell Workflows engine. This chapter helps you utilize your PowerShell skills to unleash the maximum out of Azure Automation in order to build a complex yet advanced automation platform for your Azure services and workloads.

Chapter 9: Azure RemoteApp

In this chapter, you learn about Azure RemoteApp services and its PowerShell cmdlets via a full end-to-end RemoteApp scenario. The examples show how to build an Azure RemoteApp custom template with applications and how to use the RemoteApp template image to create a RemoteApp collection and publish it. Moreover, it shows how to monitor RemoteApp usage, manage the connected user sessions, and take actions, such as disconnecting a session, logging off a session, and sending a message to the active sessions.

Chapter 10: Azure Identity and Access

"With great power comes great responsibility" is a well-known saying. And with the cloud's power comes a great security risk, if you don't do things right. Azure Active Directory (AAD) is one of the components that helps you set the right permissions to the right people on the cloud, just like Windows Server Active Directory for the on-premises infrastructure. In this chapter, you learn about the PowerShell module for Azure Active Directory, including where to download it and how to install and configure it.

Chapter 11: Azure Rights Management Services

Azure Rights Management Services is an information and content protection service that helps you ensure that data is always protected and only accessed by the right people. Usually, you have different departments, groups, and levels of employees within the same organization. This means that you have to create different RMS policies to fit the business requirements of each of these groups. This chapter demonstrates how to use the Azure RMS PowerShell module to easily manage the Azure RMS settings, as well as Azure RMS policies and protected content.

Chapter 12: Building and Managing Azure HDInsight Clusters

There is no doubt that cloud computing is a trend, and Big Data is today's technology fashion. So, imagine how powerful it would be to have the capabilities of Big Data powered by cloud computing and managed by PowerShell. This is what you read about in this chapter, and in which you learn about using PowerShell to build and manage Azure HDInsight clusters, how to manipulate and use an HDInsight cluster, as well as running Pig or Hive scripts, and automating processes for efficient resource usage.

Who Should Read this Book?

Pro PowerShell for Microsoft Azure is written for Windows professionals who are familiar with PowerShell and want to learn to build, operate, and administer their Windows workloads in the Microsoft Azure cloud. The book is packed with practical examples and scripts, with easy-to-follow explanations for a wide range of day-to-day needs and essential administration tasks.

This book assumes you have experience with Microsoft PowerShell. It will not teach you how to write PowerShell scripts. There are numerous excellent books on the market already. As an example, Apress offers a book titled *Pro Windows PowerShell* by HristoDeshev.

On the other hand, it would be great to have a hands-on experience with Microsoft Azure; this would help you progress faster. However, in some cases, we start with the basics and build on that foundation. In other cases, especially advanced topics such as virtual networking and HDInsight, the chapter entirely counts on your experience with these subjects.

If this is your first time dealing with Azure PowerShell, then I highly recommend that you follow the chapter's sequence and structure. It is very important to do this because the chapters rely on each other. However, if you have experience with Azure PowerShell and you want to jump to a specific chapter or topic in the book, then I recommend that you at least read Chapter 2 to refresh your memory and prepare your environment for other chapters.

What Do You Need for this Book?

To get the maximum benefit out of this book and to reproduce the examples, you should have the following:

- Internet connectivity.
- A Microsoft Azure subscription. You can register for a free trial or get it as a benefit of an MSDN subscription (if you have any).
- Azure PowerShell version 9.8.1.

CHAPTER 1

Azure Architecture Overview

The computer industry is the only industry that is more fashion-driven than women's fashion.

—Larry Ellison (Chairman, Oracle Corporation)

The cloud is a popular and trending term that everyone is using nowadays. Of course, the cloud that I mean has nothing to do with the weather, but with technology—cloud computing.

Today, almost everyone is using the cloud to describe a service delivered to or consumed by end users and information workers. The cloud is everywhere and it is being consumed by almost everyone on the planet—from the oldest computer geeks to the youngest tablet and game console users.

People may not even know that they are using a cloud service, but everyone who uses the Internet is using the cloud. If you have an e-mail account, then you are using the cloud. If your kids are playing video games online with their friends, then they are using the cloud. If your spouse is using iCloud, OneDrive, or any similar service to store pictures, videos, and other files, that's through the cloud too. Despite these examples, ironically, there are people still resisting the idea of using the cloud, although they are using it on a daily basis.

The cloud, in fact, is one of the fastest growing technologies in the history of the computer industry. Every day you will find a new vendor delivering a different type of cloud service; and every time you log in to your cloud service portal, you will find a brand-new feature. Therefore, to cope with the massive explosion of features and always be in control (I'll quote tire manufacturer Pirelli's slogan: "Power is nothing without control"), we have to ensure that we are using the right tools in our arsenal to help us achieve this goal.

This book spotlights PowerShell as one of the most powerful tools that you must have in your toolbox. PowerShell is not just a scripting language, but also an automation engine that makes it easy to do a complex task in less time and with minimal effort. Moreover, PowerShell plays a major role as a platform in some of Microsoft Azure's features. For example, the Azure automation engine is built on top of PowerShell's workflow feature. Don't worry—I will cover everything in more detail in the upcoming chapters.

In this chapter, and in the entire book, you will learn about the PowerShell module for Microsoft Azure and how to get it ready. Also, you will learn how to use the PowerShell modules and cmdlets to deploy, configure, manage, and automate Azure services.

What Is Microsoft Azure?

Microsoft Azure (formerly Windows Azure) is Microsoft's cloud platform—you could say Microsoft's implementation for cloud computing—that provides both Infrastructure as a Service (IaaS) and Platform as a Service (PaaS). Azure is the platform to build, deploy, deliver, and manage robust, secure, and scalable applications and services, not only using Microsoft's technologies, but other vendors' tools, operating systems, and programming languages as well.

Because it is a hybrid platform, Azure allows you to tightly integrate your on-premises services with cloud-hosted solutions as if they are both in the same datacenter. Also, it is a scalable and economical platform that easily and quickly scales up or down your services and resources when it is needed—and without paying a lot of money. You only pay for what you use and consume.

■ **Note** Azure is the only major cloud platform ranked by Gartner as an industry leader for both IaaS and PaaS.

Azure Regions

The Azure platform operates through a global network of Microsoft-managed datacenters in 17 regions (at the moment I am writing these words) around the world, with more datacenters in more regions to come soon. Microsoft has more than 1 million servers hosted in 100-plus datacenters within its cloud infrastructure portfolio. This massive infrastructure delivers 200-plus cloud services to more than 1 billion customers in 90 countries.

■ **Note** For more statistics about Microsoft's datacenters, refer to `http://download.microsoft.com/download/8/2/9/8297F7C7-AE81-4E99-B1DB-D65A01F7A8EF/Microsoft_Cloud_Infrastructure_Datacenter_and_Network_Fact_Sheet.pdf`

The global presence of Azure means a high availability of services (a 99.95% service level agreement (SLA)). It also allows you to build your disaster recovery (DR) site—geolocation-redundant replicas of your applications and services—with ease, low effort and resources, and in a cost-effective manner. Moreover, it will help you deliver world-class service performances with minimal latency by hosting at a location closest to your users' base.

Figure 1-1 shows a regional map of Azure datacenters. Azure's services availability varies from one region to another, so make sure to check the Microsoft Azure web site (`http://azure.microsoft.com/en-us/regions/#services`) for the most updated services availability list.

Figure 1-1. *Microsoft Azure regional locations*

Table 1-1 lists the Azure regions and locations, so that you can easily identify the closest one to you and your users.

Table 1-1. *Azure Regions and Locations*

Region	Location
US Central	Iowa
US East	Virginia
US East 2	Virginia
US Gov Iowa	Iowa
US Gov Virginia	Virginia
US North Central	Illinois
US South Central	Texas
US West	California
Europe North	Ireland
Europe West	Netherlands
Asia Pacific East	Hong Kong
Asia Pacific Southeast	Singapore
Japan East	Saitama Prefecture
Japan West	Osaka Prefecture
Brazil South	Sao Paulo State
Australia East	New South Wales
Australia Southeast	Victoria

In Table 1-1 you will notice that there are two regions labeled US Gov; these regions are part of Azure Government. Azure Government is the cloud platform designed and built to address the security and compliance needs of the United States government and its solution providers. Also, it is physically isolated from other non-US government datacenters and operated by screened personnel.

■ **Note** The Australia Regions are available only to customers with billing addresses in Australia and New Zealand.

Azure Content Delivery Network (CDN)

In addition to the global network of Microsoft datacenters, Azure has another global network of content delivery network (CDN) nodes. Basically, CDNs are a nodes—you can call them datacenters or servers—that are distributed globally to cache static content (such as images, videos, audios, etc.) to the closest geographical physical location of your end users.

Does it make any difference?! Yes, of course. A CDN is another way to deliver a better performance to your end users. I am pretty sure that you are now comparing CDNs to Azure regions and that you are wondering why you should use a CDN if you already have a service distributed geographically across different regions. I know, it's a little bit confusing, but I'll tell you the trick. Let's use Microsoft's web site as a real-life example. Microsoft has a dynamic web site that has a lot of files that users can download, including Windows, Office, and other products. There is no doubt that a technology giant like Microsoft has its web site hosted on different locations—and, of course, no need to say it is hosted on Azure.

With Windows 10 now available for download, can you imagine how many people have tried to access the Microsoft web site to download Windows 10? Yes, millions. You are totally right. By distributing the web site across different datacenters, users in Europe are able to download the file from datacenter locations in Ireland and the Netherlands—but wouldn't it be faster for users in France to download it from a server in Paris, and for users in Spain to download it from a server in Madrid? Of course this would be faster and more reliable, which is the beauty of a CDN. CDNs are not a replacement for regions but something to compliment them.

Table 1-2 lists the Azure Content Delivery Network nodes and their locations so that you can easily decide where to enable a CDN endpoint for your cloud storage/service according to the location of the majority of end users.

Table 1-2. *Azure CDN Node Locations*

Node Region	Location
US East	Atlanta, Miami, New York, Washington DC, Philadelphia
US West	Los Angeles, San Jose, Seattle
US North Central	Chicago
US South Central	Dallas
Europe North	Copenhagen, Helsinki, Stockholm, Vienna, Warsaw
Europe West	Amsterdam, Frankfurt, Milan, London, Madrid, Paris
Asia Pacific East	Batam, Hong Kong, Jakarta, Kaohsiung, Singapore, Seoul
Asia Pacific Southeast	Melbourne, Sydney
Japan East	Tokyo
Japan West	Osaka

■ **Note** You can keep track of Azure CDN point of presence (pop) locations at `https://azure.microsoft.com/en-us/documentation/articles/cdn-pop-locations/`

Azure Services: Back to Basics

Microsoft Azure has over 60 services—and every day a new service is being added. Every time you visit the Azure portal you will find something new. These services include infrastructure services (such as virtual machines, web sites, and mobile services), data services (such as SQL Database, HDInsight, and backup recovery), application services (such as media services, notification hubs, Active Directory, and Visual Studio Online), and network services (such as Virtual Network, ExpressRoute, and Traffic Manager). Figure 1-2 shows a sample diagram of Azure's services.

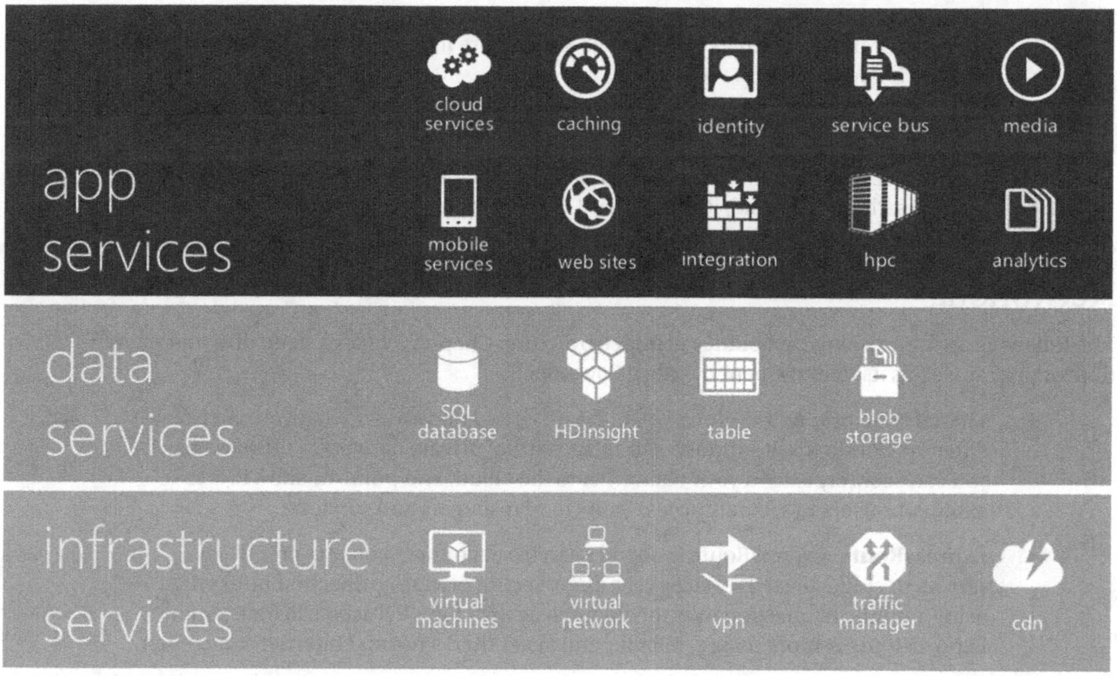

***Figure 1-2.** Microsoft Azure services architecture*

In the next section I provide a nutshell overview of the Azure services covered in this book. To be more specific, you will look at the features that can be managed by Azure PowerShell.

■ **Note** Keep track of the latest Azure services at `http://azure.microsoft.com/en-us/services/`.

Compute

The following are Azure services for hosting different workloads that require computing power (CPU and memory) in the back end to operate:

- **Virtual Machines**: Azure offers on-demand virtual machine (VM) provisioning via a group of predefined VM images and different hardware specifications (CPU and memory). The VM images gallery contains Microsoft images such as Windows, SharePoint, and SQL Server, as well as non-Microsoft images such as Linux and Oracle. You can also build your own virtual machine image. (This is discussed more in Chapter 4.)
- **Mobile Services**: Mobile services allow you to build a scalable and secure back end (storage, push notifications, and user authentications) for your mobile applications. Mobile services come with SDK that supports Windows Phone, iOS, and Android.
- **Web Apps**: Azure web apps is a service that allows you to host and deploy dynamic, flexible, and scalable web sites on Azure without the hassle of managing the infrastructure underneath. (This is covered in more detail in Chapter 6.)

- **Cloud Services**: Azure allows you to build and deploy multitier web applications that have one or more web roles. As with web sites, Azure maintains the infrastructure and service scalability on your behalf.
- **RemoteApp**: Azure RemoteApp enables you to publish a Windows Server application and deliver it virtually and seamlessly to end users, without installing it physically on their devices but with the same local experience. These devices include Windows, Windows Phone, Android, iOS, and Mac OS X. (This is covered in Chapter 9.)

Networking

The following are networking capabilities provided by Azure. Chapter 5 takes a deep dive into Azure networking, as well as its management by use of PowerShell.

- **Virtual Network**: Azure allows you to create virtual networks so that you can isolate different workloads. It supports site-to-site virtual private networks (VPNs) so that you can securely extend your datacenter to the cloud, and point-to-site VPNs to allow your users to securely access your cloud resources and services.
- **ExpressRoute**: ExpressRoute is another service to connect your on-premises servers to cloud-hosted services via a direct secure private connection rather than using a public connection over the Internet, as with the VPN scenario for example. ExpressRoute is more secure, reliable, and faster than a normal Internet connection.
- **Traffic Manager**: Traffic Manager allows you to load balance incoming traffic across multiple cloud services, whether they are running in the same or different datacenters. Traffic Manager has three load balancing methods: *failover*, *performance*, and *round robin*.

Storage and Data

The following are Azure services related to data management (cloud storage or a data platform):

- **Storage**: Azure's storage is known to have the fastest cloud storage performance in the market. It is a geo-redundant solution and highly scalable, with up to 500GB per single storage account. Moreover, its usage is not limited to Azure services but is also accessible to any application—even on-premises—through a set of REST APIs. (You will learn more about this in Chapter 3.)
- **HDInsight**: HDInsight is the Microsoft implementation for the Apache Hadoop on the cloud, or to make it simple, it is Microsoft's Big Data. (A deeply detailed guidance of this is in Chapter 12.)
- **SQL Database**: Azure provides the SQL Database as one of its PaaS services. This is SQL Server on the cloud, but as in many other cloud services, you handle only your data and Microsoft take cares of the infrastructure, patching, upgrades, backup, high availability, and all other related operational tasks. (This is discussed further in Chapter 7.)

Backup and Recovery

The following describes Azure's backup and restore, disaster recovery, and data-tiering services:

- **Backup**: Azure provides cloud backup services that you can use to back up your on-premises data to Azure cloud storage by using PowerShell or familiar tools like System Center Data Protection Manager (DPM).
- **Site Recovery**: Azure Site Recovery (ASR) is a service that allows you to automatically protect your private clouds—including applications and virtual machines—by replicating and recovering different workloads to the disaster recovery site (according to a set of predefined rules and conditions). These recovery sites could include a secondary office, an ISP/hoster site, or even an Azure site.
- **StorSimple**: StorSimple is Microsoft's hybrid cloud storage that's tightly integrated with Azure to provide and support data-tiering, archiving, and disaster recovery scenarios.

■ **Note** StorSimple is beyond the scope of this book as it requires a StorSimple appliance.

Identity and Access

The following are Azure identity and access services that allow you to secure and control access to Azure resources and services, as well as protect content, intellectual property, and sensitive data. Identity and access are covered in Chapter 10.

- **Azure Active Directory**: Azure Active Directory is a directory service for cloud-based applications that allows access and control for users, groups, applications, resources, and so forth. (This is discussed in Chapter 10.)
- **Azure Right Management Services (RMS)**: Azure RMS is the cloud-based version of the Windows Server RMS that is used mainly to prevent data leakage and unauthorized access to important files and information. (This is discussed in Chapter 11.)

Applications

Azure applications cannot be used individually without other services such virtual machines, web sites, or cloud services. However, it is very important to manage those services and it complements the story of cloud automation and management.

- **Azure Resource Manager**: Azure Resource Manager allows you to create reusable deployment templates to simplify the deployment of complex applications. In this template, you identify and describe the resources used in the service (such as web application, SQL Database, or Windows virtual machine) so that you can deploy them as a one logical unit, instead of dealing with each resource individually.
- **Azure Automation**: Azure Automation is an engine that allows you to automate the processes of creating, deploying, and maintaining Azure resources through PowerShell workflows (runbooks). You can use one of the existing workflows in the gallery or simply build your own. (We will talk more about this in Chapter 8.)

■ **Note** Make sure to get the Azure infographics. It provides an overview of Azure services and features. Visit `http://azure.microsoft.com/en-us/documentation/infographics/azure/`.

Summary

Obviously, "the sky is your limit" is no longer a valid expression; with cloud platforms like Azure, there are no limits but endless possibilities. Azure provides many services and features that make it possible for everyone to build and deliver world-class services in a more economical way.

This chapter spotlighted cloud computing with the Microsoft Azure cloud, with a brief introduction to Azure and its datacenters and services locations, as well as a quick overview of popular Azure services.

In the next chapter, we will fly to the first destination in our professional PowerShell journey. You will learn more about Azure PowerShell—how to set up, configure, and start using it.

Now, keep calm and get ready. The fun is about to start.

CHAPTER 2

Getting Started with Azure PowerShell

The cloud services companies of all sizes (...) The cloud is for everyone. The cloud is a democracy.

—Marc Benioff (CEO, Salesforce.com)

PowerShell is a great automation tool. Don't you agree? Of course you do. Don't worry—I can't read your mind (unfortunately PowerShell can't help me with that). You are reading a PowerShell book though, which means that you are using PowerShell, so I can guess!

Getting back to our topic, the reason that PowerShell became a first choice very fast is not simply due to the ease of using the language, but also because it is a complete automation platform with a scripting language, a workflows engine, Desired State Configuration (DSC), and so many other features. Also, PowerShell is used in Microsoft and non-Microsoft products. For example, VMware—one of Microsoft's biggest competitors—uses PowerShell to automate and manage VMware vSphere through the PowerShell management interface known as PowerCLI.

As with almost all Microsoft products that have a PowerShell management interface, Azure PowerShell is a module that comes as part of the Azure SDK. This module has a set of cmdlets that allow you to manage, deploy, and automate different aspects and workloads on Azure. Yet, Azure PowerShell is not the only usage for PowerShell in Azure's services. In the upcoming chapters, you learn that Azure Automation Services is built on top of PowerShell's workflow engine.

Also, there is the Azure Desired Stated Configuration (DSC) extension for virtual machines (VMs). DSC is a configuration management platform built in the Windows operating system to define how the Windows OS should be configured in your environment. In other words, DSC is built to allow you to set your own configuration standards for your servers. Starting with version 4.0, PowerShell introduced the DSC language extension so that you can configure DSC using PowerShell, which makes it super easy to build and deploy DSC. The Azure DSC extension for VMs utilizes DSC in Windows along with the PowerShell DSC extension to deploy the desired configuration while provisioning a new virtual machine. So, for example, if you are deploying a web farm that has four nodes, and each node requires Internet Information Services (IIS) to be installed, you can easily achieve this task by using the Azure DSC extension.

■ **Tip** PowerShell DSC is a great feature that you cannot afford to miss. I highly recommend reading one of the best titles on DSC, *Windows PowerShell Desired State Configuration Revealed* by Ravikanth Chaganti (Apress, 2014).

In this chapter, you will look at Azure PowerShell, what is required to install it, how to configure it, and, most importantly, how to connect it to your Azure subscription.

Azure PowerShell Jump-Start

The Azure PowerShell module is supported on Windows 7, Windows Server 2008 R2, and newer versions of Windows. It requires PowerShell 3.0 or later, .NET Framework 4.5, and an Azure subscription— so make sure to have these ready before starting.

The Azure PowerShell module is available through the *Microsoft Web Platform Installer* on the Microsoft Azure web site. To download it, go to the **Downloads** tab on the Azure home page, or simply go to `http://azure.microsoft.com/en-us/downloads/` and scroll down until you find Windows PowerShell, as shown in Figure 2-1. Click **Install** to get the prompt for saving the file.

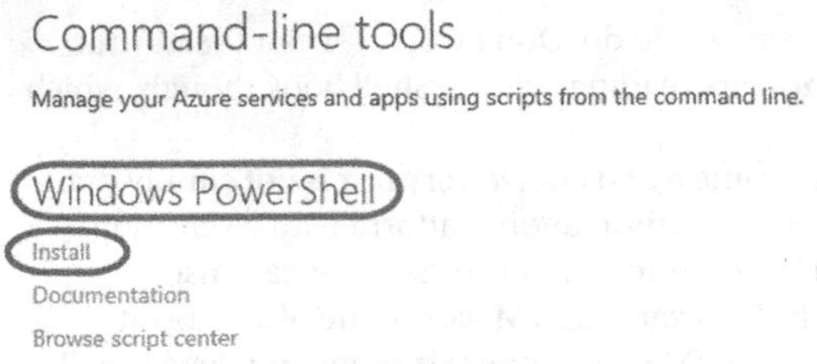

Figure 2-1. *Azure PowerShell module download*

Once the download is complete, launch the installer package and follow the setup wizard to start the Azure PowerShell installation. The installation time varies based on Internet connectivity, but it shouldn't take too much time. Azure PowerShell is part of the Azure SDK, so after finishing the installation, you will find that Microsoft Azure PowerShell has been installed along with other Azure components, as shown in Figure 2-2. We will not use any of these components in this book, but it is always good to know what we have on our machines.

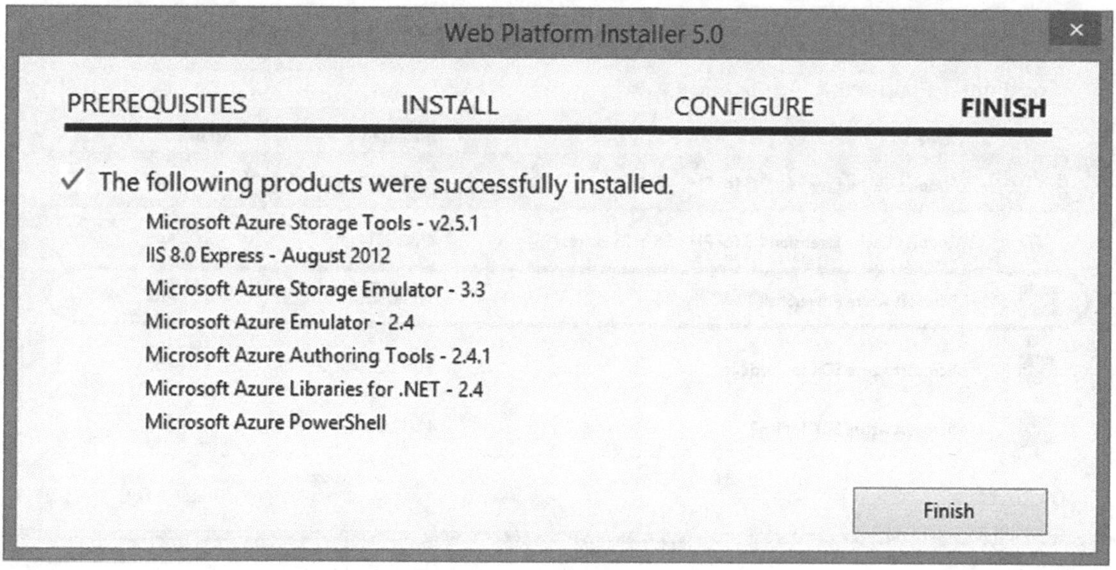

Figure 2-2. *Azure components installed with Azure PowerShell*

Azure PowerShell is the fastest-growing PowerShell module that I have ever seen, and this has been the case since the release of the first PowerShell version in 2006. There is a new version released nearly every one or two weeks, so keep your eyes on it. Azure PowerShell is an open source project available on GitHub. You can follow this project, get the source code, release installation package, and monitor the different releases and changes in every release.

■ **Note** To find Azure PowerShell on GitHub go to `https://github.com/Azure/azure-powershell`.

To update the Azure PowerShell module, launch the **Microsoft Web Platform Installer** utility on your machine, and then look for the button under the Install column in front of Microsoft Azure PowerShell, as shown in Figure 2-3.

If the button is dimmed with the word Installed inside, then you have the latest version. Otherwise, you have an update if the button is active with the word Add inside.

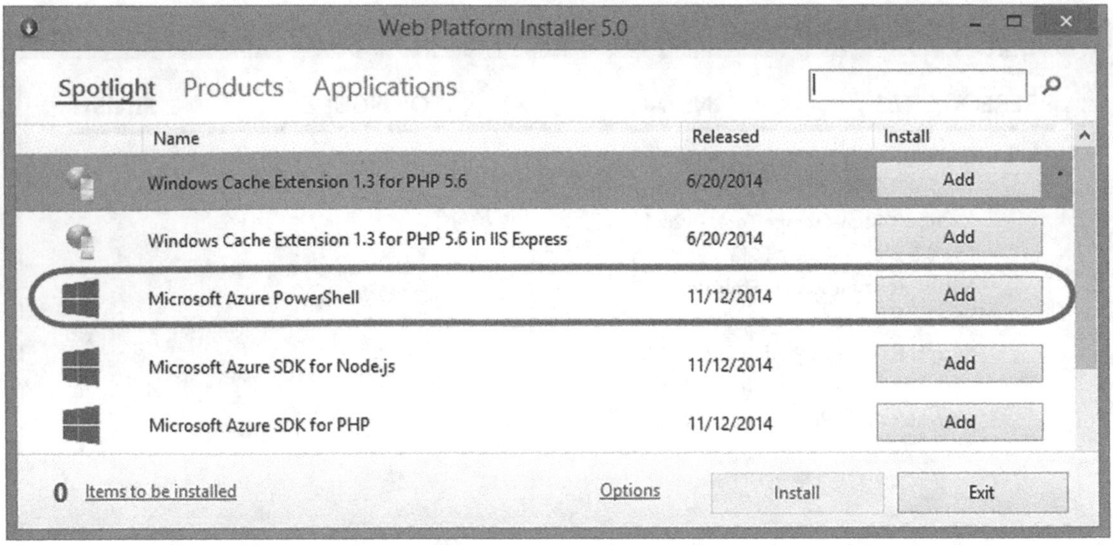

Figure 2-3. *Microsoft Azure PowerShell update in WebPI utility*

Now Microsoft Azure PowerShell is successfully installed on your machine. To open it, you can use the **Microsoft Azure PowerShell** shortcut on the desktop if you have Windows 7; it's on the Start screen if you have Windows 8 or later.

■ **Note** The Microsoft Azure PowerShell shortcut refers to this path: `C:\ProgramData\Microsoft\Windows\Start Menu\Programs\Microsoft Azure`.

Also, you can launch either the PowerShell console or the PowerShell ISE to import the Azure module by using the `Import-Module` cmdlet.

```
PS C:\> Import-Module Azure
```

You can also keep track of the module's version by using the `Get-Module` cmdlet.

```
PS C:\> Get-Module Azure | Select Version
```

To retrieve all the available cmdlets in the module, use the `Get-Command` cmdlet with the `-Module` parameter, and count them using the `Count` method.

```
PS C:\> Get-Command -Module Azure -Type Cmdlet
PS C:\> (Get-Command -Module Azure -Type Cmdlet).Count
```

If you are using PowerShell 4.0 or a later version, then you don't have to import the module manually. The reason is that starting in version 4.0, PowerShell supports module autoloading and cmdlets discovery, which automatically discovers all the modules installed on the machine and imports them.

Upcoming Changes in Azure PowerShell

Starting with Azure PowerShell version 0.8.0, the Azure PowerShell module included two sub modules: Azure Service Management (ASM) and Azure Resource Manager (ARM). These modules have a set of cmdlets that target specific Azure REST APIs. The ASM sub-module targets ASM APIs and the ARM targets ARM APIs.

Both modules can be used to create Azure resources such as storage, virtual networks, virtual machines, and so on. Also, both modules have the same cmdlets name but they work in entirely different ways. While the ASM module is for creating and managing Azure resources individually, the ARM module is capable of creating and managing a collection of different resources as a logical group or unit known as a resource group. For instance, with the ASM module you can create a web site, but with the ARM module, you can create a web site along with SQL database in the backend in a resource group and configure an access control list (ACL) for that resource group using Azure Active Directory. Later in this book, we will discuss the Azure Resource Manager in detail. Meanwhile, to understand the essence of ASM REST APIs versus ARM REST APIs, I urge you to visit the Azure Portal (`http://manage.windowsazure.com`), and the new portal (`http://portal.azure.com`, still in preview at the time of writing).

The ASM and ARM modules cannot run together in the same session. The main reason for this is that both modules have the same cmdlet names. If you want to use one of them, then you have to unload the other one. By design, the ASM module is the default module. If you want to switch between modules, use the `Switch-AzureMode` cmdlet along with the module's name—either `AzureServiceManagement` or `AzureResourceManager`.

Starting with Azure PowerShell version 0.9.2, if you are trying to use the `Switch-AzureMode` cmdlet, you will get a warning message telling you that the `Switch-AzureMode` cmdlet is deprecated and it will be removed in a future release. This is due to Microsoft making some changes in Azure PowerShell to make it possible to load both modules in the same session. They are also making ARM REST APIs the default in the Azure Portal instead of the ASM REST APIs, and the ARM Module the default module in Azure PowerShell instead of the ASM module.

As part of the change, the cmdlets in Azure Resource Manager (ARM) will be renamed from `[Verb]-Azure[Noun]` to `[Verb]-AzureRM[Noun]`. For example, the `New-AzureVM` cmdlet will become `New-AzureRMVM`. Also, the ARM module will be broken into modules by services and functionality. For example, AzureCompute, AzureStorage, AzureNetwork, and so on. The new modules for Azure and Azure Resource Manager will be distributed via PowerShell Gallery (`http://www.PowerShellGallery.com`)

■ **Note** To read the full story of deprecating the `Switch-AzureMode` cmdlet, please, refer to the following article: `https://github.com/Azure/azure-powershell/wiki/Deprecation-of-Switch-AzureMode-in-Azure-PowerShell`

In this book, we cover the ASM and ARM modules side by side in our PowerShell examples whenever possible. Thus, you don't need to worry about this change in Azure PowerShell.

Getting Azure Ready for PowerShell

After downloading, installing, and importing the Azure PowerShell module, you are very close to completing your PowerShell takeoff toward the cloud. The last step is to set up your PowerShell environment by connecting it to your Azure subscription. Since I mentioned *connection*, then I must mention *authentication*.

Azure PowerShell has two methods to get you authenticated. The first option uses a management certificate and the second option uses an Azure Active Directory account. Let's take a deeper look at each option separately.

Authentication Using a Certificate

In this method, Azure PowerShell uses Azure's Management Certificate to become authenticated and connect to the Azure subscription. To use certificate authentication, you have to first download the `PublishSettings` file, which is an XML configuration file that has your Azure subscription's unique information, such as the service endpoint URL, subscription ID, subscription name, and management certificate thumbprint. This information is used by PowerShell to reach your Microsoft Azure environment.

You can get the `PublishSettings` file easily by using the `Get-AzurePublishSettingsFile` cmdlet. This cmdlet generates a new management certificate for your subscription, and then launches the Internet browser, takes you to the Azure portal, and asks you to enter your credentials. Then you are redirected to an instructional page to generate and download your unique Microsoft Azure configuration file, which ends with the `.PublishSettings` file extension.

```
PS C:\> Get-AzurePublishSettingsFile
```

The next step is importing it to PowerShell to define your subscription information into Windows PowerShell. To import the `PublishSettings` file, use the `Import-AzurePublishSettingsFile` cmdlet.

```
PS C:\> Import-AzurePublishSettingsFile <FileName>.publishsettings
```

Once the `PublishSettings` file is imported successfully, Windows PowerShell sets your subscription as a default subscription so that every time you open Windows PowerShell and use Windows Azure cmdlets, it automatically connects to Windows Azure using the subscription defined as the default.

If you have more than one subscription in the `PublishSettings` file, the first subscription is the default one. You can easily get the list of subscriptions you have by using the `Get-AzureSubscription` cmdlet, as shown in Figure 2-4.

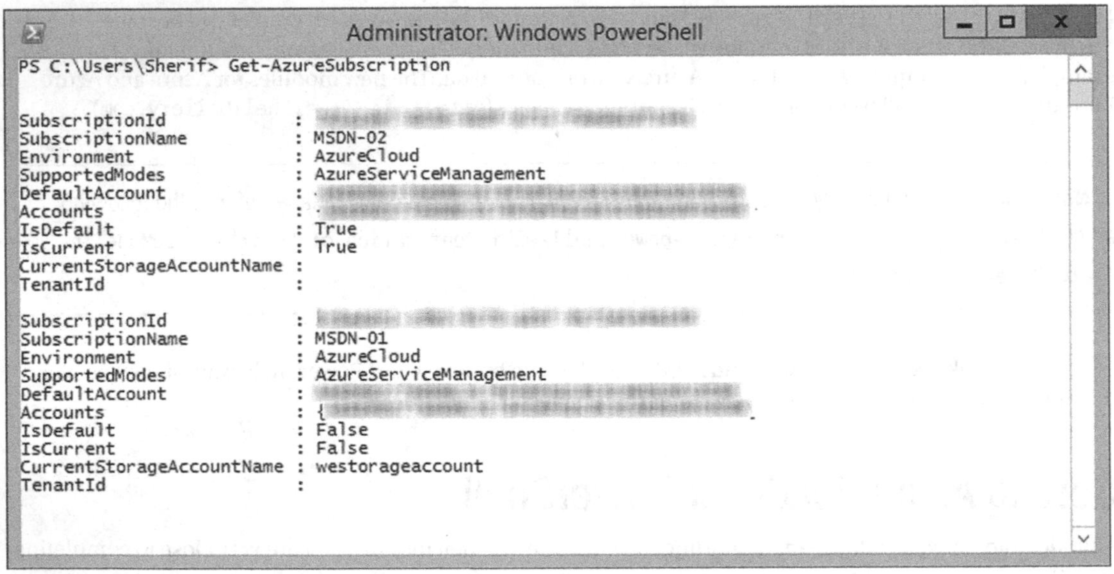

***Figure 2-4.** Get-AzureSubscription cmdlet*

You can use the Select-AzureSubscription cmdlet to move between different Azure subscriptions. To change the default subscription, use the -Default parameter.

```
PS C:\> Select-AzureSubscription -Name "MSDN-02" -Default
```

To change the current subscription temporarily without changing the default one, use the -Current parameter.

```
PS C:\> Select-AzureSubscription -Name "MSDN-02" -Current
```

Also, you can use the Remove-AzureSubscription cmdlet to remove any of your subscriptions.

Azure PowerShell also allows you to manipulate your subscription by using the Set-AzureSubscription cmdlet. It can be used to add a subscription manually to the local store, or to change the current subscription settings.

One of the most common uses for the Set-AzureSubscription cmdlet is to set up the default storage account for an Azure subscription. By setting up a default storage account, you make things easier for yourself. The next time you create a VM, a web site, or a database, Azure will select it from your subscription settings.

```
PS C:\> Set-AzureSubscription -SubscriptionName "Subscription_Name"
-CurrentStorageAccountName "Storage_Account_Name"
```

In Chapter 3, we will cover in detail the different Azure storage options and the related cmdlets. Meanwhile, for example's sake, you can use the Get-AzureStorageAccount cmdlet to list the storage accounts you have under a specific Azure subscription, or you can create a new one by using the New-AzureStorageAccount cmdlet (as shown in the following example) until we get to Chapter 3.

```
PS C:\> New-AzureStorageAccount -StorageAccountName "apresspsazure" -Label "apress1"
-Location "West Europe"
```

To verify the new default storage account name, use the Get-AzureSubscription cmdlet one more time.

```
PS C:\> Get-AzureSubscription -Name "Subscription_Name" | Select CurrentStorageAccountName

CurrentStorageAccountName
-------------------------
apresspsazure
```

Authentication Using the Azure Active Directory

Azure Active Directory authentication is done by using the Add-AzureAccount cmdlet. This cmdlet prompts a login window within PowerShell that asks for a username and password, as shown in Figure 2-5.

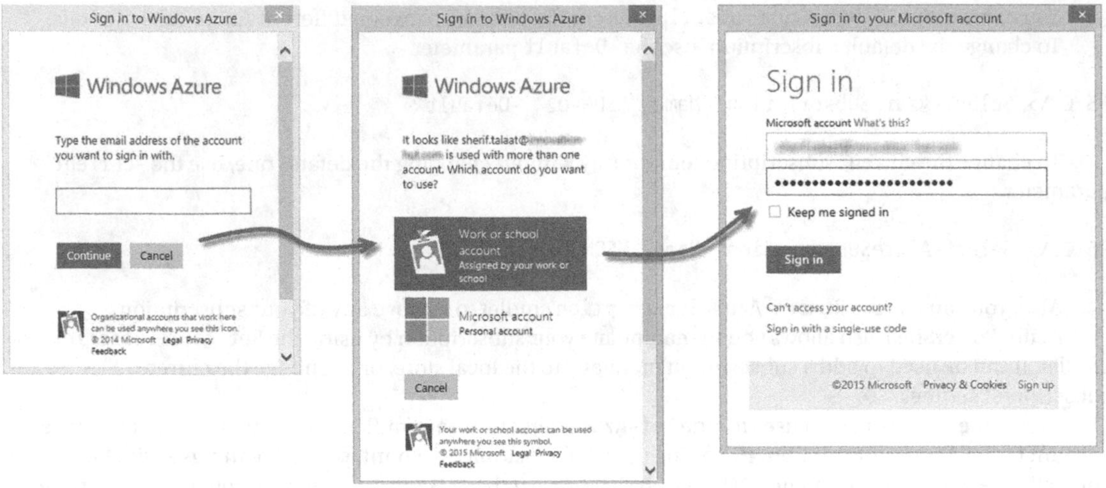

Figure 2-5. *Azure Active Directory authentication*

To get authenticated successfully, use one of the admin or co-admin accounts stored under your default Azure Active Directory tenant.

Unlike the method that uses a management certificate, Azure Active Directory authentication uses a token that is valid for 12 hours, after which you have to reauthenticate.

What I personally like about using the Azure AD authentication method is it has a `-Credential` parameter, which means that you can pass a `PSCredential` object directly to it. However, keep in mind that this feature works only for organizational accounts, not Microsoft accounts.

A Microsoft account (formerly known as Windows Live ID) is the account you create for personal use for a services like Hotmail, Xbox Live, OneDrive, and so forth. On the hand, an organizational account is the account that your company's administrator creates for you to use Microsoft cloud services like Office365, Microsoft Azure, and Microsoft Intune. The organizational account is usually in the `username@company.com` format. In Chapter 10, we cover the Azure Active Directory and how to create organizational accounts through PowerShell.

```
PS C:\> Add-AzureAccount -Credential (Get-Credential Sherif.Talaat@company123.com)
```

To list all available Azure accounts, use the `Get-AzureAccount` cmdlet.

```
PS C:\> Get-AzureAccount | Select Id
```

After finishing your tasks, you can close the session manually by using the `Remove-AzureAccount` cmdlet and passing the Azure AD account username to the `-Name` parameter.

```
PS C:\> Remove-AzureAccount -Name 'Sherif.Talaat@company123.com'
```

If you try to run any Azure cmdlet after removing the Azure account, you will get an error message, as shown in Figure 2-6.

```
Get-AzureVM : Account with name 'sherif.talaat@innovation-hut.com' does not exist.
Parameter name: accountName
At line:1 char:1
+ Get-AzureVM
+ ~~~~~~~~~~~
    + CategoryInfo          : CloseError: (:) [Get-AzureVM], ArgumentException
    + FullyQualifiedErrorId : Microsoft.WindowsAzure.Commands.ServiceManagement.IaaS.GetAzureVMCommand
```

Figure 2-6. *Account does not exist error*

Congratulations! Your Azure PowerShell environment is ready. It is time to take it to the next level.

Summary

In this chapter, you learned about Azure PowerShell and how to download, install, and configure it.

In the next chapter, you will start your tour in Azure PowerShell land by visiting Azure storage and storage accounts. Azure storage is a core component to most (if not all) Azure services and workloads. You will learn about Azure PowerShell cmdlets for different storage options, which you will practice via sets of basic and advanced scenarios and examples. Get ready for the workout!

CHAPTER 3

Managing and Maintaining Azure Storage

I don't need a hard disk in my computer if I can get to the server faster (...) carrying around these non-connected computers is byzantine by comparison.

—Steve Jobs (late chairman and co-founder, Apple)

Storage is something that we have been using since the invention of computers. Also, *cloud storage*, or Internet storage—name it whatever you want—is something that we have been using since the invention of the Internet.

In fact, cloud storage became very popular because it is useful, efficient, and cost-effective compared to local storage, especially with the huge growth in Internet speed.

Today, you can easily get hundreds of gigabytes with just a few dollars. You can access your data from anywhere, at any time, on any device. You don't have to worry about losing your drive, or crashing it, or even infecting it with a virus.

Nowadays, there is a lot of cloud storage out there that is being used either for file sharing or personal storage, including OneDrive, Dropbox, Google Drive, and so many more.

In this chapter, we are going to focus on Azure Storage since it's a major component and back end for all Azure services and workloads. As usual, the focus will be from the PowerShell point of view.

Azure Storage services go far beyond simple cloud storage for your files. It is built to work with a wide range of services that require a robust performance and massive scalability such as virtual machines and big data clusters.

Before jumping into PowerShell cmdlets for Azure Storage, it is very important to understand a few terms, components, and services related to Azure Storage.

Azure Storage Accounts

Azure Storage is simply the cloud storage where you store your Azure-hosted services, such as virtual machines, databases, web sites, and so forth. Also, it could be used as backup for your on-premises data, or it could be an archiving solution, as with the Microsoft hybrid storage solution known as StorSimple. To access services in Azure Storage, you need an Azure Storage account.

Azure provides two types of Azure storage accounts; standard and premium.

- **Standard Storage account**: This type of storage account includes storage services such as Blobs, Queues, Tables, and Files.
- **Premium Storage account**: This type of storage account is built to provide high-performance and low-latency disks for high-performance virtual machines such as D-Series VMs. Premium storage accounts provide massive performance with better IOPS and throughput per disk because it stores data on solid-state drives (SSDs), whereas standard storage accounts store it on hard disk drives (HDDs).

Moreover, an Azure storage account provides a unique namespace for working with these services. Thus, it has endpoints for those unique namespaces to access and work with the different storage services:

- **Blob endpoint**: `https://<storageaccountname>.blob.core.windows.net`
- **Table endpoint**: `https://<storageaccountname>.table.core.windows.net`
- **Queue endpoint**: `https://<storageaccountname>.queue.core.windows.net`
- **File endpoint**: `https://<storageaccountname>.file.core.windows.net`

■ **Note** Each Azure subscription can have up to 100 storage accounts, with 500TB per account.

Because data is very critical and crucial to any business, it's very important to have a backup or a replica of your data somewhere safe. Therefore, Azure offers different replication options for the data in your storage account to ensure redundancy and high availability of your data, as well as your workloads.

- **Locally Redundant Storage (LRS)**: In LRS, Azure maintains three copies of the data. The data is replicated three times within a single facility in single region.
- **Zone Redundant Storage (ZRS)**: In ZRS, Azure maintains three copies of the data, as with LRS. However, ZRS replicates the data across two to three facilities within one or two regions. ZRS supports only block blobs.

■ **Caution** Once you create a storage account with zone redundant replication, you won't be able to change it to any other replication option or vice versa.

- **Geographically Redundant Storage (GRS)**: In GRS, Azure maintains six copies of the data. The data is replicated three times across the primary region, and three times across the secondary region. GRS is the default replication option for any new storage account.
- **Read-Access Geographically Redundant Storage (RA-GRS)**: In RA-GRS, Azure maintains six copies of the data. It works like GRS replication but it provides a read access to the data in a secondary location. Thus, you can read the data from both locations in the same way, unlike the GRS that reads from the primary location and uses failover to the secondary location in case of failures.

Now you understand what an Azure storage account is, as well as its types and its different replication options. Next, you will learn how to turn this into PowerShell cmdlets to create, provision, and configure the storage accounts.

Creating a Storage Account

To create a storage account, use the `New-AzureStorageAccount` cmdlet. To complete the storage account creation, you need to pass the following parameters:

- `-StorageAccountName`: The storage account name must be 3 to 24 lowercase characters.
- `-Label`: Specify a label for the storage account. The label length may be up to 100 characters.
- `-Description`: Write a brief description for this storage account.
- `-AffinityGroup`: Specify the affinity group that will be used by the storage account. You can retrieve the list of affinity groups using the `Get-AzureAffinityGroup` cmdlet.
- `-Location`: Specify the location of the Azure datacenter that will host this storage account. You can get the list of locations by using the `Get-AzureLocation` cmdlet.
- `-Type`: Choose the type of storage account replication. The available values for the parameters are Standard_LRS, Standard_ZRS, Standard_GRS, Standard_RAGRS, and Premium_LRS. If you don't specify the `-Type` parameter, then Standard_GRS is automatically selected.

■ **Note** Use either the `-AffinityGroup` parameter or the `-Location` parameter because you cannot use both in the same command. It's better to choose the `-Location` parameter because Affinity Groups are no longer recommended by Microsoft and have been replaced by regional virtual networks.

```
## Create new Azure storage account (ASM)
New-AzureStorageAccount -StorageAccountName mylabstorageaccount -Label "My Lab Storage"
-Description "Cloud storage for Azure VMs" -Location "West Europe"
```

The preceding code sample shows how to use the `New-AzureStorageAccount` cmdlet in the ASM module to create a storage account in `mylabstorageaccount`, which is located in the West Europe region. To create a storage account using the ARM module, switch to the ARM module using the `Switch-AzureMode` cmdlet, then use the `New-AzureStorageAccount` cmdlet along with the following parameters:

- `-ResourceGroupName`: Specify the name of Azure resource group this storage account will belong to. Resource groups are a way to put all related services and components into one container for ease of management and operation.
- `-Name`: The storage account name must be 3 to 24 lowercase characters.
- `-Location`: Specify the location of the Azure datacenter that will host this storage account. You can get the list of locations with the `Get-AzureLocation` cmdlet.
- `-Type`: Choose the type of storage account replication. The available values for the parameters are Standard_LRS, Standard_ZRS, Standard_GRS, Standard_RAGRS, and Premium_LRS. If you don't specify the `-Type` parameter, then Standard_GRS is automatically selected.

```
## Create new Azure storage account (ARM)
Switch-AzureMode AzureResourceManager

#Authenticate to Azure Subscription
Add-AzureAccount

#Create New Azure Resource Group
New-AzureResourceGroup -Name "CAI-WebFarm" -Location "West Europe"

#New Storage Account
New-AzureStorageAccount -ResourceGroupName "CAI-WebFarm" -Name "mylabstorageaccount"
-Location "West Europe" -Type "Standard_LRS"
```

Listing and Removing Storage Accounts

After creating the storage account, you can easily list all the existing storage accounts under a specific Azure subscription by using the `Get-AzureStorageAccount` cmdlet. You may also get a specific storage account by storage account name, as shown in this example:

```
## Listing Azure Storage Accounts (ASM)
Get-AzureStorageAccount -StorageAccountName mylabstorageaccount

StorageAccountDescription : Storage for myAzure Lab
AffinityGroup             :
Location                  : West Europe
GeoReplicationEnabled     : True
GeoPrimaryLocation        : West Europe
GeoSecondaryLocation      : North Europe
Label                     : Azure Lab Storage
StorageAccountStatus      : Created
StatusOfPrimary           : Available
StatusOfSecondary         : Available
Endpoints                 : {https://mylabstorageaccount.blob.core.windows.net/,
                            https://mylabstorageaccount.queue.core.windows.net/,
                            https://mylabstorageaccount.table.core.windows.net/,
                            https://mylabstorageaccount.file.core.windows.net/}
AccountType               : Standard_GRS
StorageAccountName        : mylabstorageaccount
OperationDescription      : Get-AzureStorageAccount
OperationId               : 817c8dae-09e8-3d5a-baa7-bc1b739d552b
OperationStatus           : Succeeded
```

In the ARM module, use the Get-AzureStorageAccount cmdlet along with -ResourceGroupName and -Name parameters, as shown in this example:

```
## Listing Azure Storage Accounts (ARM)
Get-AzureStorageAccount -ResourceGroupName "CAI-WebFarm" -Name mylabstorageaccount

ResourceGroupName    : cai-webfarm
Name                 : mylabstorageaccount
Id                   : /subscriptions/5c6a4er1-xyz-1234-a1b7-9c72e5e9a149/resourceGroups/
coexrg/providers/Microsoft.Storage/storageAccounts/armtorageaccount
Location             : West Europe
AccountType          : StandardLRS
CreationTime         : 8/9/2015 3:51:30 AM
CustomDomain         :
LastGeoFailoverTime  :
PrimaryEndpoints     : Microsoft.Azure.Management.Storage.Models.Endpoints
PrimaryLocation      : West Europe
ProvisioningState    : Succeeded
SecondaryEndpoints   :
SecondaryLocation    :
StatusOfPrimary      : Available
StatusOfSecondary    :
Tags                 : {}
```

Also, you can remove it using the Remove-AzureStorageAccount cmdlet, as in the following example:

```
## Remove Azure Storage Account (ASM)
Remove-AzureStorageAccount -StorageAccountName mylabstorageaccount

StorageAccountName     OperationDescription         OperationId       OperationStatus
------------------     --------------------         -----------       ---------------
mylabstorageaccount    Remove-AzureStorageAccount   35371010...       Succeeded

## Remove Azure Storage Account (ARM)
Remove-AzureStorageAccount -ResourceGroupName "CAI-WebFarm" -Name mylabstorageaccount

StorageAccountName     OperationDescription         OperationId       OperationStatus
------------------     --------------------         -----------       ---------------
mylabstorageaccount    Remove-AzureStorageAccount   35371010...       Succeeded
```

Modifying Storage Account Settings

The Set-AzureStorageAccount cmdlet allows you to change the storage account's label, description, and most importantly, the replication. To change the replication option, use the -Type parameter, as in the New-AzureStorageAccount cmdlet.

Unlike, the New-AzureStorageAccount cmdlet, the -Type parameter doesn't support the Standard_ZRS value. Do you know why? Yes, because ZRS is available only while you create the storage account; it cannot be modified later. As shown in Figure 3-1, you have only three replication options, and ZRS is not one of them.

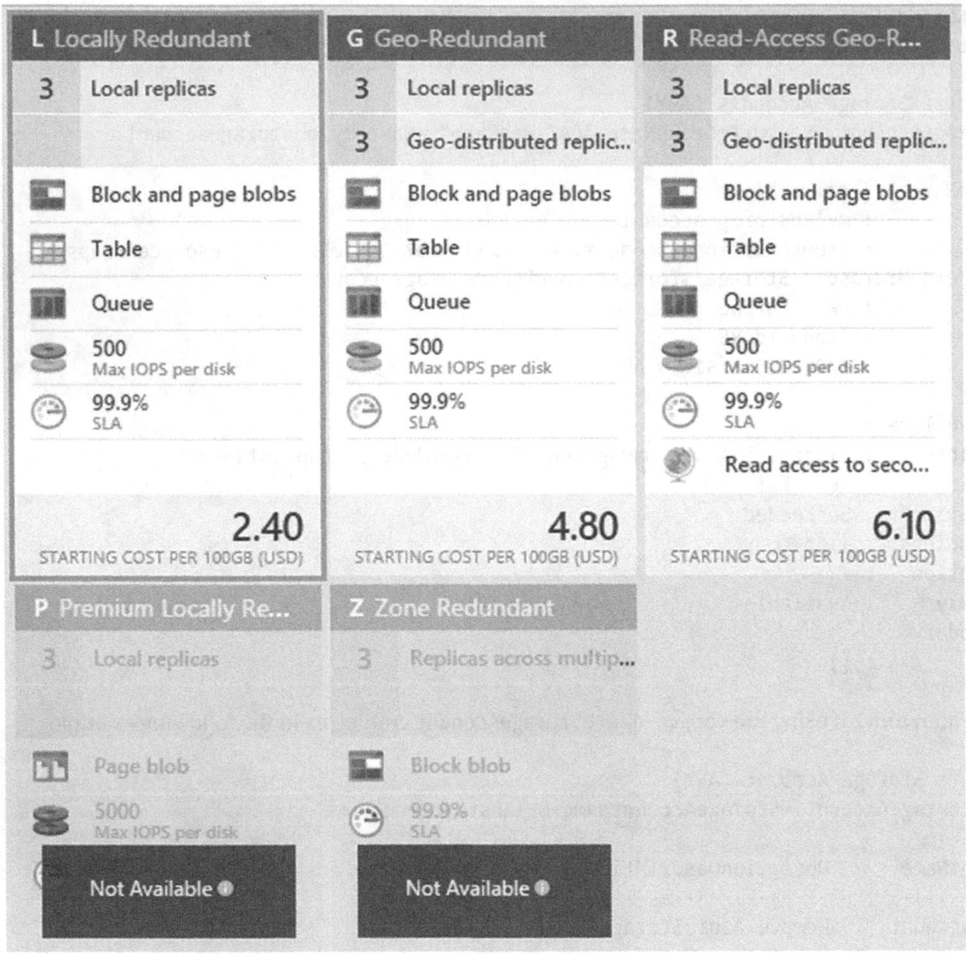

Figure 3-1. *Azure storage account replication options - New Azure Portal*

The following example shows how to change the replication option from Standard_GRS to Standard_LRS by using the `Set-AzureStorageAccount` cmdlet in the ASM module:

```
#Change Storage account replication option (ASM)
Set-AzureStorageAccount -StorageAccountName mylabstorageaccount -Type Standard_LRS
```

We can achieve the same task by using the `Set-AzureStorageAccount` cmdlet in the ARM module and replace the `StorageAccountName` parameter with `-ResourceGroupName` and `-Name` parameters.

```
## Change Storage account replication option (ARM)
Set-AzureStorageAccount -ResourceGroupName "CAI-WebFarm" -Name mylabstorageaccount -Type
Standard_LRS
```

Also, we use the `Set-AzureStorageAccount` cmdlet in the ARM module to configure a custom domain for the storage account. The custom domain allows you to use your own domain name to access storage endpoints (`storage.<custom_domain>.com`) instead of the default endpoint URL (`storageaccount.blob.core.windows.net`).

Before adding a custom domain to a storage account, we need to verify the ownership of that domain. To do so, we need to either add a CNAME record under the public DNS that refers to the original endpoint URL, or create a sub domain that refers to it. Then, use the Set-AzureStorageAccount cmdlet along with the -CustomDomainName parameter.

```
## Add Custom Domain to Storage Account (ARM)
Set-AzureStorageAccount -ResourceGroupName "CAI-WebFarm" -Name mylabstorageaccount
-CustomDomainName "storage.company123.com"
```

If you are using a sub domain for domain verification, then add the -UseSubDomain parameter to the preceding example.

Azure Storage Services

As mentioned earlier in this chapter, the standard storage account has four storage services: Blob, Table, Queue, and File. Each of these services has a different functionality and usage, as well as a set of PowerShell cmdlets that allows managing and maintaining it.

Blob Storage

A Blob provides storage for a large amount of unstructured data, such as documents, media files, backups, and so forth. Blobs are organized into containers, which assign different security policies to different blobs. Blob storage has two types of blobs:

- **Block blob**: This type is optimized for storing and streaming objects and files. The block blob can reach up to 200GB. This type is the only storage service that supports ZRS.
- **Page blob**: This type is also known as *disks* because it is optimized to support random writes and can reach up to 1TB. The Azure VM's virtual hard disks (VHDs) are stored as a page blob.

Working with Containers

Blob storage is pretty similar to the concept of folders and files, where containers represent folders and blobs represents files. Therefore, before you can start using blobs, you must ensure that you have a container to store the blobs in.

For this purpose, use the New-AzureStorageContainer cmdlet along with a couple of basic parameters -Name and -Permissions.

- -Name: Specify a unique name for the container within a storage account. The name must be between 3 and 63 lowercase characters, which may end with a number.
- -Permissions: Assign a public access level to this container. It has three different permission levels:
    - Off: Access is restricted to the storage account owner only. This is the default access level for any new containers.
    - Blob: Grants read access to blob data within a specific container, but does not grant access to the container itself.
    - Container: Grants full-read access to a specific container and its blobs.

■ **Note** You can refer to `http://msdn.microsoft.com/library/azure/dd179354.aspx` to get detailed information about which features are available to anonymous users when granting public access.

The permission level names in PowerShell have a different value than the values on the Azure portal interface, as shown in Figure 3-2.

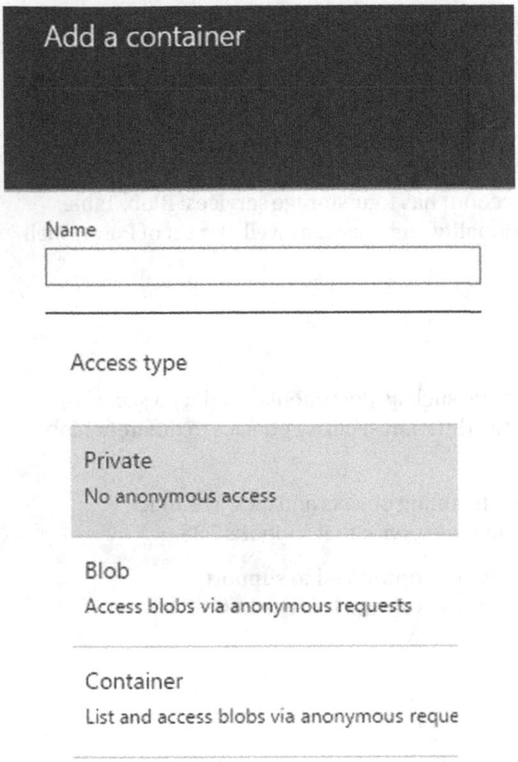

Figure 3-2. *Container permission level on the Azure portal*

Table 3-1 shows each level name and the equivalent on the portal.

Table 3-1. *Permission Levels in Azure PowerShell and Portal*

Azure PowerShell	Azure Portal
Off	Private
Blob	Public blob
Container	Public container

The following code sample shows how to create a new Azure storage container called disks that has restricted access:

```
## Create new Azure storage container (ASM)
New-AzureStorageContainer -Name disks -Permission Off
```

Did you execute the previous code? Did you notice something missing?

Usually, if you have only one storage account, you will not notice anything missing. However, if you have multiple storage accounts, mostly you will be looking for missing parameters.

C'mon, be patient. I was being mysterious but I will talk plainly now. The New-AzureStorageContainer cmdlet uses the default storage account linked to your Azure subscription— unless you define the -Context parameter (Do you remember this from Chapter 2?).

The -Context parameter is where you define the storage context for the storage operation that you are going to perform. Simply, it defines which storage account the cmdlet will use.

The -Context parameter is one of the common parameters across most of Azure PowerShell storage related cmdlets:

```
## Create new Storage Container (ASM)
New-AzureStorageContainer -Name disks -Permission Off -Context $StorageContext
```

If you want to change a container's permission later on, you can use the Set-AzureStorageContainerAcl cmdlet with the same parameters of the New-AzureStorageContainer cmdlet:

```
## Configure Container's ACL (ASM)
Set-AzureStorageContainerAcl -Name disks -Permission Container -Context $StorageContainer
```

Of course, you can list all the available containers using the Get-AzureStorageContainer cmdlet, and remove it by using the Remove-AzureStorageContainer cmdlet.

Creating New Storage Context

To create a storage context, use the New-AzureStorageContext cmdlet. The impressive thing in this cmdlet's parameters is that it is not just a parameter you use to create a storage context. Rather, it is a set of parameters that you use in combination to create a storage context based on the information that you have, the storage services that you want to use, and most importantly, the access that you have to this storage.

The following examples show part of these parameter combinations. Before you start, make sure that you have the storage account name and its access key handy and stored in the $StorageAccountName and $StorageAccessKey variables.

To get the storage access key, go to **Azure Portal**, select **Storage**, choose the desired **Storage Account** from the list, and then under **Dashboard**, click **Manage Access Key**, as shown in Figure 3-3.

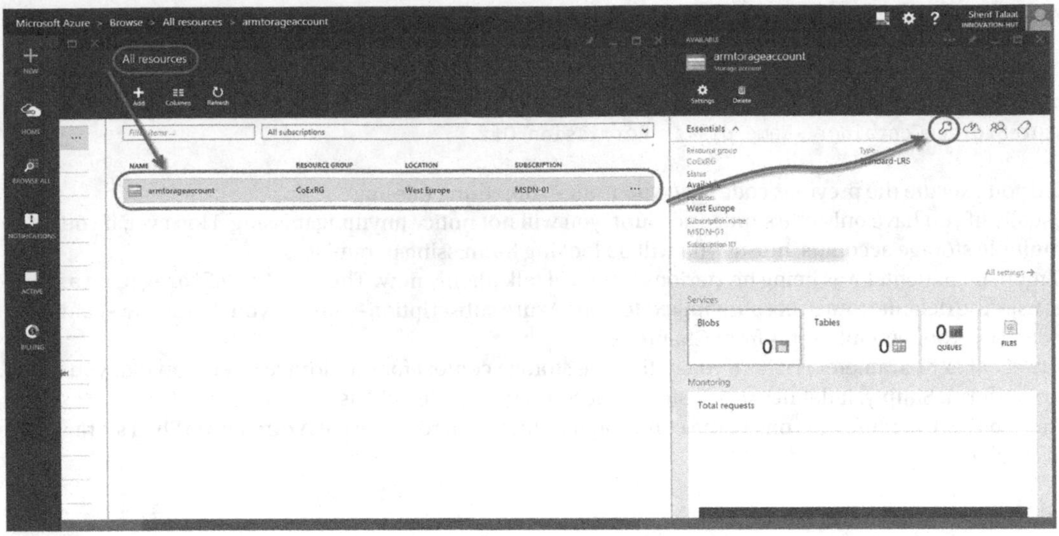

Figure 3-3. Getting to the storage access key

This pops up a window with the storage account name, primary access key, and secondary access key (see Figure 3-4). You can use any of the storage keys, and also you can regenerate them.

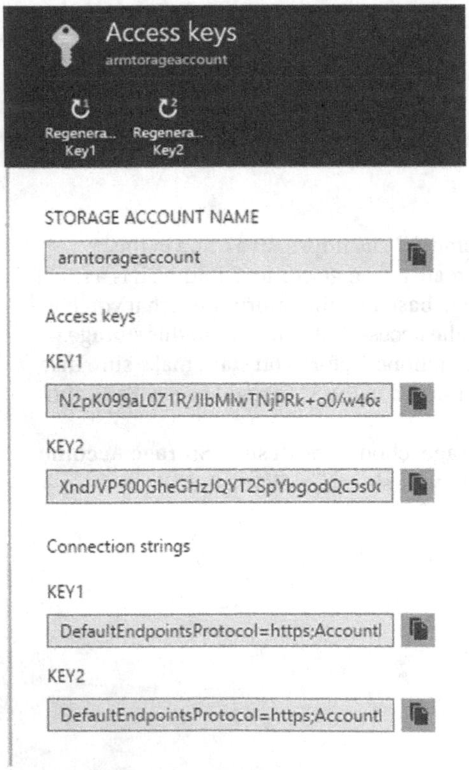

Figure 3-4. Manage Access Keys pop-up window

You can get the storage access key via PowerShell by using the Get-AzureStorageKey cmdlet in the ASM module and the Get-AzureStorageAccountKey cmdlet in the ARM module, as shown in the following examples:

```
##Generating Azure Storage Access Key (ASM)
$StorageAccountName = "mylabstroageaccount"

$StorageAccessKey = Get-AzureStorageKey -StorageAccountName $StorageAccountName | Select
-ExpandProperty Primary

## Generating Azure Storage Access Key (ARM)
$ResourceGroupName = "CAI-WebFarm"
$StorageAccountName = "mylabstroageaccount"

$StorageAccessKey = Get-AzureStorageAccountKey -ResourceGroupName $ResourceGroupName -Name
$StorageAccountName | Select -ExpandProperty Key1
```

Now, back to the creating a storage context. Again, to make the life easier, store the value in a variable:

```
$StorageAccountName = "mylabstroageaccount"
$StorageAccessKey = "<YOUR_STORAGE_ACCESS_KEY>"
```

■ **Caution** I am storing the storage access key within a variable just for the sake of example. I don't have to remind you that storing such a critical value explicitly in clear text within a script is not a best practice. However, you can keep it empty and always ask the user for the key before execution.

Example 1: Creating Storage Context by Using the Storage Account Name and Key

In this example, you create a new storage context by using very simple parameters -StorageAccountName and -StorageAccountKey along with the previously defined variables:

```
## Creating storage context using Storage Account Name and Key (ASM)
$StorageContext = New-AzureStorageContext -StorageAccountName $StorageAccountName
-StorageAccountKey $StorageAccountKey
```

Example 2: Creating Storage Context with an Anonymous Account

In this example, you create a new storage context for anonymous access. This context can be used for storage service that has public access permission, such as containers.

Use the -Anonymous parameter for anonymous access, and use -Protocol if you want use HTTP instead HTTPS, since HTTPS is the default:

```
## Creating storage context using Storage Account with Anonymous Access (ASM)
$StorageContext = New-AzureStorageContext -StorageAccountName $StorageAccountName -Anonymous
-Protocol http
```

Example 3: Creating Storage Context Using a SAS Token

In this example, you create a new storage context for a restricted container using a Shared Access Signature (SAS) token.

A SAS token is used to grant limited access to a storage account without sharing the storage access key. In order to generate a SAS token, use the New-AzureStorageContainerSASToken cmdlet along with the following parameters:

- -Name: Specify the name of the container.
- -Permission: Define the permissions of the token. The available permissions are read (r), write (w), delete (d), and list (l).
- -ExpiryTime: Define when token will expire and become no longer valid.

The following example shows how to create a SAS token for a VHD container with full permissions and that expires after five days from generating it:

```
#Generating SAS Token (ASM)
$SASToken = New-AzureStorageContainerSASToken -Name VHDs -Permission rwdl -ExpiryTime
(Get-Date).AddDays(5)

#Creating the Sotrage Context using the SAS Toekn (ASM)
$StorageContext = New-AzureStorageContext -StorageAccountName $StorageAccountName -SasToken
$SASToken
```

Then, use this token to create a new storage context.

Example 4: Creating Storage Context by Using a Connection String

In this example, you create a new storage context using a storage connection string:

```
## Creating Storage Context using Connection String (ASM)
$ConStr = "DefaultEndPointsProtocol=https;AccountName=$StorageAccountName; AccountKey=$Stor
ageAccountKey"

$StorageContext = New-AzureStorageContext -ConnectionString $ConStr
```

Working with Blobs

Previously, you created a container as a start to use blobs. Now, you are ready to go. Considering the consistency of the PowerShell cmdlet, you should be able to guess the right cmdlet to create a new blob.

I bet you are thinking of the New-AzureStorageBlob cmdlet. Right? Well, there is good news and bad news. The good news is congratulations, you are thinking PowerShell. However, the bad news is, sorry, there is no cmdlet called New-AzureStorageBlob. I understand that you may hate me, sometimes I hate myself too, but please bear with me, and I will explain things to you.

Blobs are more or less just a file; and on Azure, you cannot create files—although you can upload them. Thus, the New-AzureStorageBlob cmdlet is the Set-AzureStorageBlobContent cmdlet.

Still, you have the Get-AzureStorageBlob and Remove-AzureStorageBlob cmdlets.

Uploading and Downloading Storage Blobs

To upload a file to an Azure storage blob, use the `Set-AzureStorageBlobContent` cmdlet along with the following parameters:

- `-Blob`: The name of Azure Storage Blob.
- `-Container`: Specify which container to store this blog.
- `-Context`: Specify the storage context, unless you want to use the default storage account.
- `-File`: The local path of the file you want to upload.
- `-BlobType`: Specify either Block or Page. Block is the default blob type.
- `-Force`: Overwrites any existing blob with the same name.

So, the final command should look like the following example. In this example, we are uploading image file `PowerShell_icon.png` as the blob `PowerShell.png` to the `images` container:

```
## Uploading Local file to Azure Blob (ASM)
Set-AzureStorageBlobContent -Container images -Context $StorageContext -File .\
powershell_icon.png -Blob PowerShell.png -BlobType Block

   Container Uri: https://mylabstorageaccount.blob.core.windows.net/images

Name            BlobType  Length  ContentType           LastModified        SnapshotTime
----            --------  ------  -----------           -----------------   ------------
PowerShell.png  BlockBlob 4875    application/octet-..  12/1/2014 2:42:22   ...
```

To download an Azure blob to local storage, use the `Get-AzureStorageBlobContent` cmdlet. This cmdlet uses almost the same parameters as the `Set-AzureStorageBlobContent` cmdlet, except `-BlobType` does not exist and `-File` is replaced by `-Destination`. The following example shows how to download the blob `PowerShell.png` and save to the desktop using the `Get-AzureStorageBlobContent` cmdlet:

```
## Download Azure Blob to Local Storage (ASM)
Get-AzureStorageBlobContent -Container images -Context $StorageContext -Blob powershell.png
-Destination .\Desktop
```

Listing and Removing Storage Blobs

As said, use the `Get-AzureStorageBlob` cmdlet to list all the existing blobs within a specific container. As usual, we use the `-Context` and `-Container` parameters to specify which storage account and container to work on.

Moreover, we can use the `-MaxCount` to specify the maximum number of blobs that the cmdlet will retrieve, and `-Prefix` to get all blobs with a defined prefix like `"VM*"`. The following example shows how to get the first 25 blobs that start with `VM` under a disks container:

```
## Listing all available blobs under container (ASM)
Get-AzureStorageBlob -Container disks -Context $StorageContext -MaxCount 25 -Prefix "VM*"
```

To remove an existing blob (it is not hard to guess), use the Remove-AzureStorageBlob cmdlet. Specify the -Blob, -Container, and -Context parameters. In some cases, especially when it comes to VMs, the blob might have a snapshot that is not removed by default unless you use the -DeleteSnapshot parameter (snapshots are discussed in Chapter 4).

```
## Removing all blobs under container (ASM)
Get-AzureStorageBlob -Container disks -Context $StorageContext | Remove-AzureStorageBlob
-Force
```

Copying Storage Blobs Between Containers

Copying is one of the most basic operations that you can do on any file, including blobs. Azure PowerShell provides a couple of cmdlets that handle copying files between different storage containers. There cmdlets are Start-AzureStorageBlobCopy and Stop-AzureStorageBlobCopy.

The following code example shows how to copy a blob between two containers in two different storage accounts. Basically, the information that you need to know includes the source blob, source container, source storage context, destination blob, destination container, and destination storage context.

```
## Copying blobs between two storage accounts (ASM)
#Source Storage Information
$SrcStorageAccountName = "storage01"
$SrcStorageAccountKey = "SOURCE_STORAGE_ACCESS_KEY"
$SrcStorageContext = New-AzureStorageContext -StorageAccountName $SrcStorageAccountName
-StorageAccountKey $SrcStorageAccountKey

#Destination Storage Information
$DestStorageAccountName = "storage02"
$DestStorageAccountKey = "SOURCE_STORAGE_ACCESS_KEY"
$DestStorageContext = New-AzureStorageContext -StorageAccountName $DestStorageAccountName
-StorageAccountKey $DestStorageAccountKey

#Copy single blob from container to container
Start-AzureStorageBlobCopy -SrcBlob WI-EXCH-01-2014-11-27.vhd -SrcContainer vhds -Context
$SrcStorageContext -DestContainer vhds -DestContext $DestStorageContext

#Copy all blob from container to another container
Get-AzureStorageBlob -Container vhds -Context $SrcStorageContext | Start-
AzureStorageBlobCopy -DestContainer vhds -DestContext $DestStorageContext

#Copy blob from URI container to another container
$BlobUri = "https://Storage01.blob.core.windows.net/vhds/"

$BlobsCopy = Start-AzureStorageBlobCopy -AbsoluteUri $BlobUri -DestContainer vhds
-DestContext $DestStorageContext
```

While copying the blobs, you keep tracking the copy state by using the Get-AzureStorageBlobCopyState cmdlet. Let's build on top of the previous example and add the following line:

```
$BlobsCopy | Get-AzureStorageBlobCopyState
```

This gives you the state of each blob being copied, as shown in the following results:

```
CopyId               : 47ddcfd9-f606-42c3-824b-389d193c2d97
CompletionTime       :
Status               : Pending
Source               : https://storage01.blob.core.windows.net/vhds/xWI-EXCH-01-xWI-
EXCH-01-2014-11-27.vhd?sv=2014-02-14&sr=b&sig=C..
BytesCopied          : 8714878976
TotalBytes           : 136367309312
```

If, at any time, the copy status is still pending and you no longer want to continue this copy job, then you use the Stop-AzureStorageBlobCopy cmdlet:

```
## Stop Azure Storage Blob Copy (ASM)
Stop-AzureStorageBlobCopy -Blob Win2012R2.vhd -Container vhds -CopyId 47ddcfd9-f606-42c3-
824b-389d193c2d97
```

Blob storage is crucial to Azure, especially for critical services like virtual machines, web sites, HDInsight, and many others. So, it is very important to understand the different Azure storage options and operations. Also, master the cmdlets, because it will make your life much easier.

The next section covers the File Storage as a file share option. Although it's important to have a back-end storage to serve your critical workloads, it's also important to have storage to serve the applications and services running on those workloads.

File Storage

Azure File Storage is cloud-based standard SMB 2.1 shared storage. It can be used to share files across different Azure virtual machines and cloud services through a mounted share. Also, it can be used by on-premises applications through the File Storage REST APIs.

Working with File Storage

The file storage structure is very similar to the Windows Server share. There are a number of shares in a storage account, and each share has directories and files, as shown in Figure 3-5.

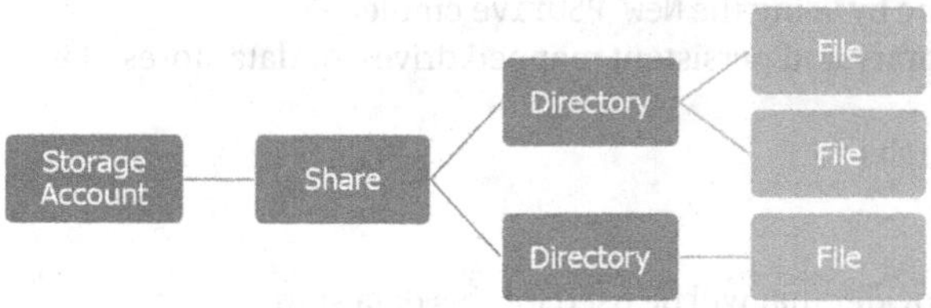

Figure 3-5. *Azure file storage structure*

Let's follow this structure and use PowerShell to build an end-to-end cloud-based file share.

First off, as stated earlier, you need to have storage context for any Azure storage services.

```
## Creating new Storage Context (ASM)
$StorageAccountName = "storage01"
$StorageAccountKey = "SOURCE_STORAGE_ACCESS_KEY"
$StorageContext = New-AzureStorageContext -StorageAccountName $StorageAccountName
-StorageAccountKey $StorageAccountKey
```

Then, you create a new share by using the `New-AzureStorageShare` cmdlet. As usual, your storage name must be lowercase characters and it may end with numbers. In the following example, you create a new share called `teamshare`:

```
## Creating new Storage Share (ASM)
New-AzureStorageShare -Name "teamshare" -Context $StorageContext
```

Next, you create a directory under the share you've just created by using the `New-AzureStorageDirectory` cmdlet, along with `-ShareName` to specify which share to use and `-Path` to specify the name of the directory:

```
## Creating new Storage Directory (ASM)
New-AzureStorageDirectory -ShareName "teamshare" -Path "Documents" -Context $StorageContext
```

Well, you have a share and a directory. Now, let's upload files to this directory. File storage is almost like blob storage because you use the `Set-AzureStorageFileContent` cmdlet to upload files, the `Get-AzureStorageFileContent` cmdlet to download them, and, of course, the `Remove-AzureStorageFile` cmdlet to delete them.

The next example shows how to upload a group of files under a specific folder to an Azure storage share:

```
## Uploading all files under Document folders (ASM)
ForEach($file in (Get-ChildItem -Path D:\Documents))
{
  Set-AzureStorageFileContent -ShareName "teamshare" -Path "documents" -Source
$file.FullName -Context $StorageContext -Force
}
```

So, if you are reading these lines, then you have successfully created a cloud-based SMB share. The last step is to mount this share to an Azure virtual machine by using the `New-PSDrive` cmdlet.

The `New-PSDrive` cmdlet is used to create temporary and persistent mapped drives, or data stores. It is the equivalent to `net use` in a command line.

The following parameters are used to mount the share:

- `-Name`: Specify the name of the drive.
- `-PSProvider`: Choose the PowerShell provider that will be used for this data store; there are different providers, such as FileSystem, Certificate, and Registry. You can get the full list by using the `Get-PSProvider` cmdlet. In this case, it is FileSystem.
- `-Root`: The location of the data store.
- `-Persist`: Used to create a Windows mapped drive.
- `-Credential`: In this case, the username is the storage account name, and the password is the storage access key.

```
## Mounting cloud-based share to Azure VM (ASM)
New-PSDrive -Name "M" -Root "\\storage01.file.core.windows.net\coexshare01" -Credential
(Get-Credential sherift) -PSProvider FileSystem -Persist
```

■ **Caution** The storage account and the virtual machines must be located in the Azure region; otherwise, you will get an error message stating that the share is no longer available.

Finally, you can easily manage your cloud-based share, directories, and files using Windows Explorer.

To remove this storage share, you can use the `Remove-AzureStorageShare` cmdlet, which will delete the share, along with any directories and files under it.

Table Storage and Queue Storage

The last two storage services in Azure storage are Table storage and Queue storage.

- **Table storage**: This is simply the Microsoft implementation for the modern database known as NoSQL, where tables consist of entities. The `New-AzureStorageTable` cmdlet is used to create a new table, the `Get-AzureStorageTable` cmdlet to list tables, and the `Remove-AzureStorageTable` cmdlet to delete them.
- **Queue storage**: This provides messaging for asynchronous communications and workflow processing between different application components. Queues consist of messages. The `New-AzureStorageQueue` cmdlet is used to create a new queue, the `Get-AzureStorageQueue` cmdlet to list queues, and the `Remove-AzureStorageQueue` cmdlet to delete them.

Unfortunately, the PowerShell cmdlets for those two services are very basic compared to the other services: Blob storage and File storage.

For example, you can create new tables and queues, but you cannot create entities and messages with PowerShell; however, you can do it using the Azure storage REST APIs. The reason is because table and queue storages are mainly for development purposes, so it makes sense to manipulate using APIs rather than PowerShell. This is unlike the blob and file storages for all the workloads, and especially the Infrastructure as a Service (IaaS) scenarios such as virtual machines, Azure Site Recovery (ASR), and so forth.

Storage Tools

In this section, we will discuss two of the Azure storage tools that you should have in your library.

Azure Storage Explorer

Azure Storage Explorer is an open source tool that you can get at `http://azurestorageexplorer.codeplex.com`. It provides a graphical user interface (GUI) to manage the different Azure storage services.

Azure Storage Explorer is similar to FTP programs. It displays all Azure storage services in a single window so you can easily discover, browse, and manage them. For example, as shown in Figure 3-6, you can select the Blob Containers item in the left-hand pane to see all the containers underneath. When you select a specific container, it will list all available blobs under it on the right-hand pane. You can also carry out different operation on the blobs such as upload, download, copy, and delete.

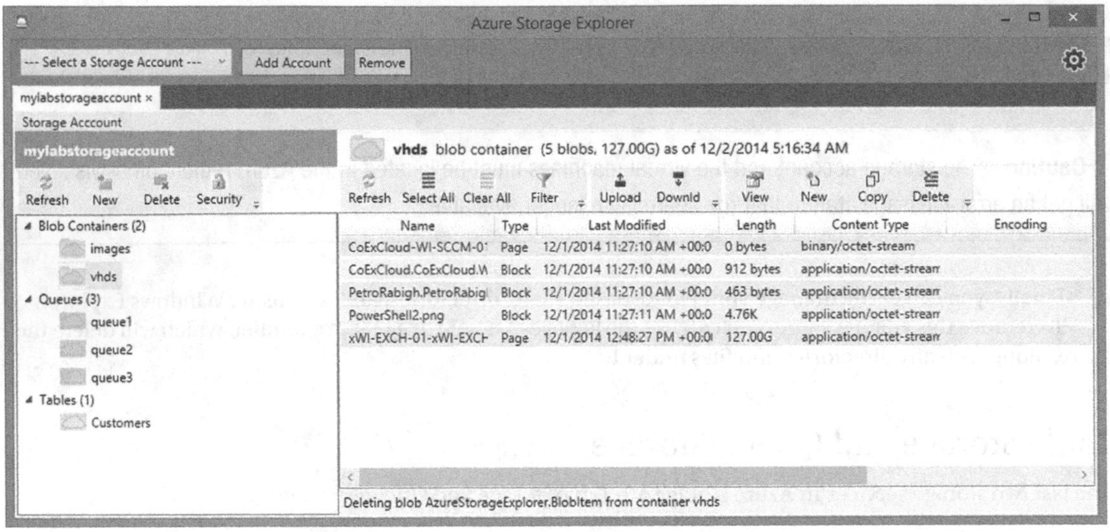

Figure 3-6. *Azure Storage Explorer*

Azure Explorer

Azure Explorer is free storage tool by Cerebrata that you can get at `http://www.cerebrata.com/products/azure-explorer/introduction`. Azure Explorer has a paid version (Azure Management Studio) that enables more management features. Unlike Azure Storage Explorer, which manages the different Azure storage services, the Azure Explorer manages only the storage blobs unless you are using the paid version.

Azure Explorer's GUI is my favorite thing about it and the reason I prefer to use it. Azure Explorer is similar to Windows Explorer. Actually, it shows Azure storage accounts as if it's a local storage resource mounted to your computer, as shown in Figure 3-7. This makes it much easier to upload and download files between Azure and local storage, and to move files between different storage accounts.

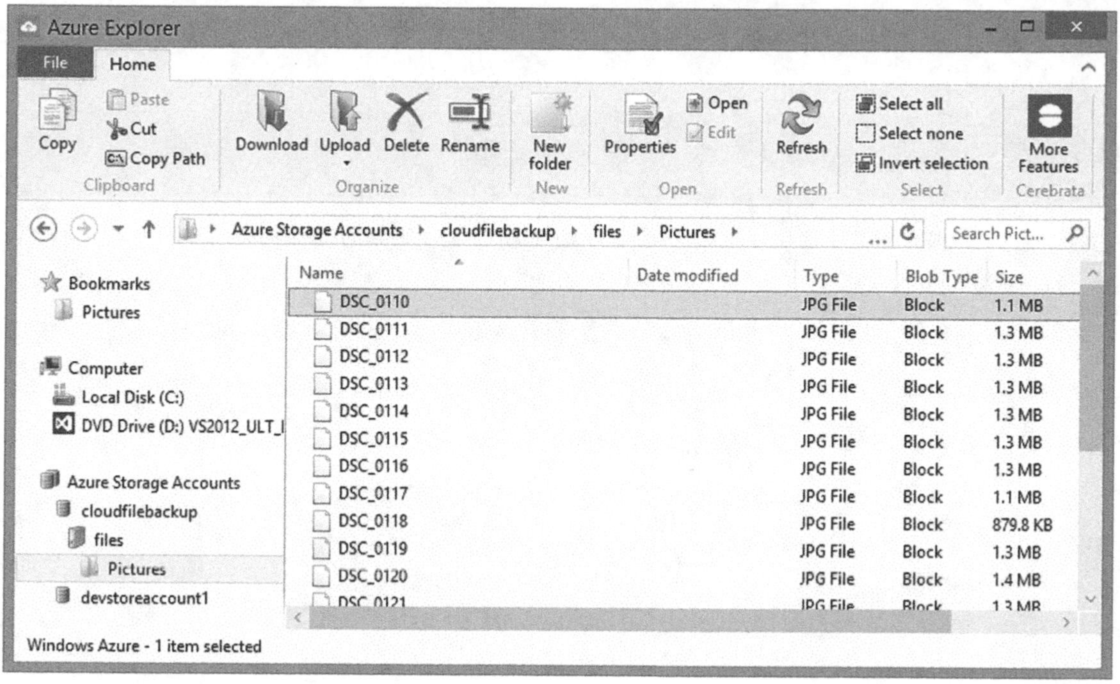

Figure 3-7. *Azure Explorer*

Summary

In this chapter, you learned about Azure Storage and its different types and services—Blob, File, Table, and Queue. Also, you learned how to use PowerShell to manage and maintain these services. Moreover, we discussed two Azure storage tools that you get use for free in order to manage Azure storage accounts and the services underneath.

In the next chapter, you start diving into the IaaS world by learning about Azure Virtual Network's capabilities as a preparation phase for Azure Virtual Machines. You will also learn how to use Azure PowerShell cmdlets to create, configure, manage, and maintain these networks.

CHAPTER 4

Virtual Machines Deployment and Management

We think everyone on the planet deserves to have their own virtual data center in the cloud.

—Lew Tucker, CTO, Sun Cloud Group

There is no doubt that virtualization technology plays a major role in cloud computing, whether private or public cloud. In fact, I'd say it's thanks to virtualization that the cloud runs at all, since it's the core of the Infrastructure as a Service (IaaS) part of the cloud.

I'm sure I don't have to tell you about the benefits of using virtualization. Instead, let's take a couple of minutes and think about it. What if the IaaS ran on top of the physical servers? I think you get my point.

This chapter addresses the virtual machine (VM) service in Azure and its respective PowerShell cmdlets. Mainly, it covers automating different tasks and operations using PowerShell.

Basic Operations: Azure Virtual Machine

The PowerShell fun is about to start, but let's warm up a little bit to get ready for it.

Since we're talking about virtual machines, the most basic operations are start, stop, and restart. Although these are basic cmdlets, they are very important, especially when you want to boot-up or shut down a number of VMs.

Again, this is just a stretching exercise. Before you start, make sure that your PowerShell session is authenticated and connected to Azure using either the `Import-AzurePublishSettingsFile` or the `Add-AzureAccount` cmdlets. Please refer to Chapter 2 for more details.

To start (turn on) a virtual machine, use the `Start-AzureVM` cmdlet.

```
## Start Azure VM (ASM)
Start-AzureVM -ServiceName DevTestFarm -Name WebApp01

## Start Azure VM (ARM)
Start-AzureVM -ResourceGroupName DevTestFarm -Name WebApp01
```

To restart (reboot) a virtual machine, use the Restart-AzureVM cmdlet.

```
## Restart Azure VM (ASM)
Restart-AzureVM -ServiceName DevTestFarm -Name WebApp01

## Restart Azure VM (ARM)
Restart-AzureVM -ResourceGroupName DevTestFarm -Name WebApp01
```

To stop (shut down) a virtual machine, use the Stop-AzureVM cmdlet. The stop cmdlet is a little different. Usually, when you shut down a virtual machine, Azure deallocates its reserved resources to free up hardware and network resources, which also saves you money. For example, the deallocation will free the IP address that was assigned to the virtual machine, so the next time you start the VM, it will acquire a new IP address—unless you assigned a static IP address to it.

Therefore, to make the resource allocated to the VM, use the -StayProvisioned parameter. Just don't forget that it will keep counting on you.

```
## Stop Azure VM (ASM)
Stop-AzureVM -ServiceName DevTestFarm -Name WebApp01 -StayProvisioned

## Stop Azure VM (ARM)
Stop-AzureVM -ResourceGroupName DevTestFarm -Name WebApp01 -StayProvisioned
```

Azure Virtual Machine (VM) Provisioning

Provisioning is the first basic step that everyone has to do to build a virtual machine. The UI looks very neat and attractive, especially with the new colorful Azure portal. It is nice for creating a single or a couple of virtual machines; however, it is not that easy when it comes to the bulk creation of VMs with advanced configurations.

Azure PowerShell provides two different ways to provision a new Azure VM. The first one is the quick provisioning that requires a minimal amount of information to create a VM; this is the PowerShell version of the Azure Portal. Provisioning a VM with the New-AzureQuickVM cmdlet has some limitations. For example, you cannot join a VM to a domain, add new endpoints, set time zones, or disable Windows Updates while creating the virtual machines.

The second way is more advanced; it requires defining each and every detail and configuration item to build a new VM. It is not complicated, but it needs a combination of two or more cmdlets together.

Provisioning a New Azure VM: Quick Configuration

Microsoft Azure allows you to choose from a set of virtual machine templates stored on Azure's gallery. Those templates are prebuilt images running different operating systems with different server products and software components.

Therefore, you need to know your image name to use it as a parameter within your PowerShell script. You can get the list of available images using the Get-AzureVMImage cmdlet. This cmdlet provides deeply detailed information on the image, which you cannot get from the Azure portal; the recommended VM size is an example.

The following line of code gets the list of available images, and then shows only the VM label, operating system, and recommended VM size.

```
## Get Azure VM images (ASM)
Get-AzureVMImage | Select Label, OS, RecommendedVmSize, PublishedDate | Sort PublishedDate | ft
```

You can also use the Get-AzureVMImage cmdlet in the Azure Resource Manager (ARM) module. The great thing about the ARM module is that it provides more capabilities and controls than the same exact cmdlets in the Azure Service Management (ASM) module. For instance, the only available parameter for the Get-AzureVMImage cmdlet in the ASM module is the -ImageName parameter. While in the ARM module, the Get-AzureVMImage cmdlet has the following parameters:

- -Location: Specifies the location of a VM image, such as Central US or West Europe, and so forth.
- -Offer: Specifies the type of a VM image offer, such as UbuntuServer or Oracle_Database_11g_R2. You can list the available VM image offers using the Get-AzureVMImageOffer cmdlet.
- -PublisherName: Specifies the name of the VM image publisher, such as Microsoft or Canonical. You can also use the Get-AzureVMImagePublisher cmdlet.
- -SKUs: Specifies the VM image SKU, such as JDK. You can also use the Get-AzureVMImageSku cmdlet.
- -Version: Specifies the VM image version, such as JDK_6 or JDK_7.

```
## Get Azure VM Images (ARM)

# Get Azure VM Image Publisher
Get-AzureVMImagePublisher -Location "West Europe" |  Group PublisherName | Select Name

# Get Azure VM Image Offer
Get-AzureVMImageOffer -Location "West Europe" -PublisherName Microsoft | Select Offer

# Get Azure VM Image Sku
Get-AzureVMImageSku -Location "West Europe" -PublisherName Microsoft -Offer "JDK" | Select SKUs

# Get Azure VM Image
Get-AzureVMImage -Location "West Europe" -PublisherName Microsoft -Offer JDK -Skus JDK_8

# Get Azure VM Image Details
Get-AzureVMImageDetail -Location "West Europe" -PublisherName Microsoft -Offer JDK -Skus
JDK_8 -Version 1.0.0
```

You have the image name. Now use the New-AzureQuickVM cmdlet to build your first Azure VM using PowerShell. The New-AzureQuickVM cmdlet is used for both Windows and Linux images with a lot of common parameters; however, a few parameters will vary according to the operating system that you are provisioning.

The following code sample shows how to provision a new Azure VM running on the Windows operating system using the New-AzureQuickVM cmdlet. In this example, you use the minimal number of parameters to provision a new VM. These parameters are as follows:

- -Name: Defines the name of the VM.
- -ImageName: Specifies which VM image will be used to provision the VM.
- -ServiceName: Enrolls the VM under an existing cloud service, or creates a new cloud service if the name doesn't exist.
- -Windows: Specifies that the VM will run on the Windows operating system.

- `-AdminUsername`: Defines the name of the local administrator.
- `-Password`: Defines the password for the local administrator with the `-AdminUsername` parameter.
- `-Location`: Specifies which region will host the VM.
- `-VNetName`: Specifies which virtual network the VM belongs to. (Azure virtual networks are discussed in more detail in Chapter 5.)
- `-AffinityGroup`: Chooses which affinity group will host the VM. The `AffinityGroup`'s properties include location, virtual network, and storage account. Thus, once you specify it, you won't have to identify parameters like `-Location` or `-VNetName`. Just remember that Microsoft's recommendation is to not use affinity groups anymore.
- `-InstanceSize`: Defines the size of the VM instance. You can refer to `https://msdn.microsoft.com/library/azure/dn197896.aspx` for a list of all the available sizes, or you can use the `Get-AzureRoleSize` cmdlet.

```
## Provision new Azure VM - Windows - (ASM)

# Windows Server 2012 R2, Datacenter Edition
$ImageName = "a699494373c04fc0bc8f2bb1389d6106__Windows-Server-2012-Datacenter-201412.01-en.
us-127GB.vhd"

New-AzureQuickVM -Windows -Name WebSrv01 -ServiceName "myPublicWebsite" -ImageName
$ImageName -Password Microsoft@123 -AdminUsername SherifT -Location "West Europe"
-InstanceSize Basic_A1
```

The previous code provisions a new VM from Windows Server 2012 R2 images. The VM named `WebSrv01` with size `A1` is part of the `myPublicWebSite` cloud service located in the West Europe datacenter and it has a local administrator called `SherifT`. Very simple and straightforward, isn't it?

Now let's provision another VM, but this time to run on a Linux operating system. You are going to use the same code from the previous example, but you will change two parameters.

Yes, you guessed right—the first parameter to change is `-Windows`, which is replaced with `-Linux`. The second parameter to change is `-AdminUsername`, which is replaced with `-LinuxUser`. Finally, don't forget to change the value of `-ImageName` with a Linux image.

```
## Provision new Azure VM - Linux - (ASM)

# SUSE Linux Server 12
$ImageName = "b4590d9e3ed742e4a1d46e5424aa335e__suse-sles-12-v20150213"

New-AzureQuickVM -Linux -Name WebSrv01 -ServiceName "myPublicWebsite" -ImageName $ImageName
-Password Microsoft@123 -Linuxuser root -Location "West Europe" -InstanceSize Basic_A1
```

The `New-AzureQuickVM` cmdlet is an ASM module cmdlet; it has no equivalent in the ARM module.

Provisioning a New Azure VM: Advanced Configuration

The other way to provision a virtual machine is to combine the `New-AzureVMConfig`, `Add-AzureProvisioningConfig`, and `New-AzureVM` cmdlets. Each one of these cmdlets handles a specific part of the provisioning process, and, of course, requires a different set of parameters.

The `New-AzureVMConfig` cmdlet takes care of creating the virtual machine configuration object, which is simply the configuration required to create the virtual machine itself. An example of the configuration is the VM name, image template, instance size, VM label, and so forth.

The `Add-AzureProvisioningConfig` cmdlet is always used with the `New-AzureVMConfig` cmdlet; it's responsible for adding the provisioning configuration to the virtual machine. The provisioning configuration defines the settings of the operating system running on the virtual machine. For example, you define the operating system—either Windows or Linux, the admin username and password, certificates, the time zone, endpoints, and so forth.

The last cmdlet is the `New-AzureVM` cmdlet that creates the virtual machine based on the config object and the provisioning config defined earlier using the `New-AzureVMConfig` and `Add-AzureProvisioningConfig` cmdlets.

The following code example shows how to combine these cmdlets to provision a Windows virtual machine. In this example, you provision a domain-joined Windows Server VM. You will find that some of the parameters are similar to the parameters of the `New-AzureQuickVM` cmdlet; however, some of them are new but look familiar, such as the following:

- `-WindowsDomain`: Provisions a Windows VM joined to the Active Directory domain.
- `-JoinDomain`: Specifies the name of the domain that the computer will join.
- `-DomainUsername`: Specifies the domain account that has access to join the machine to the domain. `-Domain` specifies the domain of the user account. Also, the `-DomainPassword` parameter specifies the password of the domain account.
- `-MachineObjectOU`: Specifies the FQDN of the organizational unit (OU) in which the computer object will be created.

As I said earlier, the combination of cmdlets gives you more config options when it comes to the operating system provisioning configuration, especially on Windows.

```
## Provision new Azure VM - Windows (Advanced) - (ASM)

# Windows Server 2012 R2, Datacenter Edition
$ImageName = "a699494373c04fc0bc8f2bb1389d6106__Windows-Server-2012-Datacenter-201412.01-en.
us-127GB.vhd"

# Create VM Config Object and Provisioning Config
$vm1 = New-AzureVMConfig -Name WebSrv01 -InstanceSize Basic_A1 -ImageName $ImageName

$vm1 | Add-AzureProvisioningConfig -AdminUsername "SherifT" -Password "P@ssw0rd"
-WindowsDomain -Domain "Corp" -JoinDomain "Corp.local" -DomainUserName "Administrator"
-DomainPassword "P@ssw0rd" -MachineObjectOU "OU=AzureVMs,DC=Corp,DC=local"
-DisableAutomaticUpdates -TimeZone "Pacific Standard Time"

# Create Azure VM using the previously created config object
New-AzureVM -ServiceName "myPublicWebsite" -VMs $vm1
```

On the other hand, to achieve the same task using the ARM module, you'd use the New-AzureVMConfig cmdlet to create the VM config object, and the New-AzureVM cmdlet to provision the virtual machine. You'd replace the Add-AzureProvisioningConfig cmdlet with the following cmdlets:

- Set-AzureVMSourceImage: Specifies the image that will be used to provision the VM.
- Set-AzureVMOperatingSystem: Sets the operating system properties and settings for the VM.
- Add-AzureVMNetworkInterface: Adds a network interface to the VM.

```
## Provision new Azure VM - Windows (Advanced) - (ARM)
# Create PSCredential Object
$Username = "Sherif"
$Password = "Master@123" | ConvertTo-SecureString -AsPlainText -Force
$Cred = New-Object System.Management.Automation.PSCredential($Username,$Password)

# Create VM Config Object
$vm1 = New-AzureVMConfig -VMName WebSrv01 -VMSize Basic_A1

# Configure VM Source Image
Set-AzureVMSourceImage -VM $vm1 -PublisherName MicrosoftWindowsServer -Offer WindowsServer
-Skus 2012-R2-Datacenter -Version 4.0.20150726

# Configure VM Operating system
Set-AzureVMOperatingSystem -VM $vm1 -Windows -ComputerName "WebSrv01" -ProvisionVMAgent
-EnableAutoUpdate -Credential $Cred

# Configure VM Network Interface
Add-AzureVMNetworkInterface -VM $vm1 -Id (Get-AzureNetworkInterface -ResourceGroupName
DevTestFarm -Name nic1).Id -Primary

# Provision VM
New-AzureVM -ResourceGroupName DevTestFarm -VM $vm1 -Location "West Europe"
```

As seen in the preceding example, ARM looks very similar to ASM from a conceptual point of view. However, ARM has more cmdlets with more parameters than ASM, which makes it more straightforward and direct. In this example, you replaced the Add-AzureProvisioningConfig cmdlet that has tons of parameters with the three cmdlets, each having three to five parameters. This is easy to remember and easy to use.

Another interesting cmdlet in the ARM module is the Add-AzureVMAdditionalUnattendContent cmdlet. Yes, it's what you were thinking! This cmdlet allows you to add extra information to the unattended Windows setup answer file (unattend.xml). Therefore, you are able to configure any operating system's settings, even if it's not available as a parameter.

Configuring Virtual Machine Endpoints

Endpoints define how the Internet inbound traffic will be directed to the virtual machine. Each endpoint has a public port, a private port, and a protocol.

The public port is used by Azure load balancers to listen for the incoming traffic from the Internet. The private port is used by the virtual machine to listen for incoming traffic from Azure load balancers. The protocol is either TCP or UDP.

As you can see, endpoints are pretty similar to the idea of networking address translation (NAT) or port forwarding capability in routers and managed switches (gamers and P2P masters can relate).

When you provision a new virtual machine, Azure creates default endpoints: RDP and PowerShell for Windows, and SSH for Linux. You can list all the configured endpoints for a specific virtual machine using the `Get-AzureEndpoint` cmdlet. The following example lists the endpoints for a VM called WI-DC-01.

```
## List configured EndPoints for VM (ASM)
# Create a VM object with the targeted VM config
$vm = Get-AzureVM -Name WI-DC-01 -ServiceName CloudFarm

# Retrieve the Endpoints list
$vm | Get-AzureEndpoint | Select Name, Protocol, Port, LocalPort
```

To add a new endpoint to an Azure VM, you use the `Add-AzureEndpoint` cmdlet. It is very straightforward: you just define the name, the protocol, and the public and private ports. The following example shows how to add an HTTPs endpoint to an existing Azure virtual machine.

First, you need to create a VM object of the target virtual machine. Then, you add the new endpoint configuration. Finally, you update the virtual machine config using the `Update-AzureVM` cmdlet.

```
## Add EndPoint to VM (ASM)
# Create a VM object with the targeted VM config (ASM)
$vm = Get-AzureVM -Name WI-DC-01 -ServiceName  CloudFarm

# Add endPoint and Update the VM
$vm | Add-AzureEndpoint -Name 'HTTPs' -Protocol TCP -LocalPort 443 -PublicPort 443 | Update-AzureVM
```

As an extra security, Azure endpoint provides access control list (ACL) capability so that you can permit/deny access to the endpoint based on the source IP address. To define the ACL rule for an endpoint, use the `-ACL` parameter with the `Add-AzureEndpoint` cmdlet.

To create a new ACL, you use the `New-AzureAclConfig` cmdlet. It is just an empty config object for the ACL, so it hasn't any parameter. Then, you use the `Set-AzureAclConfig` cmdlet to define the access rules. The `Set-AzureAclConfig` cmdlet has a different set of parameters, depending on which action you want to apply. You could add a rule, remove a rule, or update an existing rule.

The next example shows how to create a new ACL and add a rule to it.

```
## Create EndPoint ACL (ASM)
# Create new ACL Config Object
$acl = New-AzureAclConfig

# Set ACL Config - Add Rule
Set-AzureAclConfig -AddRule -ACL $acl -Action Permit -Order 1 -RemoteSubnet "10.10.0.0/8"
-Description "On-Premises vLAN"

RuleId       : 0
Order        : 0
Action       : Permit
RemoteSubnet : 10.10.0.0/8
Description  : On-Premises vLAN
```

In this example, you created the new ACL config object `$acl`. You then added a new access rule to permit all requests from the `10.10.0.0/8` subnet. Now you can just pass the `$acl` object to the `-ACL` parameter with the `Add-AzureEndPoint` cmdlet.

```
#Get VM object of VM "WI-DC-01"
$vm = Get-AzureVM -Name WI-DC-01 -ServiceName CloudFarm

#Adding Azure Endpoint to $vm
$vm | Set-AzureEndpoint -Name 'HTTPs' -Protocol TCP -LocalPort 443 -Port 443 -ACL $acl |
Update-AzureVM)
```

Virtual Machines Load Balancing

Network Load Balancing (NLB) plays a major role in any application serving users, such as web sites. In on-premises scenarios, you usually set NLB hardware in place or set up the NLB role in Windows Server.

In Azure, it's a little different; the hardware load balancers already exist as part of Azure's datacenter infrastructure. You just have to configure the NLB settings.

There are two load-balancing options in Azure, depending on the scenario you are looking for. To be more specific, it depends on the source of the incoming traffic—the Internet or an intranet.

For Internet incoming traffic, you use the load-balanced (LB) endpoints. However, for intranet incoming traffic, you use the internal load balancer (ILB) in cases like having back-end database servers that get traffic from front-end Internet-facing web servers.

Configuring NLB Using Endpoints

Using Azure endpoints for load balancing is very similar to adding an endpoint to an Azure VM; the difference is only in the parameter set that differentiates between the stand-alone and the load-balanced endpoints.

I'll explain by example. You have an Azure cloud service that hosts a web farm consisting of four Azure VM instances. You want to make sure that incoming traffic is distributed among the four VMs.

For the purpose of this task, you will use the `Add-AzureEndpoint` cmdlet along with the following parameter set:

- `-Name`: Specifies a name for the endpoint rule.
- `-Protocol`: Specifies the endpoint protocol—either TCP or UDP.
- `-LocalPort`: Specifies the endpoint local port.
- `-PublicPort`: Specifies the endpoint public port to listen to the incoming Internet requests.
- `-LBSetName`: Specifies a name for the load-balanced endpoint that will be used by different VMs.
- `-ProbeProtocol`: Specifies the protocol for the load-balanced endpoint to be probed (checked), whether HTTP or TCP.
- `-ProbePort`: Specifies the port to be used by the probes; by default, the public port is used if this parameter is not defined.
- `-ProbePath`: Specifies the URI to be used by probes; it's used only with the HTTP probe protocol.

```
## Configure NLB EndPoints (ASM)
# Get all VMs within Cloud Service
$VMs = Get-AzureVM -ServiceName  CloudFarm

# Adding Load-Balanced Azure Endpoint to $VMs
$VMs | Add-AzureEndpoint -Name "LB-Http" -Protocol tcp -PublicPort 80 -LocalPort 80
-LBSetName "LB-WebFarm" -ProbePort 80 -ProbeProtocol "http" -ProbePath "/" | Update-AzureVM
```

In this code, the added load-balanced endpoint looks similar to the stand-alone endpoint. However, I am sure that you've noticed that few parameters start with the keyword `Probe`. The probe is what Azure uses to check the health of the endpoint and its resources to make sure that it's alive and operating. If a resource didn't respond before the probing timeout, then it gets out of the rotation to avoid sending a request to a resource that is down.

Azure VM endpoints have no cmdlets in the ARM module; the reason is that the service architecture changed entirely and endpoints are no longer part of VM configuration. The endpoints are now known as *NAT rules*. Network security groups configured as part of Azure networking have their own cmdlets, which will be covered in Chapter 5.

Working with Virtual Machine Data Disks

There are three different types of VM disks in Azure: the operating system disk, the temporary storage disk, and the data disk.

There is one operating system disk per virtual machine. It's a SATA drive and has a maximum capacity of 127 GB.

The temporary storage disk is non-persistent storage that's created automatically for applications and processes. Once you restart or shut down the VM, all data is removed.

The data disk is persistent storage that is used to store application data and user files. The data disks are registered as SCSI drives. To attach a data disk to a VM, you use the `Add-AzureDataDisk` cmdlet, which supports three different parameter sets.

Attaching an Empty Data Disk

In this scenario, you are creating a new empty data disk, which you will attach to an existing Azure VM. For the purpose of this task, you will use the `CreateNew` parameter set, which uses the following parameters:

- `-CreateNew`: Creates a new data disk.
- `-DiskSizeInGB`: The size of the data disk in gigabytes.
- `-DiskLabel`: Specifies a label for this data disk.
- `-LUN`: Specifies the LUN location for the data disk in the VM. You can choose a LUN value from 0 to 15.
- `-VM`: Specifies the VM to add the data disk to.
- `-MediaLocation`: Specifies the location of the Azure storage account's blob to store the data disk on. If you didn't use this parameter, then the default location is the VHDs container under the default storage account.

```
## Attaching Empty Data Disk to VM (ASM)
# Create a VM object with the targeted VM config
$vm = Get-AzureVM -Name WI-DC-01 -ServiceName  CloudFarm

# Attach new data disk and Update the VM
$vm | Add-AzureDataDisk -CreateNew -DiskSizeInGB 50 -DiskLabel "ISOs" -LUN 0 | Update-AzureVM
```

In the previous code, you created a 50 GB data disk labeled ISOs and you attached it to the WI-DC-01 VM on LUN 0.

The Add-AzureDataDisk cmdlet could be used in combination with the Add-AzureProvisioningConfig cmdlet to add the data disk while provisioning a new VM.

You can query the data disk information using the Get-AzureDataDisk cmdlet.

```
# Query Data Disks attached to VM (ASM)
$vm | Get-AzureDataDisk
```

The equivalent to the Add-AzureDataDisk cmdlet in the ARM module is the Add-AzureVMDataDisk cmdlet along with the following parameters:

- -Caching: Specifies the caching mode of the disk, either ReadOnly or ReadWrite.
- -DiskSizeInGB: The size of the data disk in gigabytes.
- -Name: Specifies a name for the data disk.
- -LUN: Specifies the LUN location for the data disk in the VM. You can choose a LUN value from 0 to 15.
- -VM: Specifies the VM to add the data disk to.
- -VhdUri: Specifies the location of the Azure storage account's blob to store the data disk on.
- -CreationOption: Specifies whether the disk will be created as an empty disk or an attached existing disk, or created from an image. The available values are Attach, Empty, and FromImage.
- -SourceImageUri: Specifies the URI of the disk when the creation option value is Attach.

```
## Attaching Data Disk to VM (ARM)
# Create a VM object with the targeted VM config
$vm = Get-AzureVM -ResourceGroupName DevTestFarm -Name WebSrv01

#Add Azure Data Disk
$diskLocation = https://mylabstorageaccount.blob.core.windows.net/vhds/datadisk1.vhd

Add-AzureVMDataDisk -VM $VirtualMachine -Name "disk1" -VhdUri $diskLocation -LUN 2 -Caching
ReadWrite -DiskSizeinGB 1 -CreateOption Empty

# Update the VM
Update-AzureVM -ResourceGroupName DevTestFarm -Name WebSrv01 -VM $vm1
```

Attaching an Existing Data Disk

The second scenario is importing an existing data disk to an Azure VM. For example, let's say that you have a problem with an OS disk in another virtual machine and you want to troubleshoot it. Thus, you can import it as a data disk in a different VM to fix it.

To import an existing data disk, you use the `Import` parameter set with the following parameters:

- `-Import`: Imports an existing data disk.
- `-DiskName`: Specifies the name of the disk to import from the default disk library.
- `-LUN`: Specifies the LUN location for the data disk in the VM. You can choose a LUN value from 0 to 15.
- `-VM`: Specifies the VM to add the data disk to.

Before you start the attachment process, you need to detach the disk from its original VM by using the `Remove-AzureDataDisk` cmdlet, as shown in the following example.

```
## Attach an Existing Data Disk to VM (ASM)
# Detach data disk from old VM
Get-AzureVM -Name oldVM -ServiceName CloudFarm | Remove-AzureDataDisk -Lun 2 | Update-AzureVM

# Create a VM object with the targeted VM config
$vm = Get-AzureVM -Name WI-DC-01 -ServiceName CloudFarm

# Import an existing data disk and Update the VM
$vm | Add-AzureDataDisk -Import -DiskName "myISOsVHD" -LUN 1 | Update-AzureVM
```

Importing a Data Disk from a Different Location

The last parameter set is `ImportFrom`, which is similar to the `Import` parameter set, but it is mainly to import a data disk from a specific blob in an Azure storage account. Therefore, you replace the `-DiskName` parameter with the `-MediaLocation` parameter, and, of course, change the parameter set from `Import` to `ImportFrom`, as shown in the following code sample.

```
## Importing Data Disk from different Location (ASM)
# Create a VM object with the targeted VM config
$vm = Get-AzureVM -Name WI-DC-01 -ServiceName  CloudFarm

# Import an existing data disk and Update the VM
$DiskLocation = https://mystorage.blob.core.windows.net/Disks/myISOsVHD.vhd

$vm | Add-AzureDataDisk -ImportFrom -MediaLocation -DiskLabel "myISOsVHD" $DiskLocation
-LUN 1 | Update-AzureVM
```

■ **Note** If you want to importantan Azure data disk that is attached to an Azure VM, you have to detach it from that VM first using the `Remove-AzureDataDisk` cmdlet.

As you've noticed, you have used the blob endpoint URI to specify which data disk to import to the WI-DC-01 VM instance. If the disk is attached to the VM, then you can get the disk location using the Get-AzureDataDisk cmdlet, as shown in the next example, or search the storage account and underlying containers and blobs using the Get-AzureStorageContainer and Get-AzureStorageBlob cmdlets, as discussed in Chapter 3.

```
## Getting URI of Data Disk Attached to VM (ASM)
$vm = Get-AzureVM -Name WI-SQL-01 -ServiceName  CloudFarm
$diskURI = Get-AzureDataDisk -VM $vm | Select MediaLink
$diskURI.MediaLink.OriginalString

https://mystorage.blob.core.windows.net/Disks/myISOsVHD.vhd
```

Moving On-Premises VM to Azure

One popular scenario, especially for the cloud-enabled infrastructure, is moving virtual machines between on-premises and cloud sites for migration, disaster recovery, or even testing. So instead of rebuilding the entire VM on Azure, you can simply upload your on-premises VM's VHD(s) to Azure and build the Azure VM using this uploaded disk. Thus, you have two steps to do here: upload and provision.

To upload a VHD file from on-premise to the Azure blob, you use the Add-AzureVHD cmdlet. To do the reverse, you use the Save-AzureVHD cmdlet to download an Azure disk from the blob to a local file. For a simple VHD upload, you use the -Destination and -LocalFilePath parameters, as shown in the following code.

```
## Moving On-Premises VM to Azure (ASM)
# Get the Azure Storage Account for the default Azure Subscription
$StorageAccountName = (Get-AzureSubscription).CurrentStorageAccount

# Specify Local VHD file path
$LocalVHD = 'D:\Hyper-V\Virtual Hard Disks\WebSrv01.vhd'

# Specify the URI for the Windows Azure Container
$Destination = 'http://' + $StorageAccountName + '.blob.core.windows.net/vhds/ WebSrv01.vhd'

# Move VHD file from local server to Azure Storage account blob
Add-AzureVhd -LocalFilePath $LocalVHD -Destination $Destination
```

This code uploads a fixed VHD to an Azure blob; however, if you want to upload a different disk, then you need to specify the base image for the disk by using the -BaseImageUriToPatch parameter. You might also use the -overwrite parameter to replace an existing disk. Finally, you can use the -NumberOfUploaderThreads cmdlet while uploading the VHD. The default number of uploader threads is 8.

Well, you have uploaded the VHD file successfully to Azure. Because it is still just a file, you need to register it as a disk using the Add-AzureDisk cmdlet in the Azure disks repository so that you can attach it to the Azure VM. To add it to the disks repository, you use the following parameters:

- -DiskName: Specifies the name of the disk that will appear in the repository. This is the name that is used with the Import parameter set in the Add-AzureDataDisk cmdlet.
- -DiskLabel: Specifies a label for the disk.
- -MediaLocation: Specifies the URI of the blob in the Azure storage account that stores the VHD file.
- -OS: Specifies that the disk is bootable and has an operating system. You select either Windows or Linux.

Let's register the disk you uploaded in the previous example.

```
#Add the VHD file to Azure Disks Repository
Add-AzureDisk -OS Windows -DiskName "WebSrv01" -MediaLocation $Destination
```

Perfect. Now you have the WebSrv01 disk in the repository. Finally, let's provision the VM using this disk. To do this task, you use the New-AzureVMConfig cmdlet. Yes, it's the same cmdlet that you used earlier to provision a VM from an image. The New-AzureVMConfig cmdlet has two parameters sets: ImageName and DiskName.

Both parameter sets are pretty similar; you just need to replace the -ImageName parameter with the -DiskName parameter, as shown in the following example.

```
#Create VM Config Object with DiskName parameter set
$vm1 = New-AzureVMConfig -Name WebSrv01 -InstanceSize Basic_A1 -DiskName "WebSrv01"

#Create Azure VM using the previously created config object
New-AzureVM -ServiceName "myPublicWebsite" -VMs $vm1
```

Well done. The virtual machine is being provisioned and it will be ready in a couple of minutes.

Azure VM Images

Although Azure has a huge number of VM images (523 at the moment I'm writing these lines), it is still not enough. Azure VM images are very generic, but your company may require something that is customized. Therefore, Azure allows you to build your own custom images.

There are two ways to build a custom image: the first way is to capture an existing Azure VM and the second way is to use an OS VHD.

Creating a VM Image from an Existing VM

The process is very simple: you build a virtual machine using one of the existing images, and then you customize it to match your business needs and requirements. Lastly, you capture the new state of the VM with customization as a standard VM image.

To capture an existing VM, you use the Save-AzureVMImage cmdlet. This captures and saves the image of a stopped VM, and then deletes the source VM.

Before starting the capturing process, make sure to generalize your operating system by using SysPrep for Windows, or waagent for Linux.

```
## Create Azure VM Image (ASM)
Save-AzureVMImage -ServiceName CloudWebFarm -Name WebSrv01 -ImageName "WebSrvImage"
-ImageLabel "Corp Web Server Image" -OSState Generalized
```

In this code, you've captured the VM WebSrv01 under the CloudWebFarm cloud service, and then saved it to a new VM image called WebSrvImage.

The same cmdlet is available in the ARM module but with different parameters, as usual. After generalizing the operating system, you mark the VM as generalized using the `Set-AzureVM` cmdlet, as shown in the following example.

```
## Create Azure VM Image (ARM)
# Mark the VM as generalized
Set-AzureVM -ResourceGroupName CloudWebFarm -Name WebSrv01 -Generalized

# Capture the VM as VM Image
Save-AzureVMImage -ResourceGroupName CloudWebFarm -VMName WebSrv01 -VHDNamePrefix
VM01 -DestinationContainerName "VMImages"
```

Creating a VM Image from a VHD

Unlike the first method, you can build your own VM locally on Hyper-V and generalize the operating system, and then upload the VHD to Azure using the `Add-AzureVhd` cmdlet. Finally, you add it to the images repository using the `Add-AzureVMImage` cmdlet.

```
## Creating VM Image from VHD (ASM)
#Specify Local VHD file path
$LocalVHD = 'D:\Hyper-V\Virtual Hard Disks\WebSrv01.vhd'

#Specify the URI for the Windows Azure Container
$Destination = 'http://' + $StorageAccountName + '.blob.core.windows.net/vhds/ WebSrv01.vhd'

#Move VHD file from local server to Azure Storage account blob
Add-AzureVhd -LocalFilePath $LocalVHD -Destination $Destination

#Build VM image using vhd
Add-AzureVMImage -ImageName  WebSrvImage -Label "Corp Web Server Image" -OS Windows
-MediaLocation $Destination -PublishedDate (Get-Date)
```

Once you build the image, you might want to add or modify its properties. Using the `Update-AzureVMImage` cmdlet, you are able to update the following properties:

- ImageName
- Label
- EULA
- Description
- ImageFamily
- PublishedDate
- PrivacyUri
- RecommendedVMSize
- DiskConfig
- Language
- IconUri
- DontShowInGui

Generating an Azure VM RDP File

Remote Desktop Protocol (RDP) is a very important tool for managing your VM, especially if it is hosted on a remote datacenter like the cloud. Azure configures the RDP endpoint by default for each VM. There is a button on the Azure portal that allows you to save an RDP file (`*.rdp`), which has required information like the hostname and ports.

Very cool, huh? It's cool if you want to get the RDP file for one VM, but when it comes to getting the files for a number of VMs under one subscription, trust me, it gets boring very fast. Doing it in PowerShell is cooler. Azure PowerShell has the `Get-AzureRemoteDesktopFile` cmdlet that gets the RDP file for a selected VM.

In the following example, you use the cmdlet to save the RDP files for all VMs under a specific cloud service.

```
$VMs = Get-AzureVM -ServiceName CloudFarm

ForEach ($VM in $VMs)
{
    $FileName = $VM.Name + ".rdp"
    Get-AzureRemoteDesktopFile -ServiceName $VM.ServiceName -Name $VM.Name -LocalPath
    $home\Desktop\AzureRDPs\$FileName
}
```

In this code you used the `-LocalPath` parameter to specify where to save the RDP file. However, you can replace it with the `-Launch` parameter to initiate a remote connection instead of saving the file.

The same cmdlet is available in the ARM module with almost the same parameters. You just replace the `-ServiceName` parameter with the `-ResourceGroupName` parameter.

Exporting and Importing Azure Virtual Machines

How many times you have deleted and rebuilt a virtual machine because you placed it in the wrong cloud service? C'mon, don't be shy. You are not alone. This happens all the time, but thankfully PowerShell covers us. The problem is not in rebuilding the VM, but in discovering a mistake at a later stage—after finishing all the setup and configuration.

As another scenario, let's say that you have a virtual machine deployed in the Dev & Test cloud service, and you want to move it to the production cloud service without rebuilding the entire VM from scratch.

The `Export-AzureVM` cmdlet allows you to export the VM state that includes the configurations and settings of the VM. Then, using the `Import-AzureVM` cmdlet, you can import again to rebuild this VM, but under a different cloud service.

The following example shows these cmdlets moving VMs between two different cloud services.

First, you need to export the VM state using the `Export-AzureVM` cmdlet.

```
#Exporting Azure VMs State
$VMs = Get-AzureVM -ServiceName 'DevTestFarm'

ForEach ($VM in $VMs)
{
    $FileName = $VM.Name + "_VMState.xml"

    Export-AzureVM -ServiceName $VM.ServiceName -Name $VM.Name -Path $home\Desktop\VMs\$FileName
}
```

Since you are importing virtual machines that already exist, to avoid conflicts and errors during the import process, you need to remove those VMs before moving to the next step. You use the Remove-AzureVM cmdlet to remove a virtual machine.

You can add it within the ForEach loop just after the Export-AzureVM line. Thus, the new code should looks like the following.

```
#Exporting Azure VMs State
$VMs = Get-AzureVM -ServiceName 'DevTestFarm'

ForEach ($VM in $VMs)
{
    $FileName = $VM.Name + "_VMState.xml"

    Export-AzureVM -ServiceName $VM.ServiceName -Name $VM.Name -Path $home\Desktop\
VMs\$FileName

    #Removing the VM without Deleting VHD
    Remove-AzureVM -ServiceName $VM.ServiceName -Name $VM.Name
}
```

■ **Note** Removing the virtual machine only removes the VM object without deleting the virtual machine's disks, unless you use the -DeleteVHD parameter. Keep in mind that Import-AzureVM is just creating a new VM object using the exported virtual machine's disk.

Finally, import the VM's state file using the Import-AzureVM cmdlet, and build the virtual machine using the New-AzureVM cmdlet.

```
#Importing Azure VMs States
$VMs = Get-ChildItem $home\Desktop\VMs\

ForEach ($VM in $VMs)
{
    Import-AzureVM -Path $VM.Name | New-AzureVM -ServiceName 'ProductionFarm'
}
```

Azure VM Extensions

Azure VM Extensions are software components (add-ons) that extend the virtual machine's capabilities and simplify the management of IaaS resources. For example, there is a VMAccess extension that allows you to reset the password of the VM. VMCustomerScriptExtension allows the execution of a PowerShell script. There are so many more on the list, which grows every day. You can list all the available VM Extensions by using the Get-AzureVMAvailableExtension cmdlet.

```
#List all Available VM Extensions
Get-AzureVMAvailableExtension | Select ExtensionName, Description, Publisher,
Version | Out-GridView
```

How Does the VM Extension Work?

When provisioning a virtual machine, Azure installs a VM Agent that is responsible for handling the extension on the operating system. By default, the VM Agent is installed unless you manually disabled it while configuring the virtual machine.

The following line of code checks the `ProvisionGuestAgent` VM property to determine if the agent is installed or not.

```
## Check VM Guest Agent Status (ASM)
(Get-AzureVM -ServiceName 'DevTestFarm' -Name 'WebSrv01').VM.ProvisionGuestAgent

## Check VM Guest Agent Status (ARM)
(Get-AzureVM -ResourceGroupName 'DevTestFarm' -Name 'WebSrv01').OSProfile.
WindowsConfiguration.ProvisionVMAgent
```

Installing and Enabling a VM Agent

If you disabled the VM Agent, for any reason, while building your virtual machine and now you want to enable it again, you need to download and install the VM Agent package on the target virtual machine.

■ **Note** The VM Agent MSI Installer is available at `http://go.microsoft.com/fwlink/?LinkID=394789&clcid=0x409`.

Then change the value of the `ProvisionGuestAgent` property to `$True`, as shown in the following code.

```
#Get the VM object
$VM = Get-AzureVM -ServiceName 'DevTestFarm' -Name 'WebSrv01'

#Update the ProvisionGuestAgent Property
$VM.VM.ProvisionGuestAgent = $True

#Commit the changes on the VM
$VM | Update-AzureVM
```

Now the VM Agent is installed and the VM Extensions are ready to be enabled.

Working with VM Extensions

As I said, there are a lot of VM Extensions that serve different needs. If you have a virtual machine in which a VM Agent is installed by default, then you will find the BGInfo tool installed. The BGInfo on an Azure virtual machine is actually an Azure VM Extension called `VMBGInfo`.

You can query the virtual machine's installed VM Extension by using the `Get-AzureVMExtension` cmdlet, as follows.

```
#Listing all enabled VM Extensions
Get-AzureVM -ServiceName 'DevTestFarm' -Name 'WebSrv01' | Get-AzureVMExtension | Select
Name, Publisher, Version
```

If you want enable an extension for a virtual machine, then use the set-* cmdlet for this extension. For example, use the Set-AzureVMAccessExtension cmdlet to enable the VMAccess extension. You could also use the Set-AzureVMExtension cmdlet along with the ExtensionName, Publisher, and Version parameters.

```
#Enable VMAccess Extension
$VM = Get-AzureVM -ServiceName 'DevTestFarm' -Name 'WebSrv01'

$VM | Set-AzureVMAccessExtension | Update-AzureVM
```

This code enables the VMAccess extension of VM WebSrv01.

To use the extension capabilities in this case, reset the local administrator's password. You will use the Set-AzureVMAccessExtension cmdlet along with the respective parameters, which are -Username and -Password.

```
#Reset Local Admin Password using VMAccess Extension
$VM = Get-AzureVM -ServiceName 'DevTestFarm' -Name 'WebSrv01'

$VM | Set-AzureVMAccessExtension -Username SherifT -Password 'P@ssw0rd123' | Update-AzureVM
```

If you want to disable or uninstall the extension, use the same code and add the -Disable or -Uninstall parameters.

```
#Disable VMAccess Extension
$VM = Get-AzureVM -ServiceName 'DevTestFarm' -Name 'WebSrv01'

$VM | Set-AzureVMAccessExtension -Disable | Update-AzureVM

#Uninstall VMAccess Extension
$VM = Get-AzureVM -ServiceName 'DevTestFarm' -Name 'WebSrv01'

$VM | Set-AzureVMAccessExtension -Uninstall | Update-AzureVM
```

■ **Note** Uninstalling a VM Extension will totally remove the extension resource from the virtual machine; however, the Disable option keeps the resource installed by simply changing the state to disabled.

Perfect! Now, you have enabled the extension and you were able to reset the local admin's password. This concept applies to all VM Extensions.

Summary

In this chapter, you learned about one of the most important components of the Azure IaaS: Azure virtual machines (VM). The chapter covered almost all the PowerShell cmdlets available for Azure VMs. You learned about VM provisioning, VM endpoints, and load balancing, and how to work with VM disks. Then, you moved to more advanced topics, like moving VMs between on-premises and Azure, and building custom Azure VM images. The chapter closed by discussing Azure VM Extensions.

In the next chapter, you jump to another IaaS component: the Azure virtual network. You will learn about its different capabilities. You'll also learn how to use Azure PowerShell cmdlets to create and configure virtual networks and VPNs, and to manage and maintain virtual networks and other services and components.

CHAPTER 5

Virtual Networking Configuration

With the cloud, individuals and small businesses can snap their fingers and instantly set up enterprise-class services.

—Roy Stephan (Director of IT architecture and engineering, Intelligent Decisions)

You are still within the Infrastructure as a Service (IaaS) area in Microsoft Azure. Starting with storage in Chapter 3, then moving to virtual machines in Chapter 4, you are now here in Chapter 5 to learn about the virtual networking component.

An Azure virtual network (a.k.a. VNet) is a network overlay that can be configured for Azure VMs and other services to either connect them or isolate them. Moreover, Azure virtual networks can be used to extend on-premises datacenters and services to Azure via cross-premises connectivity, such as a site-to-site VPN.

This chapter sheds light on creating, configuring, and managing the Azure virtual network (VNet) service using PowerShell. As with the rest of this book, this chapter assumes that you already know how to configure an Azure VPN and that you want to learn how to do it using PowerShell.

Virtual Network Categories

Before telling you how to use PowerShell to create an Azure virtual network, it's important to understand the different virtual network configurations categories (or types) available in Azure.

Azure has three types of virtual networks: No VNet, Cloud-only VNet, and Cross-Premises VNet.

- **No VNet**: This is the network configuration for Azure services. You don't have to assign a virtual network to a service, and all the services remain isolated. For example, if you create a couple of virtual machines without choosing a virtual network, those virtual machines will still operate and have valid IP addresses, but they won't be able to communicate with each other.

- **Cloud-only VNet**: This is the virtual network you create for services hosted on Azure to connect them as if they are physically connected.

- **Cross-Premises VNet**: This type of virtual network configuration is used to connect different networks. It could be used for extending the on-premises network to Azure, or even connecting two Azure virtual networks. The latter scenario is known as VNet-to-VNet.

Cross-Premises VNet is similar to Cloud-only VNet, but it has a virtual network gateway to allow communication back and forth with other networks. Cross-Premises VNet supports three types of network connectivity.

- **Site-to-Site**: Site-to-Site VPN allows the local VPN device to communicate directly and securely with an Azure virtual network gateway. Once the connection is established, both local and Azure resources can communicate as if they are located in the same network.
- **Point-to-Site:** Point-to-Site VPN allows individual client devices to access an Azure virtual network. It's similar to using VPN to access a corporate network when you are at home or traveling.
- **ExpressRoute**: ExpressRoute allows you to have a direct secure private connection between an on-premises datacenter and an Azure datacenter without using a public Internet network. This means that you have a more secure and reliable connection with lower latency and faster speed than normal Internet connectivity; but keep in mind that this is also more expensive.

Perfect! Now you know the different types and configurations of an Azure virtual network. Let's move on to building and creating them.

Creating an Azure Virtual Network

To create a virtual network via PowerShell, use the `Set-AzureVNetConfig` cmdlet along with the `-ConfigurationPath` parameter.

The `-ConfigurationPath` parameter specifies the path of the network configuration file. The network configuration file is an XML-based file that ends with the `.netcfg` file extension and contains information about the Azure virtual network.

The following XML code is an example of an Azure virtual network configuration file. The code in the example creates a virtual network called `CloudVNet` with a `10.0.0.0/8` address space, and a `Subnet-1` subnet with an address space of `10.0.0.0/26`; it also has a DNS server called `CloudDNS` with an IP address of `10.0.0.4`.

```
<?xml version="1.0" encoding="utf-8"?>
<NetworkConfiguration xmlns:xsd="http://www.w3.org/2001/XMLSchema"
xmlns:xsi="http://www.w3.org/2001/XMLSchema-instance"
xmlns="http://schemas.microsoft.com/ServiceHosting/2011/07/NetworkConfiguration">
  <VirtualNetworkConfiguration>
    <Dns>
      <DnsServers>
        <DnsServer name="CloudDNS" IPAddress="10.0.0.4" />
      </DnsServers>
    </Dns>
    <VirtualNetworkSites>
      <VirtualNetworkSite name="CloudVNet" Location="West US">
        <AddressSpace>
          <AddressPrefix>10.0.0.0/8</AddressPrefix>
        </AddressSpace>
```

```
        <Subnets>
          <Subnet name="Subnet-1">
            <AddressPrefix>10.0.0.0/26</AddressPrefix>
          </Subnet>
        </Subnets>
        <DnsServersRef>
          <DnsServerRef name="CloudDNS" />
        </DnsServersRef>
      </VirtualNetworkSite>
    </VirtualNetworkSites>
  </VirtualNetworkConfiguration>
</NetworkConfiguration>
```

So, going back to creating a virtual network using PowerShell, save the previous XML code to a file with an .netcfg extension and pass it to the Set-AzureVNetConfig cmdlet, as follows.

```
#Creating Azure VNet (ASM)

Set-AzureVNetConfig -ConfigurationPath C:\Azure\VNet.netcfg

OperationDescription    OperationId                            OperationStatus
--------------------    -----------                            ---------------
Set-AzureVNetConfig     c20acb46-4c61-9c91-a410-7402a6d09bf3   Succeeded
```

The XML in the previous example is just a sample for basic network configuration. You can configure more options by adding more XML tags. For example, if you want to add a virtual network gateway, use the <Gateway></Gateway> tag. If the virtual network is point-to-site cross-premises, then use the <VPNClientAddressPool> </VPNClientAddressPool> tag within the gateway tag, as follows.

```
<VirtualNetworkSite>
        <Gateway>
                <VPNClientAddressPool>
                        <AddressPrefix>172.16.0.0/24</AddressPrefix>
                </VPNClientAddressPool>
        </Gateway>
</VirtualNetworkSite>
```

This is not everything. There are more tags to configure the local network site, the site-to-site VPN, the ExpressRoute, and other tags. You can read more about the Azure virtual network configuration schema and the network configuration elements in the MSDN article at https://msdn.microsoft.com/en-us/library/azure/jj157100.aspx.

If you don't want to rebuild your network configuration XML file from scratch, you can use the Get-AzureVNetConfig cmdlet to export the configuration of the existing VNet and customize this file.

```
#Exporting Azure VNET Configuration (ASM)

Get-AzureVNetConfig -ExportToFile C:\Azure\VNets\
```

Using the Get-AzureVNetConfig along with the -ExportToFile parameter, you are able to export the virtual network configuration to the .netcfg file, which can be used later to restore the network in case of accidental changes, or even to replicate the same virtual network configuration with your DR-site.

Although the Set-AzureVNetConfig cmdlet does the task and creates an Azure virtual network, the way it works is very old-fashioned, inefficient, and complicated. You know, it's not just fitting the smoothness of PowerShell. That's why I prefer to use the New-AzureVirtualNetwork cmdlet, which is part of the ARM module.

```
#Creating Azure vNET (ARM)
Switch-AzureMode AzureResourceManager

New-AzureVirtualNetwork -ResourceGroupName "DevTestRG" -Location "West Europe" -Name
"DevTestvNET" -AddressPrefix "10.0.0.0/16" -DnsServer "10.0.0.4"
```

You just created an Azure virtual network called DevTestvNET; its address prefix is 10.0.0.0/16 and it is located in the West Europe region. To add a network subnet to this virtual network, use the Add-AzureVirtualNetworkSubnetConfig cmdlet.

```
#Adding subnet to Azure virtual network (ARM)
$vNET = Get-AzureVirtualNetwork -ResourceGroupName "DevTestRG"  -Name "DevTestvNET"

$vNET | Add-AzureVirtualNetworkSubnetConfig -Name "subnet-1" -AddressPrefix "10.0.0.0/24" |
Set-AzureVirtualNetwork
```

To commit any changes to an Azure virtual network, use the Set-AzureVirtualNetwork cmdlet, as shown in the preceding code.

Working with Network Security Groups

By design, all network traffic between virtual machines in the same virtual network is allowed. For instance, if you have two subnets, Internal and DMZ, the network traffic is allowed in both directions between those subnets. You can control the traffic on the operating system level using Windows Firewall. So, you can allow only HTTPS traffic from the VMs in the DMZ subnet to the VMs in the Internal subnet. You can also deny Internal subnet access to the Internet.

With the network security groups, you can set network-level rules to control the network traffic between different subnets. Network security groups can allow or deny traffic based on direction (inbound/outbound), protocol, source port, source address, destination port, and destination address.

To create a network security group in classic mode (a.k.a. ASM), use the New-AzureNetworkSecurityGroup cmdlet, and use the Set-AzureNetworkSecurityRule cmdlet to configure the network security group rules.

```
#Creating Network Security Group (ASM)
$NSG = New-AzureNetworkSecurityGroup -Name 'DevTestNSG' -Location 'West Europe' -Label
'NSG for West Europe'

$NSG = Get-AzureNetworkSecurityGroup -Name "DevTestNSG"

$NSG | Set-AzureNetworkSecurityRule -Name rdp-access-rule -Action Allow -Protocol
TCP -Type Inbound -Priority 100 -SourceAddressPrefix '10.0.1.0/24'  -SourcePortRange
'*' -DestinationAddressPrefix '*' -DestinationPortRange '3389'
```

■ **Tip** For the -SourceAddressPrefix and -DestinationAddressPrefix parameters in ASM, you can assign the following values: INTERNET to refer to inbound/outbound traffic from/to the Internet, VIRTUAL_NETWORK to refer to inbound/outbound traffic from/to an Azure virtual network, and AZURE_LOADBALANCER to refer to inbound/outbound traffic from/to an Azure load balancer.

Once you have the network security group created and the security rules configured, you can assign this network security group to a network subnet using the Set-AzureNetworkSecurityGroupToSubnet cmdlet, or assign it to a VM using the Set-AzureNetworkSecurityGroupConfig cmdlet.

```
#Assign Network Security Group to Subnet (ASM)
$NSG = Get-AzureNetworkSecurityGroup -Name "DevTestNSG"
Set-AzureNetworkSecurityGroupToSubnet -NetworkSecurityGroup $NSG -VirtualNetworkName
'DevTestvNET' -SubnetName 'Internal'

#Assign Network Security Group to VM (ASM)
$NSG = Get-AzureNetworkSecurityGroup -Name "DevTestNSG"
$VM = Get-AzureVM -ServiceName DevTest -Name VS2015
Set-AzureNetworkSecurityGroupConfig -NetworkSecurityGroupName "$NSG" -VM $VM |
Update-AzureVM -VM $VM
```

To work with network security groups using the ARM module, use the New-AzureNetworkSecurityRuleConfig cmdlet to configure the security rules, and use the New-AzureNetworkSecurityGroup cmdlet to create the network security group.

```
#Creating Network Security Group (ARM)
$secRule1 = New-AzureNetworkSecurityRuleConfig -Name rdp-access-rule -Access Allow -Protocol
Tcp -Direction Inbound -Priority 100 -SourceAddressPrefix '10.0.1.0/24' -SourcePortRange '*'
-DestinationAddressPrefix '*' -DestinationPortRange '3389'

$NSG = New-AzureNetworkSecurityGroup -ResourceGroupName 'DevTestRG' -Location 'West Europe'
-Name 'DevTestNSG' -SecurityRules $secRule1
```

■ **Tip** For the -SourceAddressPrefix and -DestinationAddressPrefix parameters in ARM, you can assign the following values: INTERNET to refer to inbound/outbound traffic from/to the Internet, AZUREVIRTUALNETWORK to refer to inbound/outbound traffic from/to the Azure virtual network, and AZURELOADBALANCER to refer to inbound/outbound traffic from/to the Azure load balancer.

To assign a network security group to a subnet using ARM, use the Set-AzureVirtualNetworkSubnetConfig cmdlet.

```
#Assign Network Security Group to Network subnet (ARM)
$vNET = Get-AzureVirtualNetwork -ResourceGroupName "DevTestRG"  -Name "DevTestvNET"
Set-AzureVirtualNetworkSubnetConfig -VirtualNetwork $vNET -Name Internal -AddressPrefix
10.0.0.0/24 -NetworkSecurityGroup $NSG
```

You can modify existing network security rules by using the Set-AzureNetworkSecurityRuleConfig cmdlet.

User Defined Routes (UDR)

As I said in the preceding section, by design, Azure handles the network communication between virtual machines within virtual networks, as well as between virtual machines in different virtual networks, and even between virtual networks and the Internet.

Azure maintains a huge network infrastructure that automatically facilitates the traffic flow. You don't need to define your own routes because all is configured via a set of system routes that take care of the network communication. Although in some cases, you need to define control of the outbound traffic flow.

For instance, let's say that you have an application proxy or a firewall virtual appliance and you want to make sure that all traffic from your VM is being forwarded to this proxy or appliance. Or, another example is that you want Azure VMs to access the Internet via the on-premises infrastructure connected through a site-to-site VPN gateway. There are a lot of other scenarios in which you want to define your own routing table.

In Azure, the static routing table is known as *user defined routes* (UDR). To create a route table using classic mode (ASM), use the `New-AzureRouteTable` cmdlet, and the `Set-AzureRoute` cmdlet to define the static routes. One of the parameters that works with the `Set-AzureRoute` cmdlet is the `-NextHopType` parameter, which defines the type of the next hop in the route. This parameter accepts the following values: `VPNGateway`, `VNETLocal`, `Internet`, `VirtualAppliance`, and `Null`.

```
#Create Azure Route Table (ASM)
$RT = New-AzureRouteTable -Name DevTestRT -Location 'West Europe'

Set-AzureRoute -RouteName InternaltoFirewall -RouteTable $RT -AddressPrefix 10.0.0.0/24
-NextHopType VirtualAppliance -NextHopIpAddress 10.10.10.254
```

■ **Note** You can read more about UDR at `https://azure.microsoft.com/en-us/documentation/articles/virtual-networks-udr-overview/`.

Now, you have the route table ready. Let's assign it to an existing virtual network subnet using the `Set-AzureSubnetRouteTable` cmdlet.

```
#Assign Route Tablet to Subnet (ASM)
Set-AzureSubnetRouteTable -VirtualNetworkName DevTestvNET -SubnetName Internal
-RouteTableName DevTestRT
```

Alright, the route table is configured and assigned to a subnet. The last step is to make sure that whatever is marked as the next hop (a firewall virtual appliance in this case) is configured to receive traffic addressed to other destinations. To do so, you have to enable the IP forwarding for the appliance's VM.

```
#Enable IP Forwarding on the Virtual Appliance VM (ASM)
Get-AzureVM -ServiceName DevTestFarm -Name WAP | Set-AzureIPForwarding -Enable
```

To configure UDR using the ARM module, use the `New-AzureRouteTable` cmdlet to create a route table, the `New-AzureRouteConfig` cmdlet to define static routes, and the `Set-AzureVirtualNetworkSubnetConfig` cmdlet to assign the route table to a subnet.

```
#Create Azure Route Table (ARM)
$route1 = New-AzureRouteConfig -Name InternaltoFirewall -AddressPrefix 10.0.0.0/24
-NextHopType VirtualAppliance -NextHopIpAddress 10.10.10.254
```

```
$RT = New-AzureRouteTable -ResourceGroupName DevTestRG -Location 'West Europe' -Name
DevTestRT -Route $route1

$vNet = Get-AzureVirtualNetwork -ResourceGroupName DevTestRG -Name DevTestvNet

Set-AzureVirtualNetworkSubnetConfig -VirtualNetwork $vNet -Name Internal -AddressPrefix
10.0.0.0/24 -RouteTable $RT |Set-AzureVirtualNetwork
```

To enable IP forwarding on a virtual appliance in the ASM module, you can enable it on the VM directly. However, in ARM, you cannot do it directly; instead, you have to enable it on the NIC (network interface controller) assigned to the VM, as shown in the following code.

```
#Enable IP Forwarding on the Virtual Appliance VM (ARM)
$NICWAP1 = Get-AzureNetworkInterface -ResourceGroupName DevTestRG -Name NICWAP1

$NICWAP1.EnableIPForwarding = 1

Set-AzureNetworkInterface -NetworkInterface $NICWAP1
```

Azure Virtual Network Gateway

The difference between the cloud-only virtual network and the cross-premises virtual network is that the cross-premises requires a gateway to send traffic between virtual networks, whether on-premises or on the cloud. This communication could be in the form of a point-to-site VPN, a site-to-site VPN, or even an ExpressRoute. Therefore, until you create a virtual network gateway, you won't be able to set up a cross-premises virtual network.

The Azure virtual network gateway has three different SKUs: Basic, Standard, and High Performance. Each SKU has a different throughput, a maximum number of IPsec tunnels, and, of course, different prices.

Moreover, the virtual network gateway has two types: static routing (a.k.a. policy-based VPN) and dynamic routing (a.k.a. route-based VPN). Each of these supports different scenarios, based on the different SKUs. Therefore, make sure to consult the VPN gateway table at `https://azure.microsoft.com/en-us/documentation/articles/vpn-gateway-about-vpngateways/`.

Configuring an Azure Site-to-Site VPN

In this section, you will create an Azure site-to-site VPN that requires a virtual network gateway. This will help you to better understand the concept and how to use the respective cmdlets.

To configure a site-to-site VPN between Azure and your on-premises network, you have to have a compatible VPN device configured with a public IP address. The public IP address must be directly assigned on the VPN device interface and not located behind a NAT (network address translation). This VPN device could be a server running Windows Server 2012 R2 with a Routing and Remote Access Service (RRAS) role configured.

■ **Note** Refer to `https://azure.microsoft.com/en-us/documentation/articles/vpn-gateway-about-vpn-devices/` for a list of Azure-compatible VPN devices. You will also find a sample configuration file for each device.

Once you have the VPN device ready, you can start running the following commands to set up the site-to-site configuration. First off, make sure that you have an Azure virtual network with at least two subnets, one of them for the gateway network. Earlier in this chapter, you created a virtual network, DevTestvNET, with subnet Subnet-1; use the following code to add another subnet for the gateway.

```
#Add Gateway subnet to existing vNET (ARM)
$vNET = Get-AzureVirtualNetwork -ResourceGroupName "DevTestRG" -Name "DevTestvNET"
$vNET | Add-AzureVirtualNetworkSubnetConfig -Name "GatewaySubnet" -AddressPrefix
"10.0.1.0/24" | Set-AzureVirtualNetwork
```

■ **Note** The Virtual Network Gateway can only be created in a subnet with the name GatewaySubnet.

Azure "site-to-site" means that you have a cloud site that you want to connect to an on-premises (local) site. You already have the cloud virtual network that represents the cloud site. Now, you need to create the local virtual network to represent your on-premises network. To achieve this task, use the New-AzureLocalNetworkGateway cmdlet along with the -GatewayIpAddress parameter to specify the IP address of the local VPN gateway, and the -AddressPrefix parameter to specify your on-premises network address space.

```
#Create Local network site (ARM)
New-AzureLocalNetworkGateway -Name CorpNet -ResourceGroupName DevTestRG -Location 'West
Europe' -GatewayIpAddress '197.53.16.82' -AddressPrefix '192.168.10.0/24'
```

So far, you have the cloud virtual network and the local network ready and configured. The next step is to create the VPN gateway configuration and the Azure virtual network gateway using the New-AzureVirtualNetworkGateway cmdlet. Before you create the gateway, make sure that you have a public IP address to assign to this gateway. You will need this public IP address later when you configure the local VPN device. To create a public IP address, use the New-AzurePublicIpAddress cmdlet.

```
#Create Azure Public IP Address (ARM)
$GWPIP = New-AzurePublicIpAddress -Name GWPIP -ResourceGroupName DevTestRG -Location
'West Europe' -AllocationMethod Dynamic

#Get Azure Public IP Address (ARM)
Get-AzurePublicIpAddress -Name GWPIP-ResourceGroupName DevTestRG
```

Then, create the gateway IP address configuration using the New-AzureVirtualNetworkGatewayIpConfig cmdlet.

```
#Create Azure Gateway IP configuration (ARM)
$vNET = Get-AzureVirtualNetwork -ResourceGroupName "DevTestRG"  -Name "DevTestvNET"

$subnet = Get-AzureVirtualNetworkSubnetConfig -Name 'Gateway' -VirtualNetwork $vNet

$GWipconfig = New-AzureVirtualNetworkGatewayIpConfig -Name GWIPCONFIG -SubnetId $subnet.Id
-PublicIpAddressId $GWPIP.Id
```

Finally, create the gateway using the `New-AzureVirtualNetworkGateway` cmdlet.

```
#Create Azure Gateway
New-AzureVirtualNetworkGateway -Name S2SGW -ResourceGroupName DevTestRG -Location
'West Europe' -IpConfigurations $GWipconfig -GatewayType Vpn -VpnType RouteBased
```

At this stage, you are just one step away from having your site-to-site VPN ready. The last step is to create a connection between the local network site and the gateway that you just created by using the `New-AzureVirtualNetworkGatewayConnection` cmdlet.

```
#Create Azure VPN connection (ARM)
$Gateway = Get-AzureVirtualNetworkGateway -Name S2SGW -ResourceGroupName DevTestRG
$LocalvNET = Get-AzureLocalNetworkGateway -Name CorpNet -ResourceGroupName DevTestRG

New-AzureVirtualNetworkGatewayConnection -Name CorpNetToAzure -ResourceGroupName DevTestRG
-Location 'West Europe' -VirtualNetworkGateway1 $Gateway -LocalNetworkGateway2 $LocalvNET
-ConnectionType IPsec -RoutingWeight 10 -SharedKey 'powerShellRocks!'
```

Now, complete the local VPN device configuration. Use the public IP address that you created earlier for the Azure VPN gateway, and the secret share key that you created during the virtual network gateway connection.

Congratulations, you just finished building an Azure site-to-site VPN! It takes a couple of minutes for the connection to be established. Very well done!

You can validate that the status of your site-to-site is working, either from the Azure portal or by using the `Get-AzureVirtualNetworkGatewayConnection` cmdlet, which shows the status of the connection (connected or disconnected).

```
#Get Virtual Network Gateway Connection (ARM)
Get-AzureVirtualNetworkGatewayConnection -Name CorpNetToAzure -ResourceGroupName DevTestRG
```

Make sure to disconnect the gateway connectivity if you are not utilizing the connection, as it counts money as long as it's open. Also, keep in mind that the virtual network gateway costs money too. So, remove it if you no longer need it.

Azure Traffic Manager

Azure Traffic Manager is a cloud load-balancing service that allows you to control how user traffic (inbound traffic) will be distributed to your services' endpoints. The endpoints could be an Azure cloud service, an Azure web app, or other endpoints, such as an external web site hosted on a different Azure subscription.

Azure Traffic Manager supports three routing methods:

- `Failover`: In this method, you have two or more endpoints hosted in different Azure regions, and you want to use one of them as a primary or main endpoint that accepts all users' traffic, while the other endpoints act as backup in case the primary endpoint is not available.
- `Performance`: In this method, again, you have two or more endpoints hosted in different Azure regions. This time you want to provide the users with the best possible performance. In this case, Traffic Manager redirects the user's request to the endpoint nearest to the user's location in terms of low latency.
- `RoundRobin`: In this method, Azure Traffic Manager distributes user traffic equally across the available endpoints.

■ **Note** You can read more about Azure Traffic Manager routing methods at `https://azure.microsoft.com/en-us/documentation/articles/traffic-manager-routing-methods/`.

Creating an Azure Traffic Manager

Azure Traffic Manager has two main components: the Traffic Manager profile, which defines the properties of the traffic manager, and the Traffic Manager endpoints, which specifies the endpoints that serve the traffic manager.

Creating a Traffic Manager Profile

As mentioned, the Traffic Manager profile defines how the traffic manager should work. It defines properties such the domain, routing methods, monitoring protocols, monitoring ports, and so on.

To create a Traffic Manager profile, you use the `New-AzureTrafficManagerProfile` cmdlet with the following parameters:

- `-Name`: Specifies the name of the Traffic Manager profile.
- `-DomainName`: Specifies the domain name of the Traffic Manager profile. The domain must be a subdomain of `trafficmanager.net` such as `company123.trafficmanager.net`. You can check the availability of domain names using the `Test-AzureTrafficManagerDomainName` cmdlet.
- `-LoadBalancingMethod`: Specifies the routing method that will be used to distribute the traffic. It should one of these values: `Failover`, `Performance`, or `RoundRobin`.
- `-MointorProtocol`: Specifies the protocol to monitor the endpoint health status. It should be either HTTP or HTTPS.
- `-MointorPort`: Specifies the port to monitor the endpoint health status. It could be any integer from 1 to 65353.
- `-MointorRelativePath`: Specifies the relative path to the endpoint domain name to probe for health state.
- `-Ttl`: Specifies the DNS Time-to-Live (TTL) value. It accepts any value between 30 and 999999.

So, the final code in creating a new Azure Traffic Manager profile should look like the following:

```
#Create New Azure Traffic Manager Profile (ASM)
New-AzureTrafficManagerProfile -Name DevTestTM -DomainName 'DevTestLab.trafficmanager.net'
-LoadBalancingMethod RoundRobin -MonitorProtocol Http -MonitorPort 80 -Ttl 30
-MonitorRelativePath '/'

TimeToLiveInSeconds     : 30
MonitorRelativePath     : /
MonitorPort             : 80
MonitorProtocol         : Http
LoadBalancingMethod     : RoundRobin
Endpoints               : {}
```

```
MonitorStatus                 : Inactive
Name                          : DevTestTM
DomainName                    : DevTestLab.trafficmanager.net
Status                        : Enabled
```

To create an Azure Traffic Manager profile using the ARM module, you use the New-AzureTrafficManagerProfile cmdlet, similar to the one in the ASM module, along with the following parameters:

- -Name: Specifies the name of the Traffic Manager profile.
- -ResourceGroupName: Specifies the name of the Azure resource group to add this traffic manager to.
- -RelativeDnsName: Specifies the domain name of Traffic Manager profile. You can check the availability of the domain name using the Test-AzureTrafficManagerDomainName cmdlet.
- -TrafficRoutingMethod: Specifies the routing method that used to distribute the traffic. It should one of these values: Priority, Performance, or Weighted.
- -MointorProtocol: Specifies the protocol to monitor the endpoint health status. It should be either HTTP or HTTPS.
- -MointorPort: Specifies the port to monitor the endpoint health status. It could be any integer from 1 to 65353.
- -MointorRelativePath: Specifies the relative path to the endpoint domain name to probe for health state.
- -Ttl: Specifies the DNS Time-to-Live (TTL) value. It accepts any value between 30 and 999999.
- -ProfileStatus: Chooses the status of the profile to be created—either enabled or disabled. This is unlike the New-AzureTrafficManagerProfile cmdlet in ASM, which enables the profile by default.

```
#Create New Azure Traffic Manager Profile (ARM)
New-AzureTrafficManagerProfile -Name DevTestTM -ResourceGroupName DevTestRG -ProfileStatus
Enabled -Ttl 30 -RelativeDnsName 'DevTestLab' -TrafficRoutingMethod Weighted
-MonitorProtocol HTTP -MonitorPort 80 -MonitorPath '/'

Name                     : DevTestTM
ResourceGroupName        : DevTestRG
RelativeDnsName          : DevTestLab.trafficmanager.net
Ttl                      : 30
ProfileStatus            : Enabled
TrafficRoutingMethod     : Weighted
MonitorProtocol          : HTTP
MonitorPort              : 80
MonitorPath              : /
Endpoints                : {}
```

The output of the New-AzureTrafficManagerProfile cmdlet shows whether the status of the new profile is enabled. You can disable the Traffic Manager profile by using the Disable-AzureTrafficManagerProfile cmdlet. You can re-enable it using the Enable-AzureTrafficManagerProfile cmdlet.

Add a Traffic Manager Endpoint

In the preceding step, you created an Azure Traffic Manager profile, which means that you now have a traffic manager ready. However, it's not functioning yet because you don't have any endpoints configured.

To add an Azure Traffic Manager endpoint to the Traffic Manager profile, you use the Add-AzureTrafficManagerEndpoint cmdlet with the following parameters:

- -DomainName: Specifies the domain name of the endpoint.
- -Location: Specifies the location of the endpoint; it must be an Azure region. This parameter is required for endpoints of type Any.
- -Status: Specifies the status of the endpoint, whether enabled or disabled.
- -TrafficManagerProfile: Specifies the Traffic Manager profile to add endpoints to.
- -Type: Specifies the type of endpoint: CloudService, AzureWebsite, TrafficManager, or Any.
- -Weight: Specifies the weight of the endpoint. It accepts values from 1 to 1000. This parameter is required only for endpoints under the traffic manager configured for round-robin load balancing.
- -MinChildEndPoints: Specifies the minimum number of online endpoints in a nested profile to be considered online and healthy. This parameter is required when adding an endpoint of type TrafficManager.

```
#Adding Endpoint to Traffic Manager Profile (ASM)
$EP1 = 'website-ca.azurewebsites.net'
$EP2 = 'website-ea.azurewebsites.net'

$ATMP = Get-AzureTrafficManagerProfile -Name DevTestTM

Add-AzureTrafficManagerEndpoint -TrafficManagerProfile $ATMP -DomainName $EP1 -Type
AzureWebsite -Status Enabled

Add-AzureTrafficManagerEndpoint -TrafficManagerProfile $ATMP -DomainName $EP2 -Type
AzureWebsite -Status Enabled

Set-AzureTrafficManagerProfile -TrafficManagerProfile $ATMP
```

To add an Azure Traffic Manager endpoint using the ARM module, you use the Add-AzureTrafficManagerEndpointConfig cmdlet along with the following parameters:

- -EndpointName: Specifies the name of the endpoint.
- -EndpointLocation: Specifies the location of the endpoint; it must an Azure region. This parameter is required for endpoints of type ExternalEndpoints.
- -Target: Specifies the domain name of the endpoint.

- `-EndpointStatus`: Specifies the status of endpoint, whether enabled or disabled.
- `-TrafficManagerProfile`: Specifies the Traffic Manager profile to add endpoints to.
- `-Type`: Specifies the type of endpoint: `AzureEndpoints`, `ExternalEndpoints`, or `NestedEndpoints`.
- `-Weight`: Specifies the weight of the endpoint. It accepts values from 1 to 1000. This parameter is required only for endpoints under the Traffic Manager configured for `Weighted`.
- `-Priority`: Specifies the priority of the endpoint. It accepts values from 1 to 1000. A lower value represents a higher priority. This parameter is required only for endpoints under the Traffic Manager configured for `Priority`.
- `-MinChildEndPoints`: Specifies the minimum number of online endpoints in a nested profile to be considered online and healthy. This parameter is required when adding endpoint of type `TrafficManager`.

```
#Adding Endpoint to Traffic Manager Profile (ARM)
$T1 = 'website-ca.azurewebsites.net'
$T2 = 'website-ea.azurewebsites.net'

$ATMP = Get-AzureTrafficManagerProfile -Name DevTestTM -ResourceGroupName DevTestRG

Add-AzureTrafficManagerEndpointConfig -EndpointName "web-ca" -EndpointStatus Enabled -Target
$T1 -TrafficManagerProfile $ATMP -Type ExternalEndpoints  -Priority 1

Add-AzureTrafficManagerEndpointConfig -EndpointName "web-ea" -EndpointStatus Enabled -Target
$T2 -TrafficManagerProfile $ATMP -Type ExternalEndpoints  -Priority 2

Set-AzureTrafficManagerProfile -TrafficManagerProfile $ATMP
```

In the preceding code, you added two endpoints to an existing Traffic Manager profile by using the `Add-AzureTrafficManagerEndpoint` cmdlet in the ASM module and the `Add-AzureTrafficManagerEndpointConfig` cmdlet in the ARM module. Then, you used the `Set-AzureTrafficManagerProfile` cmdlet, for both ASM and ARM, to save and commit the changes to the traffic manager profile.

Modifying Azure Traffic Manager Profile Settings

The `Set-AzureTrafficManagerProfile` cmdlet could also be used to modify the properties of the Traffic Manager profile. You can change any of the Traffic Manager profile's properties except the domain name, which cannot be modified. The following examples show how to change the load balancing method for an existing traffic manager.

```
#Modify Azure Traffic Manager Profile Properties (ASM)
$ATMP = Get-AzureTrafficManagerProfile -Name DevTestTM
Set-AzureTrafficManagerProfile -TrafficManagerProfile $ATMP -LoadBalancingMethod Performance
```

Also, you can change the properties of the Traffic Manager endpoint using the Set-AzureTrafficManagerEndpoint cmdlet.

```
#Modify Azure Traffic Manager Endpoint Properties (ASM)
$EP1 = 'website-ca.azurewebsites.net'
$ATMP = Get-AzureTrafficManagerProfile -Name DevTestTM

Set-AzureTrafficManagerEndpoint -TrafficManagerProfile $ATMP -DomainName $EP1 -Status
"Disabled" -Type "AzureWebsite" | Set-AzureTrafficManagerProfile
```

Removing Traffic Manager

To remove Azure Traffic Manager, you have to remove the Traffic Manager profile and any configured Traffic Manager endpoints linked to this profile. Of course, you have to start by removing the endpoints, otherwise, you get an error message informing you that the Traffic Manager profile can't be deleted until you remove the endpoints.

To remove Traffic Manager endpoints, you use the Remove-AzureTrafficManageEndpoint cmdlet along with the -TrafficManagerProfile parameter to specify that the Traffic Manager profile has this endpoint, and the -DomainName parameter to specify the domain name of the endpoint.

```
#Removing Endpoint to Traffic Manager Profile (ASM)
$EP1 = 'website-ca.azurewebsites.net'
$EP2 = 'website-ea.azurewebsites.net'

$ATMP = Get-AzureTrafficManagerProfile -Name DevTestTM
Remove-AzureTrafficManagerEndpoint -TrafficManagerProfile $ATMP -DomainName $EP1
Remove-AzureTrafficManagerEndpoint -TrafficManagerProfile $ATMP -DomainName $EP2
Set-AzureTrafficManagerProfile -TrafficManagerProfile $ATMP
```

For the ARM module, you use the Remove-AzureTrafficManagerEndpointConfig cmdlet along with the -TrafficManagerProfile and -EndpointName parameters.

```
#Removing Endpoint to Traffic Manager Profile (ARM)
$ATMP = Get-AzureTrafficManagerProfile -Name DevTestTM -ResourceGroupName DevTestRG

Remove-AzureTrafficManagerEndpointConfig -EndpointName "web-ca" -TrafficManagerProfile $ARMP

Remove-AzureTrafficManagerEndpointConfig -EndpointName "web-ea" -TrafficManagerProfile
$ARMP -ProfileName $ARMP

Set-AzureTrafficManagerProfile -TrafficManagerProfile $ATMP
```

Now, you have a Traffic Manager profile without any endpoints. To remove the Traffic Manager profile, you use the Remove-AzureTrafficManagerProfile cmdlet along with the -Name parameter to specify the name of the profile.

```
#Removing Traffic Manager Profile (ASM)
Remove-AzureTrafficManagerProfile -Name DevTestTM -Force

#Removing Traffic Manager Profile (ARM)
Remove-AzureTrafficManagerProfile -Name DevTestTM -ResourceGroupName DevTestRG  -Force
```

At this stage, you successfully removed the Azure Traffic Manager, including the profile and endpoints.

Azure DNS

Azure DNS was in introduced in May 2015 during the Microsoft Ignite event. With this new feature, you can host domains in Azure. You are able to manage your DNS zones and records from a single place. It may sound normal to have DNS on Azure, because you probably have a DNS service with your domain. However, the real benefit of Azure DNS is when you have workloads or apps hosted on Azure. Azure DNS can seamlessly integrate with Azure-based services.

As shown in Figure 5-1, the Azure DNS is similar to a DNS hosted by any ISP, or even hosted locally. The DNS consists of zones that represents your domain names, and each DNS zone has record sets that represent the relative names of the domain, such as `www`, `mail`, or `sts`. Each record set has a name and type, where the type specifies the types of DNS records created within this record set. You also create a DNS record and assign it a value in the record set.

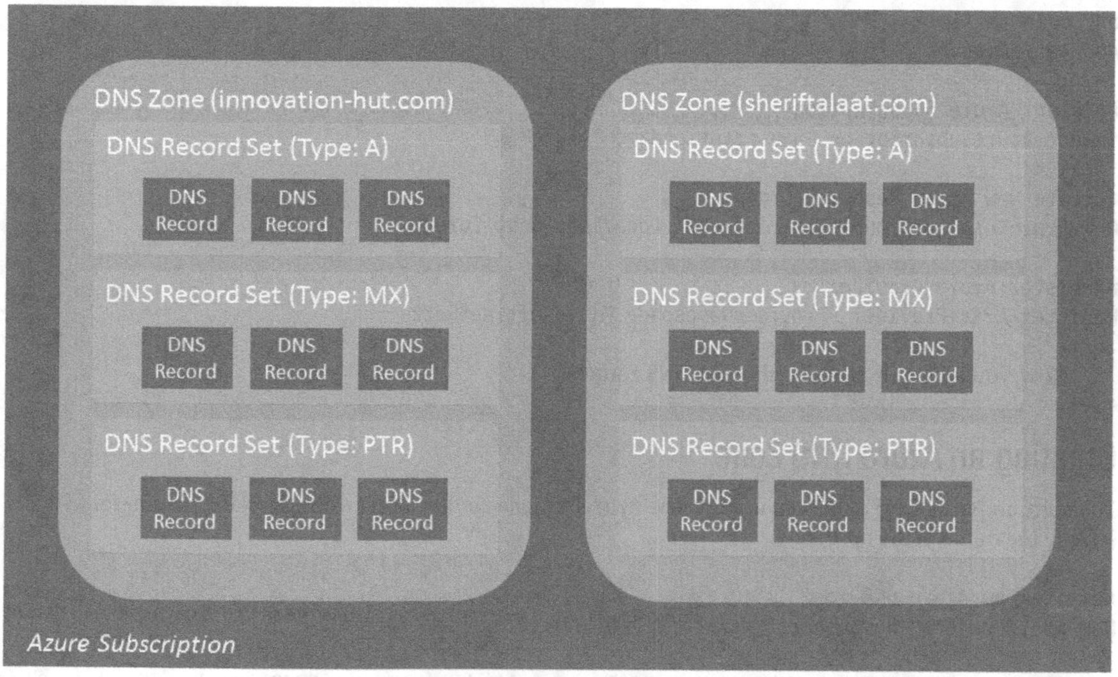

***Figure 5-1.** Azure DNS architecture*

You may find that the DNS record set and DNS record concepts are a little bit confusing; I totally agree with you. However, don't judge too quickly. Let's try the following scenario and then decide. In this scenario, you will create a DNS for a domain name, `sheriftalaat.com`; feel free to use a domain of your choice. For this domain, you need to use `www` and `mail` as relative names, so you need to create a DNS record set. Finally, you need to assign a value to those relative names; so whenever the user types **`www.sherif.talaat.com`** or **mail.sheriftalaat.com**, the request is redirected to the right destination. For the purpose of this task, you will create DNS records within the respective DNS record set.

Setting up Azure DNS

It is worth mentioning that an Azure DNS can be only managed via PowerShell. I know that some people will hate it, but personally, I believe that it's an advantage for Azure DNS. Anyway, Azure DNS uses the Azure Resource Manager (ARM), which means that you will be using the Azure PowerShell ARM module to manage Azure DNS.

Before creating your first DNS zone, you need to first log in to an Azure account using the `Add-AzureAccount` cmdlet, and then after a successful authentication, make sure to select the right Azure subscription (if you have more than one) using the `Select-AzureSubscription` cmdlet. Also, because you are using the ARM module, you should have an Azure resource group; if you don't have one, create one using the `New-AzureResourceGroup` cmdlet. Finally, since the Azure service is managed by the Microsoft.Network resource provider, you have to register your selected Azure subscription to use this resource provider. The provider registration is a one-time process, per subscription.

```
## Login to Azure
Add-AzureAccount

##Select Azure Subscription
Select-AzureSubscription -SubscriptionName "AzureMSDN"

#Create New Azure Resource Group
New-AzureResourceGroup -Name AzureRG -Location "West Europe"

#Register Azure Provider
Register-AzireProvider -ProviderNamespace Microsoft.Network
```

Now, you are ready to create the first DNS zone.

Creating an Azure DNS Zone

To create an Azure DNS zone, you use the `New-AzureDnsZone` cmdlet along with the `-Name` parameter to specify the name of the new zone.

```
#Create New Azure DNS zone
New-AzureDnsZone -Name sheriftalaat.com -ResourceGroupName AzureRG
```

The `New-AzureDnsZone` cmdlet creates a DNS zone and it also creates two DNS records:

- A start of authority (SOA) record, which appears at the root of every DNS zone.
- An authoritative name server (NS) record that shows which name servers are hosting the DNS zone. Make sure to delegate the domain to the Azure DNS to make it the authoritative source for name resolution in your zone. Otherwise, you have to specify the name server address for your zone explicitly.

To view the information in these records, use the Get-AzureDnsRecordSet cmdlet.

```
#Get Azure DNS Zone Record Sets
Get-AzureDnsRecordSet -ZoneName sheriftalaat.com -ResourceGroupName AzureRG

Name                    : @
ZoneName                : SHERIFTALAAT.COM
ResourceGroupName       : AzureRG
Ttl                     : 3600
Etag                    : 18cc728f-58d6-4bca-b72f-7ac38cdff640
RecordType              : SOA
Records                 : {[ns1-05.azure-dns.com,msnhst.microsoft.com,3600,300,2419200,300]}
Tags                    : {}

Name                    : @
ZoneName                : SHERIFTALAAT.COM
ResourceGroupName       : AzureRG
Ttl                     : 3600
Etag                    : 3d295814-f0ce-41ae-b842-99c22344e6a4
RecordType              : NS
Records                 : {ns1-05.azure-dns.com, ns2-05.azure-dns.net, ns3-05.azure-dns.org,
                           ns4-05.azure-dns.info}
Tags                    : {}
```

The record sets at the root of the DNS zone use @ as the name of the record set. To test this newly create DNS zone, you can use the nslookup.exe cmdlet or the Resolve-DnsName cmdlet.

```
#Resolve DNS zone
Resolve-DnsName -Name sheriftalaat.com -Type SOA

Name                    : ns1-05.azure-dns.com
QueryType               : A
TTL                     : 3600
Section                 : Additional
IP4Address              : 208.76.47.5
```

Alright, you have the DNS zone ready. Let's go to the next step and create DNS record sets.

Creating Azure DNS Record Sets and Records

As I mentioned earlier, the fully qualified name includes the zone name, whereas a relative name does not. Therefore, the relative record name with www in the sheriftalaat.com zone gives a fully qualified record named www.sheriftalaat.com; the record sets are what defines the relative name.

To create an Azure DNS record set, you use following: the New-AzureDnsRecordSet cmdlet along with the -Name parameter to specify the name of the record set; the -ZoneName parameter to specify the name of the DNS zone that will host this record set; -Ttl to specify the time to live for this record set; and -RecordType to specify the type of DNS records that will be created in this record set.

■ **Note** Use the `@` as the value for the `-Name` parameter to create a record at the root zone. It's very common for MX (mail exchanger) records.

For the DNS record types, you can choose from the following: A, AAAA, CNAME, MS, NS, PTR, SRV, and TXT.

```
#Create new Azure DNS Record Set
$rs = New-AzureDnsRecordSet -Name "www" -RecordType "A" -ZoneName "sheriftalaat.com"
-ResourceGroupName AzureRG
```

So far, you have an empty record set that you need to add records to. To add a DNS record, use the `Add-AzureDnsRecordConfig` cmdlet along with the `-RecordSet` parameter to specify which DNS record set to add the record to. In this case, you want to create a DNS record of type A, so you will add the `-Ipv4Address` parameter.

```
#Add A Record to DNS Record Set
Add-AzureDnsRecordConfig -RecordSet $rs -Ipv4Address 65.52.121.5
```

Although you added the DNS record, it won't reflect on the DNS record set unless you commit this change using the `Set-AzureDnsRecordSet` cmdlet.

```
#Commit changes to the DNS Record Set
Set-AzureDnsRecordSet -RecordSet $rs
```

Once you commit the change, you use the `Get-AzureDnsRecordSet` cmdlet once more to list all the records within the record set, or you query the record using the `Resolve-DnsName` cmdlet.

```
#List DNS records within a Record set
Get-AzureDnsRecordSet -Name www -RecordType A -ZoneName sheriftalaat.com -ResourceGroupName
AzureRG

Name                 : www
ZoneName             : sheriftalaat.com
ResourceGroupName    : AzureRG
Ttl                  : 3600
Etag                 : 68e78da2-4d74-413e-8c3d-331ca48246d9
RecordType           : A
Records              : {65.52.121.5}
Tags                 : {}
```

In the preceding example, I showed you how to create a record set with a DNS record. The next few code samples show you how to create the different types of record sets.

```
#Create new Azure DNS Record Set - Type AAAA
New-AzureDnsRecordSet -Name "www" -RecordType AAAA -ZoneName "sheriftalaat.
com" -ResourceGroupName AzureRG -Ttl 60 | Add-AzureDnsRecordConfig -Ipv6Address
"2607:f8b0:4009:1803::1005"  | Set-AzureDnsRecordSet
```

```
#Create new Azure DNS Record Set - Type MX
New-AzureDnsRecordSet -Name "@" -RecordType MX -ZoneName "sheriftalaat.com"
-ResourceGroupName AzureRG  -Ttl 60 | Add-AzureDnsRecordConfig -Exchange
"mail.sheriftalaat.com" -Preference 5 | Set-AzureDnsRecordSet

#Create new Azure DNS Record Set - Type CName
New-AzureDnsRecordSet -Name "test" -RecordType CNAME -ZoneName "sheriftalaat.com"
-ResourceGroupName AzureRG  -Ttl 60 | Add-AzureDnsRecordConfig -Cname "www.sheriftalaat.com"
| Set-AzureDnsRecordSet
```

As shown in the previous code samples, the same code is used for all the records. You just change the record set type along with the respective parameter that represents its value.

Updating an Existing Record Set

To modify an existing record within a record set, you retrieve the record using the `Get-AzureDnsRecordSet` cmdlet, modify the respective value, and commit the changes using the `Set-AzureDnsRecordSet` cmdlet. In this example, you modify the record that you created earlier for the `www` record set in the `sheriftalaat.com` zone.

```
#Update existing Record Set
$rs = Get-AzureDnsRecordSet -Name www -RecordType A -ZoneName sheriftalaat.com
-ResourceGroupName AzureRG
$rs.Records[0].Ipv4Address = "192.168.1.1"
Set-AzureDnsRecordSet -RecordSet $rs
```

Azure DNS uses Etags to handle concurrent changes to the same DNS resource. Each DNS resource has an Etag associated with it. Whenever a resource is retrieved, its Etag is also retrieved. When updating a resource, you have the option to pass back the Etag so that Azure DNS can verify that the Etag on the server matches. The `Set-AzureDnsRecordSet` cmdlet uses Etag checks to ensure that concurrent changes are not overwritten. Use the `-Overwrite` flat to suppress these checks.

Removing DNS Zone, Record Set, and Record

Removing an Azure DNS record is similar to updating it. The only different is that instead of updating the record, you use the `Remove-AzureDnsRecordConfig` cmdlet.

```
# Removing DNS Record
$rs = Get-AzureDnsRecordSet -Name "www" -RecordType AAAA -ZoneName imaginecupegypt.com
-ResourceGroupName DevTestRG
Remove-AzureDnsRecordConfig -RecordSet $rs -Ipv6Address "2607:f8b0:4009:1803::1005"
Set-AzureDnsRecordSet -RecordSet $rs
```

To remove a DNS record set, you use the `Remove-AzureDnsRecordSet` cmdlet.

```
# Removing DNS Record Set
Remove-AzureDnsRecordSet -Name "www" -RecordType A -ZoneName imaginecupegypt.com
-ResourceGroupName DevTestRG -Force
```

To remove a DNS zone, you use the Remove-AzureDnsZone cmdlet.

```
# Removing DNS Zone
Remove-AzureDnsZone -Name imaginecupegypt.com -ResourceGroupName DevTestRG -Force
```

Don't forget to remove the nested records in each resource before removing it. For instance, remove all the records in the record set, and then remove all the record sets in the zone.

Summary

Here, at the end of this chapter, I can say congratulations—you have learned about the last component of Azure IaaS covered in this book. In this discussion on Azure virtual networks (VNets), you learned about the different Azure virtual networks types and configurations. You learned how to create a virtual network. The chapter covered exporting and backup, and extending the on-premises networks to Azure virtual networks via an Azure virtual gateway. You also learned how to use Azure DNS to host your DNS services and serve your Azure-hosted workloads. Moreover, the chapter covered how to configure Azure Traffic Manager to control and distribute the traffic across different regions to provide a better end-user experience.

In the next chapter, you move to Azure and Platform as a Service (PaaS). You will learn about Azure web sites, and how to automate deployment and configuration using PowerShell.

CHAPTER 6

Deploying Azure Web Apps

Since the invention of the World Wide Web in 1990, web sites have been hosted on servers, or web servers to be more specific. A web site is hosted on either an on-premises server or a server hosted by a service provider. So it seems that cloud computing was here since day one of the Internet, and it's not entirely a new concept. It's the same idea of hosting a web site on a service provider's server, but it was developed and enhanced to expand from just a web site to virtual machines, virtual networks, databases, and so on. So, if you want to compare traditional hosting methods to today's cloud computing, think of them as similar to Infrastructure as a Service (IaaS) and Platform as a Service (PaaS).

Azure has both options: on-premises hosting, where you create a virtual machine and install a server operating system with an enabled web server role (like Windows Server with IIS or Linux with Apache) and service provider hosting. Azure Web Apps gives you this latter platform and takes care of the underlying infrastructure; you just manage the web site code and content.

This chapter focuses on the second option, which is Azure Web Apps. You will use PowerShell to deploy, manage, configure, and control Azure Web Apps.

Creating an Azure Web App

Azure Web Apps is a powerful service that allows developers and IT pros to smoothly build, deploy, and manage web sites and web apps. Azure Web Apps is not only for those developers who use .NET, but also those who use PHP, Python, Java, and NodeJS.

Azure Web Apps has a gallery—similar to VM gallery—that provides a set of web app templates to build your web apps, including blogs, forums, and wikis, but many other types as well.

Caution Don't get confused: Azure Web Apps is the new name of Azure Websites service. It began a long time after the release of Azure PowerShell. That's why it uses "web app" although the cmdlets still use "web site".

To create an Azure Web App using PowerShell, you use the `New-AzureWebsite` cmdlet along with the `-Name` parameter to specify the name of the web site you want to create. Also, you can use the `-Location` parameter to specify which region to host your web site; remember that you can get the list of locations that support web site services by using the `Get-AzureWebsiteLocation` cmdlet.

With the following example, let's create an Azure web app; let's name it SherifTalaatBlog.

```
## Create new Azure Website (ASM)
New-AzureWebsite -Name SherifTalaatBlog

Instances                        : {}
NumberOfWorkers                  : 1
DefaultDocuments                 : {Default.htm, Default.html, Default.asp, index.htm...}
NetFrameworkVersion              : v4.0
PhpVersion                       : 5.4
RequestTracingEnabled            : False
HttpLoggingEnabled               : False
DetailedErrorLoggingEnabled      : False
PublishingUsername               : $SherifTalaatBlog
PublishingPassword               : qjcOvGR8SxokoCxR6bkZXXXXXXXXXXXXXhe38AvdjeJWqM9enJN6grE
AppSettings                      : {WEBSITE_NODE_DEFAULT_VERSION}
Metadata                         : {}
ConnectionStrings                : {}
HandlerMappings                  : {}
Name                             : SherifTalaatBlog
State                            : Running
HostNames                        : {sheriftalaatblog.azurewebsites.net}
WebSpace                         : NorthEuropewebspace
SelfLink                         : https://waws-prod-db3-021.api.azurewebsites.windows.
net:454/subscriptions/7d2a1de7-b03b-460f-b752-fdeda1d7144c/webspaces/NorthEuropeweb
                                   space/sites/SherifTalaatBlog
RepositorySiteName               : SherifTalaatBlog
Sku                              : Free
UsageState                       : Normal
Enabled                          : True
AdminEnabled                     : True
EnabledHostNames                 : {sheriftalaatblog.azurewebsites.net}
SiteProperties                   : Microsoft.WindowsAzure.Commands.Utilities.Websites.
Services.WebEntities.SiteProperties
AvailabilityState                : Normal
HostNameSslStates                : {sheriftalaatblog.azurewebsites.net}
AzureDriveTraceEnabled           :
AzureDriveTraceLevel             : Error
AzureTableTraceEnabled           :
AzureTableTraceLevel             : Error
AzureBlobTraceEnabled            :
AzureBlobTraceLevel              : Error
ManagedPipelineMode              : Integrated
WebSocketsEnabled                : False
RemoteDebuggingEnabled           : False
RemoteDebuggingVersion           : VS2012
RoutingRules                     : {}
Use32BitWorkerProcess            : True
AutoSwapSlotName                 :
SlotStickyAppSettingNames        : {}
SlotStickyConnectionStringNames : {}
```

After successfully creating the web app, the New-AzureWebsite cmdlet feeds your PowerShell console's screen with information about the web app, including the hostname, .NET Framework version, PHP version, SKU, publishing username, FTP URL, and other important information.

To browse this newly created web app, you can use the hostname, which is <WEBAPP_NAME>.azurewebsites.net, or you can simply use the Show-AzureWebsite cmdlet, which opens the web app directly in the browser on the default web page (see Figure 6-1).

```
## Open Azure Website using PowerShell (ASM)

Show-AzureWebsite -Name SherifTalaatBlog
```

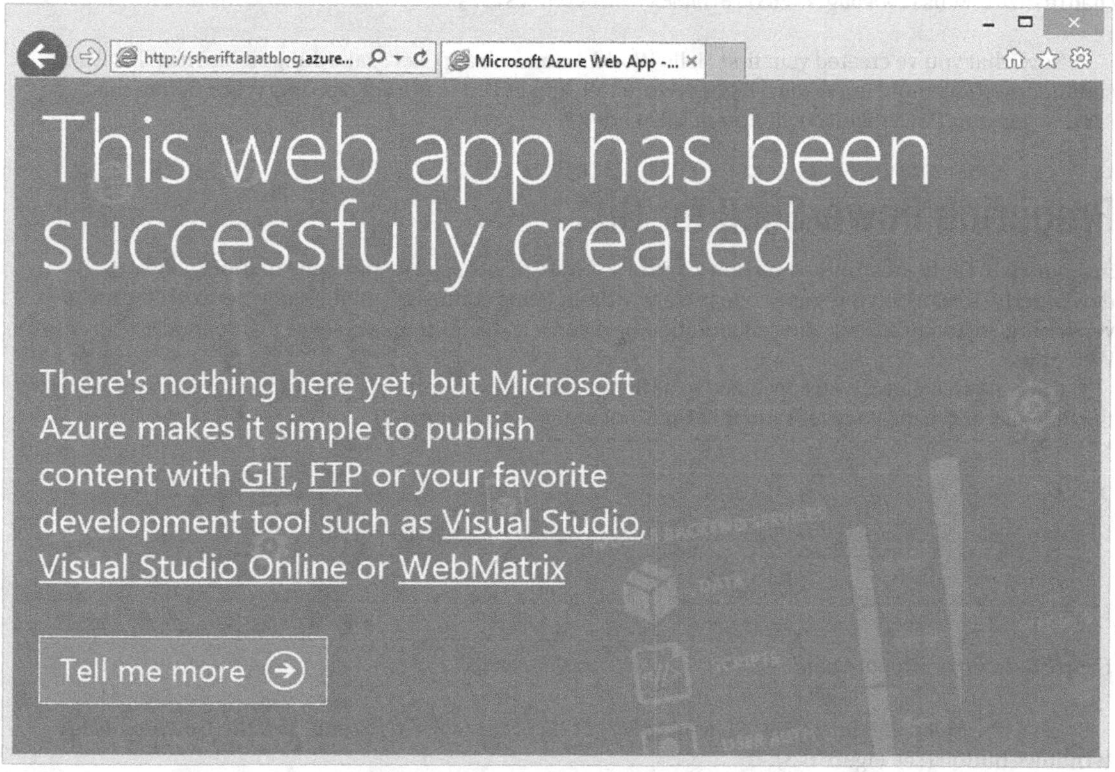

Figure 6-1. *Azure Web App default page*

You can also pipe the New-AzureWebsite cmdlet to the Show-AzureWebsite cmdlet to open the web app once you create it. But in this case, you will not get any information about your web app; however, you can still get it using the Get-AzureWebsite cmdlet.

```
New-AzureWebsite -Name <WEBSITE_NAME> | Show-AzureWebsite
```

An interesting thing happens with the Show-AzureWebsite cmdlet when you combine it with the Get-AzureWebsite cmdlet. This opens all the web apps in your Azure subscription in multiple tabs in an Internet browser.

Like any web app, the one just created might require some basic operations, such as restarting it, stopping it, or even removing it. I know that you can easily guess these cmdlets, but let me share them quickly. To stop an Azure web app, use the `Stop-AzureWebsite` cmdlet; to start an Azure web app, use the `Start-AzureWebsite` cmdlet; to restart an Azure web app, use the `Restart-AzureWebsite` cmdlet; and finally to remove an Azure web app, use the `Remove-AzureWebsite` cmdlet. These cmdlets have a common parameter, `-Name`, which you use to specify the name of the web app that you want to apply the action to.

Also, you can enable remote debugging for an Azure web app by using the `Enable-AzureWebsiteDebug` cmdlet along with the `-Version` parameter to define the Visual Studio version, either `VS2012` or `VS2013`. Use the `Disable-AzureWebsiteDebug` cmdlet to turn it off.

```
#Enable Remote Debugging
Enable-AzureWebsiteDebug <WEBSITE_NAME> -Version VS2013
```

Now, that you've created your first Hello World Azure web app. Let's take things to the next level and create something more interesting, like an Azure web app linked to the Git repository. But before that, you need to get your PowerShell environment Git-ready.

Preparing PowerShell for Git

In a nutshell, Git is a distributed version-control software that is used to allow one or more software developer(s) to work on the same code project without being connected on the same network. It provides versioning, history tracking, and collaboration between a team. So, it makes sense to integrate it with Azure Web Apps.

If you try to create a web app linked to a Git repository via PowerShell, you will get an error message; the first part of the message tells you that Git is not found (see Figure 6-2).

```
New-AzureWebsite : Git not found. Please install git and place it in your command line path.
At line:1 char:1
+ New-AzureWebsite -Name myWebsitewithGithub -GitHub -GithubRepository SherifTalaa ...
+ ~~~~~~~~~~~~~~~~~~~~~~~~~~~~~~~~~~~~~~~~~~~~~~~~~~~~~~~~~~~~~~~~~~~~~~~~~~~~~~~~~
    + CategoryInfo          : CloseError: (:) [New-AzureWebsite], Exception
    + FullyQualifiedErrorId : Microsoft.WindowsAzure.Commands.Websites.NewAzureWebsiteCommand
```

Figure 6-2. *Error Git not found*

Let's download and install Git. Go to `http://git-scm.com/downloads` and click the **Downloads for Windows** button (see Figure 6-3).

Figure 6-3. Download Git for Windows

Save the package and install it. It's a very straightforward installation that you can complete with a few clicks. Git is a command-line tool, which was clarified in the preceding error message: "and place it in your command line path." This placement is done as part of the installation process in which Git configures your command-line environment to understand Git commands.

However, since we are talking about PowerShell, you need to configure the PowerShell environment. To achieve this task, you use Posh-Git.

Posh-Git (or PowerShell-Git) is a PowerShell module that integrates PowerShell and Git to provide a Git-aware PowerShell environment in which you can use Git commands. You can get Posh-Git from `https://github.com/dahlbyk/posh-git`, or you get it directly from PsGet using the upcoming code.

In case you don't know about PsGet, it is repository for PowerShell modules that allows the streamlined installation of them; PsGet is available at `http://psget.net`.

To install Posh-Git via PsGet, you need to first install the PsGet module.

```
## Install PsGet module (ASM)
(new-object Net.WebClient).DownloadString("http://psget.net/GetPsGet.ps1") |
Invoke-Expression

#Install Posh-Git Module
Install-Module Posh-Git
```

At this stage, you should have successfully configured PowerShell to understand Git. Now, restart your PowerShell console to apply the new configuration. Let's do an initial configuration, which is basically helping Git to identify you by setting your name and e-mail address. Use the following commands to do that.

```
#Config Name
Git config --global user.name = "YOUR NAME"

#Config Email Address
Git config --global user.email = Email@Domain.com
```

Now, get ready to create an Azure web app associated with Git.

Create an Azure Web App with Git

In this scenario, you will create an Azure web app associated with a local Git repository. So, you will work on your project locally and push your files directly to the Azure web app from the local Git repository instead of uploading the files manually via FTP.

For the purpose of this task, you will use `New-AzureWebsite`, which is the same cmdlet that you used earlier to create the Azure web app, along with the `-Name` parameter. You'll also use the `-Git` parameter to specify that the web app will be linked to the Git repository.

In the following code sample, you will...

- Create a new directory to be used as a local Git repository using the `New-Item` cmdlet, and then move to this directory using the `Set-Location` cmdlet.
- Create (initiate) an empty Git repository using the `git init` command.
- Create an Azure web app using the `New-AzureWebsite` cmdlet along with the `-Git` parameter.

```
## Create new directory (ASM)
New-Item c:\Projects\Websites\AzureWebsiteWithGit -type directory | Set-Location

#Initiate git repository in the created directory
git init .

#Create Azure Website
New-AzureWebsite -Name WebsiteWithGit -Git
```

OK, your Git repository is now ready. What happened in the background while creating the web app? By using the `-Git` flag, Azure created a Git repository on the cloud linked to your web app and configured the URL of this remote Git repository on your local PowerShell environment. So, you push your files from the local repository to the remote one, and then the Azure web app pulls them from the remote repository.

Azure web apps that are linked to Git repositories must have a deployment credential so that you can push the files from the local repository to the remote one. Unfortunately, the `New-AzureWebsite` cmdlet doesn't create deployment credentials; but the Azure portal does. Therefore, before creating a web app with a Git repository via PowerShell, you should have at least one web app created using the Azure portal; otherwise, you get the error shown in Figure 6-4.

```
New-AzureWebsite : You must create your first web site using the Microsoft Azure portal.
Please follow these steps in the portal:
1. At the bottom of the page, click on New > Web Site > Quick Create
2. Type WebsiteWithGit in the URL field
3. Click on "Create Web Site"
4. Once the site has been created, click on the site name
5. Click on "Set up Git publishing" or "Reset deployment credentials" and setup a publishing username and password.
   Use those credentials for all new websites you create.
6. Back in the console window, rerun this command by typing "New-AzureWebsite <site name> -Git"
At line:3 char:1
+ New-AzureWebsite -Name WebsiteWithGit -Git
+ ~~~~~~~~~~~~~~~~~~~~~~~~~~~~~~~~~~~~~~~~~~
    + CategoryInfo          : CloseError: (:) [New-AzureWebsite], Exception
    + FullyQualifiedErrorId : Microsoft.WindowsAzure.Commands.Websites.NewAzureWebsiteCommand
```

Figure 6-4. *New-AzureWebsite error*

Once, you successfully execute the New-AzureWebsite cmdlet with a -Git flag, the directory you are browsing becomes a local Git repository. Note that [master] appears beside the directory path, like in the following example; this means that your web app files will be fetched to this folder, and any changes in this folder will be pushed to the remote repository.

```
c:\Projects\Websites\AzureWebsiteWithGit [master]>
```

You can list all the available remote repositories using the git remote show command, which in this case shows only one remote repository, called azure. You can also get the URL of the repository by adding its name to the same command, as shown in the following example.

```
PS \> git remote show azure

Password for 'https://admin@websitewithgit.scm.azurewebsites.net':
* remote azure
  Fetch URL: https://admin@websitewithgit.scm.azurewebsites.net/WebsiteWithGit.git
  Push  URL: https://admin@websitewithgit.scm.azurewebsites.net/WebsiteWithGit.git
  HEAD branch: (unknown)
  Remote branch:
```

You also get the repository URL; you can reset its deployment credentials on the Azure portal by going to Websites, selecting the desired web app with Git, and selecting the Deployments tab (see Figure 6-5).

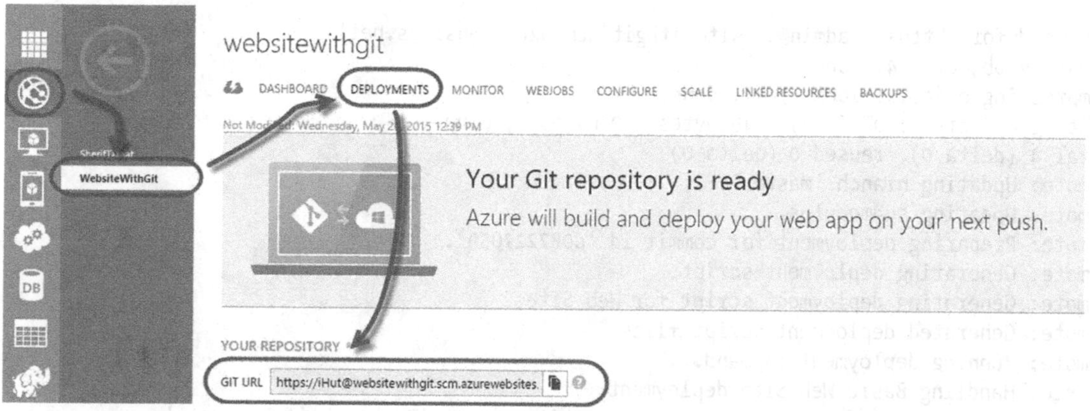

Figure 6-5. *Git URL on Azure portal*

Is it time to upload some files to your web app? Alright, let's do it. Do you remember your local Git repository? Copy your web app files to the directory labeled with [master]. Or you can just copy the following sample HTML page to Notepad and save it to default.htm under the same directory.

```
<html>
        <body>
                <h1>Hello World! PowerShell Rocks!</h1>
        </body>
</html>
```

Awesome. Let's add this new file to the local Git repository and then push it to the remote Git using the `git add .` command. Notice that `[master]` changes to `[master +1 ~0 -0]`, where `+1` indicates that you added 1 new file, `~0` indicates that no files were modified, and `-0` means that no files were removed.

```
c:\Projects\Websites\AzureWebsiteWithGit [master +1 ~0 -0]>
```

After adding files, you need to commit those changes on the repository using the `git commit` command. You might use the `-m` parameter to place a message on this commit task, so the final command should look like the following.

```
c:\Projects\Websites\AzureWebsiteWithGit [master +1 ~0 -0]> git commit -m"initial draft"

[master 5f21dbf] initial draft
 0 file changed, 1 insertion(+), 0 deletion(-)
```

Finally, push those committed changes to the remote Git repository using the `git push <Remote_GIT> <Local_GIT>` command.

```
c:\Projects\Websites\AzureWebsiteWithGit [master +1 ~0 -0]> git push azure master
```

The previous command prompts you to enter the password for the remote Git repository, which is the deployment credential for your Azure web app. Once you are authenticated, the files are pushed and you get the following log.

```
Password for 'https://admin@websitewithgit.scm.azurewebsites.net':
Counting objects: 4, done.
Compressing objects: 100% (3/3), done.
Writing objects: 100% (4/4), 346 bytes | 0 bytes/s, done.
Total 4 (delta 0), reused 0 (delta 0)
remote: Updating branch 'master'.
remote: Updating submodules.
remote: Preparing deployment for commit id 'd082227059'.
remote: Generating deployment script.
remote: Generating deployment script for Web Site
remote: Generated deployment script files
remote: Running deployment command...
remote: Handling Basic Web Site deployment.
remote: KuduSync.NET from: 'D:\home\site\repository' to: 'D:\home\site\wwwroot'
remote: Deleting file: 'hostingstart.html'
remote: Copying file: '.gitignore'
remote: Copying file: 'Default.html'
remote: Finished successfully.
remote: Deployment successful.
To https://admin@websitewithgit.scm.azurewebsites.net/WebsiteWithGit.git
```

■ **Note** Read more about Git commands at `http://git-scm.com/docs`.

If you go the Deployments tab again on the Azure portal for your web app, you can get to the deployment history; you can easily see the deployment that you just made from the message "initial draft" that you noted earlier while committing the changes (see Figure 6-6).

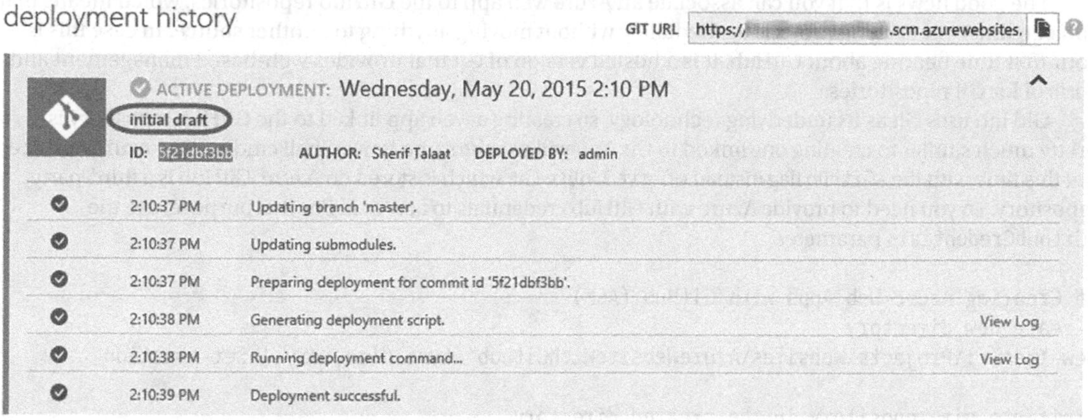

Figure 6-6. *Web site deployment history*

You can get deployment information using the `Get-AzureWebsiteDeployment` cmdlet. You can specify the name of the web app using the `-Name` parameter.

```
## Get Azure Website Deployment information (ASM)
Get-AzureWebsiteDeployment -Name <Azure_Website_Name>
```

Well, if everything went perfectly, your web app should look like Figure 6-7.

Figure 6-7. *Web site new default page after deployment*

Congratulations! The new web app is up and running. Using a local repository for the web app, along with a local repository for version control sounds like a cool idea. But, what about associating the Azure web app with your favorite repository that has a management interface? I think that sounds even cooler. Anyway, let's see what Azure Web Apps has in store for you in the next section.

Azure Web Apps and GitHub

In the previous section, you associated an Azure web app with a Git repository, which is hosted on Azure. You can easily see this by checking the remote repository that ends with `scm.azurewebsites.net`.

The good news is that you can associate an Azure web app to the GitHub repositories, which means that you can link your existing projects immediately without moving anything to another source. In case this is your first time hearing about GitHub, it is a hosted version of Git that provides web-based management and control for Git repositories.

GitHub uses Git as its underlying technology, so creating a web app linked to the GitHub repository is pretty much similar to creating one linked to Git. You will use the same PowerShell cmdlet, `New-AzureWebsite`, but this time with the `-Github` flag instead of `-git`. Unlike Git, which is stored on Azure, GitHub is a third-party repository, so you need to provide Azure with GitHub credentials to access it. For this purpose, use the `-GithubCredentials` parameter.

```
## Creating Azure Web Apps with GitHub (ASM)
#Create new directory
New-Item c:\Projects\Websites\AzureWebsiteWithGithub -type directory | Set-Location

#Initiate git repository in the created directory
git init .

#Github Credentials
$Cred = Get-Credential <GitHub_Username>

#Create Azure Website
New-AzureWebsite -Name WebsiteWithGithub -Github -GithubCrednetials $Cred
```

Perfect! You have created an Azure web app associated with GitHub. Now, you need to add the remote repository address to your PowerShell environment so that later on you can push files to it. Unfortunately, it is not like `-git`, which automatically configures the remote repository for Azure.

To define a new remote repository, use the `git remote add` command, as follows.

```
#Define new remote repository (a.k.a origin)
PS \> git remote add <Remote_Respository_Name> <https://github.com/user/repo.git>

PS \> git remote add GithubProject https://github.com/SherifTalaat/AzureWebsite.git
```

As I was saying, GitHub is an implementation of Git, so the same commands you used to push files in the previous section will work here too. However, this time it changes the remote repository from `azure` to `githubproject`, which means that you get authenticated against GitHub, not Azure.

```
#Add news file to the local repository
c:\Projects\Websites\AzureWebsiteWithGithub [master +1 ~0 -0]> git add .

#Commit changes
c:\Projects\Websites\AzureWebsiteWithGithub [master +1 ~0 -0]> git commit -m"update
homepage"

[master 5f21dbf] initial draft
 0 file changed, 1 insertion(+), 0 deletion(-)
```

```
#Push files from local "Master" to Remote "GitHubProject" Repository
c:\Projects\Websites\AzureWebsiteWithGithub [master +1 ~0 -0]> git push GithubProject master
Username for 'https://github.com': Github_Username
Password for 'https://Github_Username@github.com':
```

You should expect what happens next. The files are pushed from the local repository to the Azure web app via the GitHub repository in the middle. A few seconds later, your new web app is up and running.

Configuring Azure Web Apps

Until this point, you have learned how to create Azure web apps. However, the New-AzureWebsite cmdlet seems not to be enough since it only creates a web app and specifies its location. That's why there is the Set-AzureWebsite cmdlet to do the web app configuration.

The Set-AzureWebsite cmdlet sets configurations such as the app settings, connections strings, .NET Framework version, PHP version, default documents, handler mapping, and more.

■ **Note** You can read more about the Set-AzureWebsite cmdlet at https://msdn.microsoft.com/en-us/library/azure/dn495207.aspx.

Let's look at how you can set the app settings for an Azure web app. In this example, you define the SiteName and SiteTitle as appSettings and set their values. First, you define the settings and their values within a hash table, and then use these hash tables as input for the -AppSettings parameter.

```
#define appSettings in Hashtable
$AppSettings = @{"SiteName" = "Sherif Talaat"; "SiteTitle" = "Sherif Talaat's Blog"}

#Set App Settings
Set-AzureWebsite myWebSite -AppSettings $AppSettings

#Verify App Settings Configuration
(get-AzureWebsite WebsiteWithGit).AppSettings

Name                                Value
----                                -----
SiteTitle                           Sherif Talaat's Blog
SiteName                            Sherif Talaat
```

A more advanced example would define the connection string setting for a web app. You are still using the Set-AzureWebsite cmdlet, but this time with the -ConnectionString parameter. The reason I say "advanced" is because this time you won't create a string or a hash table, but an object—an object of type ConnStringInfo, and then you'll set its properties (name, connection strings, and type), and pass it to the -ConnectionString parameter.

```
#Create object of type ConnStringInfo
$ConnStr = New-Object ` Microsoft.WindowsAzure.Commands.Utilities.Websites.Services.
WebEntities.ConnStringInfo

#Set Name Property
$ConnStr.Name = "MyWebsiteConnStr"
```

```
#Set Connection String Property
$ConnStr.ConnectionString = 'Data Source=tcp:server_name.database.windows.net,1433;Initial
Catalog=<DB_NAME>;User Id=<Admin@Server>;Password=<Password>;'

#Set Type Property
$ConnStr.Type = [Microsoft.WindowsAzure.Commands.Utilities.Websites.Services.WebEntities.
DatabaseType]::SQLAzure

#Set Connection String
Set-AzureWebsite WebsiteWithGit -ConnectionStrings $ConnStringInfo
```

In this code, you used `SQLAzure` as a connection string type because you are using an SQL database hosted on Azure. You also use the following values: `SQLServer`, `MySQL`, and `Custom`.

Before moving on to another PowerShell cmdlet for Azure web apps, the last example in this area enables some logging features for the web app. You will use the following parameters with the `Set-AzureWebsite` cmdlet:

- `-DetailedErrorLoggingEnabled` to log detailed IIS errors.
- `-RequestTracingEnabled` to enable request tracing.
- `-HttpLoggingEnabled` to enable HTTP logging.

```
#Enable logging and requests tracing for Azure websites.
Set-AzureWebsite WebsiteWithGit -DetailedErrorLoggingEnabled $true
-RequestTracingEnabled $true -HttpLoggingEnabled $true
```

Well, since you've just enabled web app logging and request tracing, let's now learn how to get these logs using PowerShell.

Working with Web App Logs

In the last example, you enabled logging for a web app. You need to find a way to read them because they are very important; that's why you enabled them in the first place. Makes sense, huh? OK, there are two ways (or actually cmdlets) to get the log.

The first method is the `Save-AzureWebsiteLog` cmdlet along with the `-Output` parameter to save a local copy of the log on your computer.

```
#Save Azure Website Log (ASM)
Save-AzureWebsiteLog WebSiteName -Output C:\Website-Log.zip
```

The second method is the `Get-AzureWebsiteLog` cmdlet that connects you to the log streaming service to keep tracing the web app. Do you remember the request tracing that you enabled in the previous section? Now you can use it.

With the `Get-AzureWebsiteLog` cmdlet, you specify the name of the web app to be traced and the `-Tail` parameter to stream the log. You might use the `-Message` parameter to trace only logs that contain a specific string. Also, you can use the `-Path` parameter to specify from which path the log is retrieved. If you didn't use it, then the default path would be used, which is the root.

```
#Get Azure Website Log - Log Streaming
Get-AzureWebsiteLog WebSiteWithGit -Tail
```

Figure 6-8 shows a sample of log streaming for the WebSiteWithGit web app.

Figure 6-8. *Log streaming sample*

To try the `Get-AzureWebsiteLog` cmdlet to get some real tracing information, I suggest using the free load-testing tools available on the Internet; you should get some great information. I used the tool at `https://loadimpact.com` to generate the logs shown in Figure 6-8.

Another type of Azure Web Apps log is the application diagnostic log, which supports four log levels: `Error`, `Information`, `Verbose`, and `Warning`. To enable the application diagnostic log, you use the `Enable-AzureWebsiteApplicationDiagnostic` cmdlet along with the `-Name` parameter to specify the name of the web app and `-LogLevel` to specify which one of the four log levels to enable. You can store the log on the file system so that you can access via FTP or you can store it directly to Azure blob storage. The following code samples show how to achieve both tasks.

```
## Enable App Diagnostic Log - File System (ASM)
Enable-AzureWebsiteApplicationDiagnostic -Name WebsiteWithGit -LogLevel Verbose -File

## Enable App Diagnostic Log - Storage Account (ASM)
Enable-AzureWebsiteApplicationDiagnostic -Name WebsiteWithGit -LogLevel Verbose
-StorageAccountName mystorageaccount -StorageBlobContainerName logs -BlobStorage
```

Azure Web App Metrics

Are you familiar with the Monitor tab for a web app on the Azure portal? It's the one that has a graph so that you can keep an eye on specific web site metrics, like the number of requests, CPU time, average response time, and others. Of course, you know this. I am just refreshing your memory.

Well, the data is presented in a colorful graph, which can also appear on your PowerShell console using the `Get-AzureWebsiteMetric` cmdlet. This cmdlet allows you to get data on one or more metric(s) within a specific time period.

The following example shows how to get the metrics information of a specific web app during the last seven days.

```
#Getting Website Metrics Information (ASM)
$MetricsInfo = Get-AzureWebsiteMetric -Name WebsiteWithGit -StartDate (Get-date).addDays(-7)
-InstanceDetails

ForEach ($Metric in $MetricsInfo)
{
     $Metric.Data
}

Name                    : AverageResponseTime
Unit                    : Milliseconds
StartTime               : 5/23/2015 3:00:00 AM
EndTime                 : 5/30/2015 3:27:19 AM
TimeGrain               : PT1H
PrimaryAggregationType : Instance
Values                  : {Time:5/23/2015 11:00:00 AM, Total:667, Min:, Max:, Time:5/23/2015
6:00:00 PM, Total:671, Min:, Max:, Time:5/23/2015 7:00:00 PM, Total:0, Min:,
                          Max:, Time:5/28/2015 11:00:00 AM, Total:6151, Min:, Max:...}
```

You can also get information on specific metric(s) by specifying the metric name using the -MetricName parameter.

```
#Gettings Request & Cpu Time Metrics
$MetricsInfo = Get-AzureWebsiteMetric -Name WebsiteWithGit -StartDate (Get-date).addDays(-7)
-MetricNames @("Requests","CpuTime") -InstanceDetails

ForEach ($Metric in $MetricsInfo)
{
     $Metric.Data
}
```

If you don't know the name of the metric, or you know it but you don't know the equivalent value in PowerShell, then the following code gives you the list of available metrics.

```
#Getting Metrics Names
$MetricsInfo = Get-AzureWebsiteMetric -Name WebsiteWithGit

ForEach ($Metric in $MetricsInfo)
{
     $Metric.Data | Group Name | Select Name
}
```

Once you know which metric(s) you want to keep track of within a period, you can use the Get-AzureWebsiteMetric cmdlet along with Excel COM (Component Object Model) add-ins to generate a rich visual report, as shown in the following code. In this example, the script extracted the information for the CpuTime, Requests, and AverageResponseTime metrics. Then, it created a detailed Excel worksheet for each metric (see Figure 6-9).

```
## Exporting Web App Metrics to Excel Sheet
#Create object of the Excel.Application
$Excel = New-Object -comobject Excel.Application

#Make this instance visible
$Excel.visible = $True

#Create Excel Workbook
$ExcelWB = $Excel.Workbooks.Add()

$MetricsInfo = Get-AzureWebsiteMetric -Name WebsiteWithGit -StartDate (Get-date).addDays(-7)
-MetricNames @("Requests","CpuTime","AverageResponseTime")

    ForEach ($Metric in $MetricsInfo)
    {
        $Item = 1

        #Create 1 Excel Worksheet
        $ExcelWS = $ExcelWB.Worksheets.Item($Item)
        $ExcelWS.Name = $Metric.Data.Name

        #Define Report Title
        $ExcelWS.Cells.Item(1,1) = $Metric.Data.Name.ToString()
        $ExcelWS.Range("A1","B1").Cells.Merge()

        $ExcelWS.Range("A1","B1").Interior.ColorIndex = 41
        $ExcelWS.Range("A1","B1").Font.ColorIndex = 2
        $ExcelWS.Range("A1","B1").Font.Size = 18
        $ExcelWS.Range("A1","B1").Font.Bold = $True

        $ExcelWS.Cells.Item(2,1) = "Metric Start Date"
        $ExcelWS.Cells.Item(2,2) = $Metric.Data.StartTime

        $ExcelWS.Cells.Item(3,1) = "Metric End Date"
        $ExcelWS.Cells.Item(3,2) = $Metric.Data.EndTime

        $ExcelWS.Cells.Item(4,1) = "Metric Unit"
        $ExcelWS.Cells.Item(4,2) = $Metric.Data.Unit

        #cell background, font color, and boldness of the header
        $ExcelWS.Range("A7","E7").Interior.ColorIndex = 41
        $ExcelWS.Range("A7","E7").Font.ColorIndex = 2
        $ExcelWS.Range("A7","E7").Font.Bold = $True

        [reflection.assembly]::loadWithPartialname("Microsoft.Office.Interop.Excel")
        $xlConstants = "microsoft.office.interop.excel.Constants" -as [type]
        $ExcelWS.Range("B8","E10").HorizontalAlignment = $xlConstants::xlCenter

        #Metric Values Table Header
        $ExcelWS.Cells.Item(7,1) = "Time Created"
        $ExcelWS.Cells.Item(7,2) = "Total"
        $ExcelWS.Cells.Item(7,3) = "Minimum"
```

```
        $ExcelWS.Cells.Item(7,4) = "Maximum"
        $ExcelWS.Cells.Item(7,5) = "Count"

        $row = 8
        ForEach($v in $Metric.Data.Values)
        {
            #Fill the rows with Metric Values information
            $ExcelWS.Cells.Item($row,1) = $v.TimeCreated
            $ExcelWS.Cells.Item($row,2) = $v.Total
            $ExcelWS.Cells.Item($row,3) = $v.Minimum
            $ExcelWS.Cells.Item($row,4) = $v.Maximum
            $ExcelWS.Cells.Item($row,5) = $v.Count

            $row++
        }

        #Table Column Autofit
        $ExcelWS.UsedRange.EntireColumn.AutoFit()

        #Create new Excel Worksheet
        $ExcelWB.Worksheets.Add()
        $Item++
    }
```

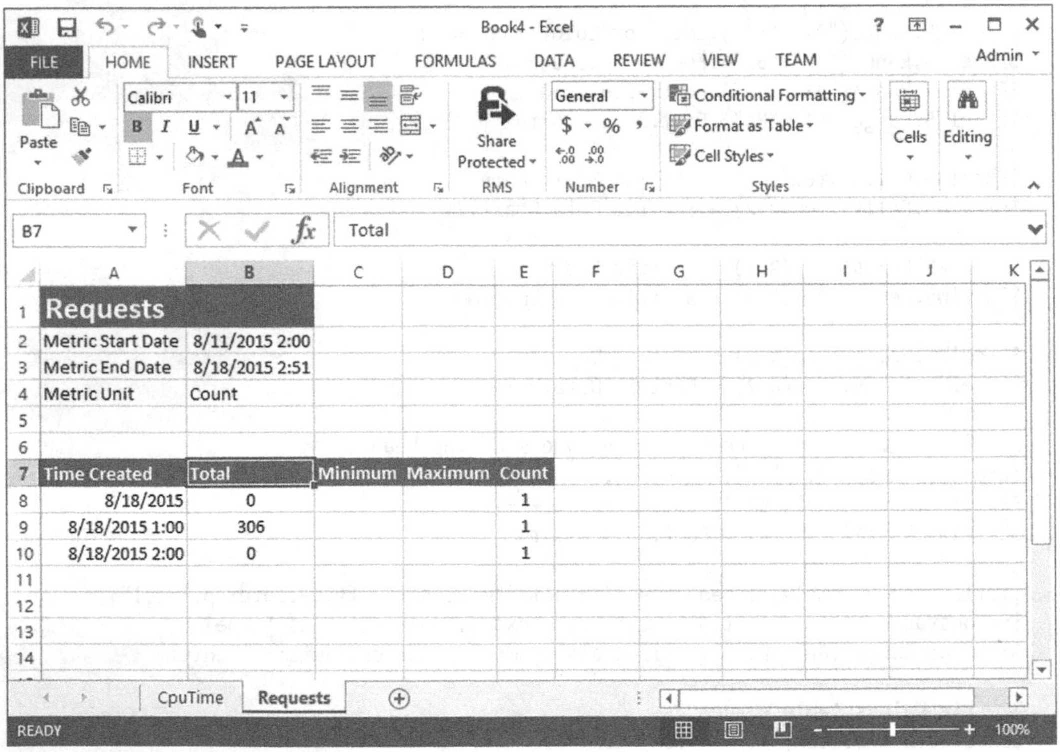

Figure 6-9. *Web app metric exported to Excel*

If you wonder why you would use PowerShell when you already have a monitoring graph on the Azure portal, then I must remind you that the maximum period for a graph on Azure is seven days. If you need a greater time span, then you must ask your friend PowerShell.

Managing Azure WebJobs

Azure WebJobs allows you to run a program or a script as a background process in your Azure web apps. WebJobs can be written using PowerShell, Bash, NodeJS, Java, Python, PHP, or even Windows CMD. WebJobs can run continuously or triggered (on demand or scheduled).

Azure WebJobs provides a solution for a lot of problems. I remember a project that I worked on in 2009. I was building a web-based monitoring dashboard for an ISP in Egypt that had just acquired four other companies. The challenge was collecting data from four different systems running on different platforms.

To overcome this issue, I configured a scheduled task to run PowerShell to collect the data from those systems and store it in a back-end SQL database for the dashboard. Although, this solution worked perfectly, the drawback was dedicating a server to run the scheduled task. It would have been easier and gone more smoothly if I had WebJobs at the time.

Anyway, to create a WebJobs from the Azure portal, go to the **WEBJOBS** tab on your Azure web app, click **ADD A JOB**, and fill in the required fields (see Figure 6-10).

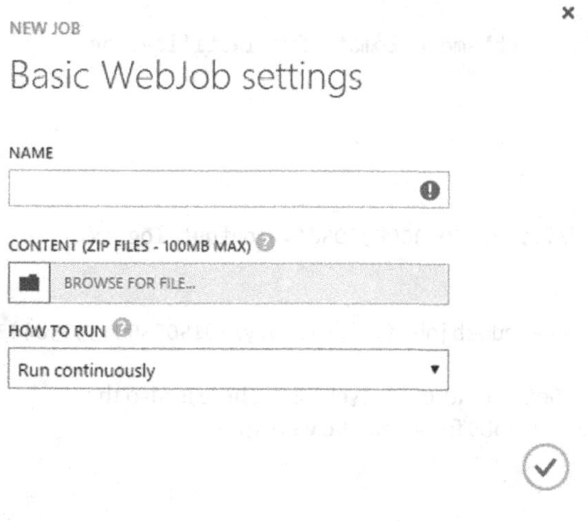

***Figure 6-10.** Adding WebJob settings*

To do the same task using PowerShell, you need the same input, but this time you use the `New-AzureWebsiteJob` cmdlet along with the following parameters:

- `-Name`: Specifies which web site to create the WebJob for.
- `-JobName`: Specifies a name for the WebJob.
- `-JobFile`: Specifies the path of the script or program to run within the WebJob. The file must use the `.zip` extension and contains the script or program.
- `-JobType`: Specifies how the job runs (Triggered or Continuous).

The following example creates a WebJob AutomatedEmailNotification for the WebsiteWithGit web site to run on demand. This WebJob is simply a PowerShell script that sends e-mail notifications using Send-MailMessage cmdlet. Another example is to create a web job that checks the unactivated users in your database and sends them a reminder to activate their account. In the next chapter, you learn about the Azure SQL Database and it will be easy to implement such a scenario. The point here is that you can create a script to do whatever you want and upload it as a WebJob.

```
#Create Azure WebJob
New-AzureWebsiteJob -Name WebsiteWithGit -JobName AutomatedEmailNotification -JobFile
C:\WebJobs\AutomatedEmail.zip -JobType Triggered
```

Conversely, to remove a WebJob, you use the `Remove-AzureWebsiteJob` cmdlet.

To start a WebJob, use the `Start-AzureWebsiteJob` cmdlet; to stop a running WebJob, use the `Stop-AzureWebsiteJob` cmdlet.

```
#Start Azure WebJob
Start-AzureWebsiteJob -Name WebsiteWithGit -JobName AutomatedEmailNotification -JobType
Triggered
```

Also, you get the history of WebJobs by using the `Get-AzureWebsiteJobHistory` cmdlet.

```
#Getting WebJobs History
Get-AzureWebsiteJobHistory -Name WebsiteWithGit -JobName AutomatedEmailNotification

Duration  : 00:00:05.2499176
EndTime   : 5/30/2015 4:33:11 AM
Id        : 201505300433058442
JobName   : AutomatedEmailNotification
OutputUrl : https://website.scm...../triggered/.../201505300433058442/output_log.txt
StartTime : 5/30/2015 4:33:05 AM
Status    : Success
Url       : https://websitewithgit...t/api/triggeredwebjobs/.../history/201505300433058442
```

The `Get-AzureWebsiteJobHistory` is not the only `Get-*` cmdlet for WebJobs. There is also the `Get-AzureWebsiteJob` cmdlet, which retrieves all available jobs for a specific web app.

Summary

In this chapter, you tackled the Azure Web Apps service. You started by creating a basic Azure web app, and then you created a web site associated with the Git repository. You learned how to prepare PowerShell to work with Git to serve associated web sites.

After that, you moved to the advanced configuration of a web site, such as setting connection strings, app settings, managing logs, and monitoring metrics. Finally, you closed the chapter with creating and managing Azure WebJobs.

The next chapter discusses PaaS components and spotlights the Azure SQL Database (formerly SQL Azure). As usual, you learn how to achieve different SQL database tasks, like database creation, backup and restore, configuration, and other tasks using PowerShell.

CHAPTER 7

Azure SQL Database

In the pre-cloud era, the cost of building software was so high that we often have to define a scope and leave out functionality, which we feel doesn't fetch the ROI for automation. [The] cloud makes whatever was previously left out of scope a candidate for automation now! Thanks to simplification, access, and affordability brought by IaaS and PaaS.

—Suresh Sambandam (Founder & CEO, OrangeScape)

There is no doubt that the database is a core and irreplaceable component in a software application, regardless of the database's type or format. Taking Microsoft as an example, you clearly see that SQL Server services its products, such as System Center, CRM, SharePoint, and so many more. So, whether you are a developer or an IT pro, you will find yourself dealing with SQL Server, which makes it a platform rather than just software.

Everyone understands how challenging it is to manage and maintain a platform such as SQL Server. Because one component services other software, losing it will bring everything down. So, you need to take care of performance, security, high availability, backup, patches, updates, and so on. This is the beauty of a cloud computing Platform as a Service (PaaS) solution; and this is where the Azure SQL Database becomes useful. You can read more about the differences between Azure SQL Database and SQL Server in Azure VM in the articles located at the following URLs:

- `https://azure.microsoft.com/en-us/documentation/articles/data-management-azure-sql-database-and-sql-server-iaas/`
- `http://azure.microsoft.com/blog/2012/06/26/data-series-sql-server-in-windows-azure-virtual-machine-vs-sql-database/`

As mentioned earlier in this book, in PaaS, you manage only the application and data, while the vendor manages the underlying infrastructure. This is unlike IaaS, where you manage the application, the data, the operating system, patches, updates, and backups.

In Azure, you have two options for SQL Server. You can have it as IaaS, where you install SQL Server on Azure VM (in which there is already a VM template image for SQL Server). You can also have it as PaaS, on what is called Azure SQL Database.

In this chapter, you learn how to manage Azure SQL Database services using Azure PowerShell.

What Is Azure SQL Database?

Azure SQL Database is simply a database engine in the cloud that is managed, maintained, and patched by Microsoft. The user has nothing to worry about except creating the database and using it. There are currently three tiers offered, based on the size of the workload.

- **Basic**: This tier is designed for applications with a light transactional workload. The typical use case is an application that needs a small database with a single operation at any given point in time. It has 5 DTUs (database throughput units); the database size cannot exceed the 2 GB. A database can be restored to any point in time during the last seven days.
- **Standard**: This tier is the best option for getting started with transactional workloads. It offers better performance and better built-in business continuity features than the Basic tier. The typical use case is an application with multiple concurrent transactions. It allows many database sizes, reaching up to 250 GB; it has up to 100 DTUs. The point-in-time restore is 14 days.
- **Premium**: This tier is designed for mission-critical applications. It offers the best level of performance and access to advanced business continuity features, including active geo-replication in up to four Azure regions of your choice. A typical use case is a mission-critical application with high transactional volume and many concurrent users. It offers up to 1750 DTUs and the database size can be up to 1 TB. The point-in-time recovery is for any millisecond during the last 35 days.

The pricing and SLAs differ on every schema. Users should select what's appropriate for their workload and convenient from a cost perspective.

Creating Your First Database

Now, let's create your first Azure SQL Database. First, authenticate your Azure subscription. Then start the creation process, as follows.

```
## Azure Subscription Authentication
Add-AzureAccount
```

To create an Azure SQL Database, you first need to create an Azure SQL Server instance. For the purpose of this task, use the `New-AzureSqlDatabaseServer` cmdlet along with the following parameters:

- `-AdministratorLogin`: Specifies the username of the server administrator.
- `-AdministratorLoginPassword`: Specifies the administrator's account password. It must be a strong and complex password.
- `-Location`: Specifies the region in which the Azure SQL Database server will be created.
- `-Version`: Specifies the version of the server. Use `2.0` for version 11.0 and `12.0` for version 12.

```
## Creating Azure SQL Database Server (ASM)
$AzureDatabaseServer = New-AzureSqlDatabaseServer -AdministratorLogin "SherifT"
-AdministratorLoginPassword "pass@word1" -Location "West US" -Version "12.0" -verbose
```

After the command has been executed, no results appear on the screen. And you must have noticed that you didn't choose the database server name. That is because the Azure management layer picks a name and creates the server with it. To learn the name, you can print the `$AzureDatabaseServer` object.

```
$AzureDatabaseServer | fl

ServerName          : s5m8t9ssp5
Location            : West US
AdministratorLogin : SherifT
Version             : 12.0
```

As you can see, the database server name is `s5m8t9ssp5`. This name is used if you want to log in from SQL Server Management Studio or identify your server on the Azure portal.

The equivalent of the `New-AzureSqlDatabaseServer` cmdlet in the ARM module is the `New-AzureSqlServer` cmdlet. The advantage of using `New-AzureSqlServer` is that the `-ServerName` parameter allows you to specify the name of the Azure SQL Database server rather than creating a random name, as with the `New-AzureSqlDatabaseServer` cmdlet.

```
## Creating Azure SQL Database Server (ARM)

# Create PSCredential Object
$Username = "SherifT"
$Password = "pass@word1" | ConvertTo-SecureString -AsPlainText -Force
$Cred = New-Object System.Management.Automation.PSCredential($Username,$Password)

# Create Azure SQL Database Server
$AzureDatabaseServer = New-AzureSqlServer -ResourceGroupName "DevTestFarm" -ServerName
"DevTestSQLServer" -SqlAdministratorCredentials $Cred -Location "West US" -ServerVersion
"12.0" -verbose
```

If you create an Azure SQL Database server in version 11.0, but you want to upgrade it to version 12.0, you can use the `Start-AzureSqlServerUpgrade` cmdlet. You can use the `-ScheduleUpgradeAfterUtcDateTime` parameter to start the upgrade on a specific date and time.

```
## Upgrade Azure SQL Database Server Version (ARM)
$UpgradeSchedule = (Get-Date).AddDays(1).TouniversalTime()

Start-AzureSqlServerUpgrade -ResourceGroupName "DevTestFarm" -ServerName "devtestfarm-sql-01"
-ServerVersion 12.0 -ScheduleUpgradeAfterUtcDateTime $UpgradeSchedule
```

Now the server is ready. Let's create a database on it. The database will be called `DemoDB`, which you'll put on the server that you've just created. To create an Azure SQL Database, use the `New-AzureSqlDatabase` cmdlet along with the following parameters:

- `-ServerName`: Specifies the name of the Azure SQL Server to create the database on.
- `-DatabaseName`: Specifies the name of the Azure database.
- `-Edition`: Specifies the database edition (offering): Basic, Standard, or Premium. Remember that the edition defines the disaster recovery backward recovery time, the database size, and it affects the cost as well.
- `-MaxSizeGB`: Specifies the size of the database in gigabytes. The maximum size depends on the database edition.

- -Collation: Specifies the collation for the new database. If not specified, then the default SQL_Latin1_General_CP1_CI_AS collation will be used.
- -ServiceObjective: Specifies the object that defines the service objective (performance level) of the new database. For example, if it's a standard database, then it is S0, S1, S2, or S3. You can get the service objective information using the Get-AzureSqlDatabaseServiceObjective cmdlet.

```
## Creating New Azure SQL Database (ASM)
# Ceating Service Objective Object
$so = Get-AzureSqlDatabaseServiceObjective -ServerName $AzureDatabaseServer.ServerName -
ServiceObjectiveName S2

# Creating Azure SQL Database
New-AzureSqlDatabase -ServerName $AzureDatabaseServer.ServerName -DatabaseName
DemoDB -Edition "Standard" -MaxSizeGB 50 -ServiceObjective $so

Name                                        : DemoDB
CollationName                               : SQL_Latin1_General_CP1_CI_AS
Edition                                     : Standard
MaxSizeGB                                   : 250
MaxSizeBytes                                : 268435456000
ServiceObjectiveName                        : S2
ServiceObjectiveAssignmentStateDescription :
CreationDate                                : 8/23/2015 5:09:25 AM
RecoveryPeriodStartDate                     : 8/23/2015 5:20:26 AM
```

The New-AzureSqlDatabase cmdlet is the same in the ARM module, but the parameters are a little different. The New-AzureSqlDatabase cmdlet under the ARM module has the following parameters:

- -ResourceGroupName: Specifies the resource group that the Azure SQL Database server is in.
- -ServerName: Specifies the name of the Azure SQL Server to create the database on.
- -DatabaseName: Specifies the name of the Azure database.
- -Edition: Specifies the database edition (offering): Basic, Standard, Premium, or Default.
- -MaxSizeBytes: Specifies the size of the database in bytes. The maximum size depends on the database edition.
- -CollationName: Specifies the collation for the new database.
- -CatalogCollation: Specifies the collation of the database catalog.
- -RequestedServiceObjectivename: Specifies the object that defines the service objective (performance level) of the new database. For example, if it's a standard database, then it is S0, S1, S2, or S3. You can specify the name directly as a string, unlike the equivalent parameter in the ASM module that requires you to get service objective information using the Get-AzureSqlDatabaseServiceObjective cmdlet.
- -ElasticPoolName: Specifies the name of the elastic pool that the new database will be a part of. If you don't know what an elastic pool is, then just remember this parameter because it's discussed shortly.

```
## Creating New Azure Database (ARM)
# Creating Azure SQL Database
New-AzureSqlDatabase -ResourceGroupName "DevTestFarm" -ServerName $AzureDatabaseServer.
ServerName -DatabaseName "DevTestDB" -Edition Standard -MaxSizeBytes 50gb
-RequestedServiceObjectiveName s2
ResourceGroupName                  : DevTestFarm
ServerName                         : devtestfarm-sql-01
DatabaseName                       : DevTestDB
Location                           : West US
DatabaseId                         : cb496337-69e4-4229-aab8-be6c48eb3002
Edition                            : Standard
CollationName                      : SQL_Latin1_General_CP1_CI_AS
CatalogCollation                   :
MaxSizeBytes                       : 53687091200
Status                             : Online
CreationDate                       : 8/22/2015 5:41:00 AM
CurrentServiceObjectiveId          : 455330e1-00cd-488b-b5fa-177c226f28b7
CurrentServiceObjectiveName        : S2
RequestedServiceObjectiveId        : 455330e1-00cd-488b-b5fa-177c226f28b7
RequestedServiceObjectiveName      :
ElasticPoolName                    :
EarliestRestoreDate                :
Tags                               :
```

■ **Tip** PowerShell understands memory units such as KB, MB, GB, and so on. Whenever you type a memory unit in your code, it returns the equivalent value in bytes. For example, if you type `1mb` and hit Enter, 1048576 is returned. That's why in the preceding code I used `50gb` as a value for the `-MaxSizeBytes` parameter instead of 53687091200, which would mess up the code's readability.

So far, you have successfully created the Azure SQL Database server and database. Eventually, it is very common to find yourself in need to modify some of the properties in those resources. To modify an Azure SQL Database server's properties, you use the `Set-AzureSqlDatabaseServer` cmdlet in ASM and the `Set-AzureSqlServer` cmdlet in ARM. The only available modification to the database servers is the admin password.

For modifications in Azure SQL Database's properties, you use the `Set-AzureSqlDatabase` cmdlet in both the ASM and the ARM modules. The database properties that can be modified are the database edition, the maximum database size, and the service object. You can change the database name in only in the ASM module; you can change the elastic pool property in only the ARM module.

Managing an Azure SQL Database Server Firewall

Security is always a concern with data, especially if the data is stored on a cloud service. In general, databases are a popular target for hackers or intruders because everything they could want is in a database.

Microsoft invests a lot in the latest technologies to ensure the security of its services, and applies best practices to provide its customers with the most secure experience. For example, one of those practices is preventing access to an Azure SQL Database server unless it is opened explicitly via a *firewall rule*.

A firewall rule lets you define which computer or IP address has access to your Azure SQL Database server. To create a firewall rule using the ASM module, you use the `New-AzureSqlDatabaseServerFirewall` cmdlet along with the `-StartIpAddress` and `-EndIpAddress` parameters to define the range of the IP addresses allowed to access the server. Also, you can use the `-AllowAllAzureServices` parameter to allow access from all Azure services.

```
## Creating New Azure SQL Database Server Firewall Rule (ASM)
$AzureDatabaseServer = Get-AzureSqlServer -ServerName "s5m8t9ssp5"

# Create Firewall Rule for single IP Address
New-AzureSqlDatabaseServerFirewallRule -ServerName $AzureDatabaseServer.ServerName -RuleName
"myHomeComputer" -StartIpAddress "167.200.188.210" -EndIpAddress "167.200.188.210"

# Create Firewall Rule for Azure Services
New-AzureSqlDatabaseServerFirewallRule -ServerName $AzureDatabaseServer.ServerName -RuleName
"AllowAzureServices" -AllowAllAzureServices
```

To create a firewall rule using ARM, you use the `New-AzureSqlFirewallRule` cmdlet. Like the `New-AzureSqlDatabaseServerFirewall` cmdlet, you use the `-StartIpAddress` and `-EndIpAddress` parameters to define the range of the IP addresses, and you use the `-AllowAllAzureIPs` parameter to allow access from all Azure IP addresses.

```
## Creating New Azure SQL Database Server Firewall Rule (ARM)
$AzureDatabaseServer = Get-AzureSqlServer -ResourceGroupName "DevTestFarm" -ServerName
"DevTestSQLServer"

# Create Firewall Rule for single IP Address
New-AzureSqlServerFirewallRule -ResourceGroupName "DevTestFarm" -ServerName
$AzureDatabaseServer.ServerName -FirewallRuleName "myHomeComputer" -StartIpAddress
"167.200.188.210" -EndIpAddress "167.200.188.210"

# Create Firewall Rule for Azure IP Addresses
New-AzureSqlServerFirewallRule -ServerName $AzureDatabaseServer.ServerName -FirewallRuleName
"AllowAzureIPs" -AllowAllAzureIPs
```

You can define a certain IP to open the database, but connecting from any other IP will fail. The following code opens the full range of IP addresses for a connection. Keep in mind that this is for testing purposes only—never do this on a production server.

```
# Create Firewall Rule - Full Range (ASM)
New-AzureSqlDatabaseServerFirewallRule -ServerName $AzureDatabaseServer.ServerName -RuleName
"FullRange" -StartIpAddress "0.0.0.0" -EndIpAddress "255.255.255.255"

RuleName             : FullRange
StartIpAddress       : 0.0.0.0
EndIpAddress         : 255.255.255.255
ServerName           : s5m8t9ssp5
OperationDescription : New-AzureSqlDatabaseServerFirewallRule
OperationId          : d3dc2ea2dfd304718ff3d86c1b869997
OperationStatus      : Success
```

```
# Create Firewall Rule - Full Range (ARM)
New-AzureSqlServerFirewallRule -ResourceGroupName "DevTestFarm" -ServerName
$AzureDatabaseServer.ServerName -FirewallRuleName "FullRange" -StartIpAddress "0.0.0.0"
-EndIpAddress "255.255.255.255"

ResourceGroupName : DevTestFarm
ServerName        : DevTestSQLServer
StartIpAddress    : 0.0.0.0
EndIpAddress      : 255.255.255.255
FirewallRuleName  : FullRange
```

Once you create the right firewall rule, the database can be accessed from any application—even through the SQL Server Management Studio (SSMS). The connection string can be found on the portal. First, let's access the management portal and log on to the database.

Logging on to the portal for the database server gives you six tabs, as shown in Figure 7-1.

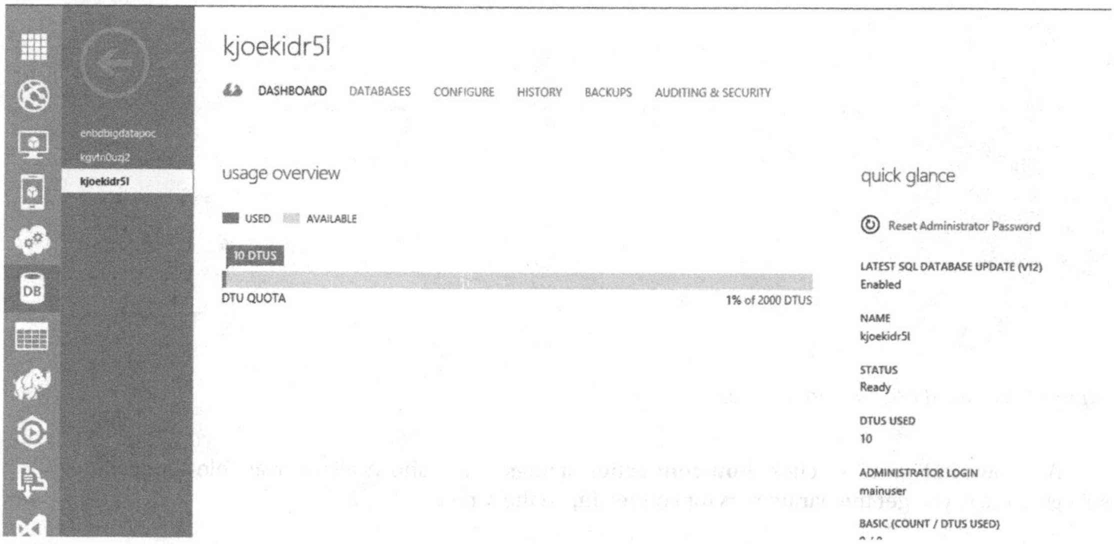

***Figure 7-1.** Azure portal access to the Azure SQL Database server*

The following describes the six tabs.

- **Dashboard**: Shows the current DTU usage on the server and what is available.
- **Databases**: Shows the current databases on the server.
- **Configure**: Configures the server for the allowed IPs.
- **History**: Shows the history of imports and exports on the database, after the user supplies his or her username and password.
- **Backups**: Shows the backups of the databases hosted on Azure SQL database server. Also, shows backup strategies used for an export from the database in the Standard version. Only databases that are Geo-Redundant can be restored.
- **Auditing & Security**: Sets up the security and auditing settings for the server.

Connecting to the Database

Later in the chapter you'll take a look at how to manage some of the functionalities through PowerShell. But to make sure that the database is accessible from any normal SQL client, you need to connect to it. But first you need to have the connection string.

Log on to the portal. In the Databases tab, click **DemoDB**. In the Dashboard tab, you'll find a monitoring trace of the activities on the database. On the lower right-hand side of the page, you'll find a lot of useful links. One of them is especially for the connection string, as shown in Figure 7-2.

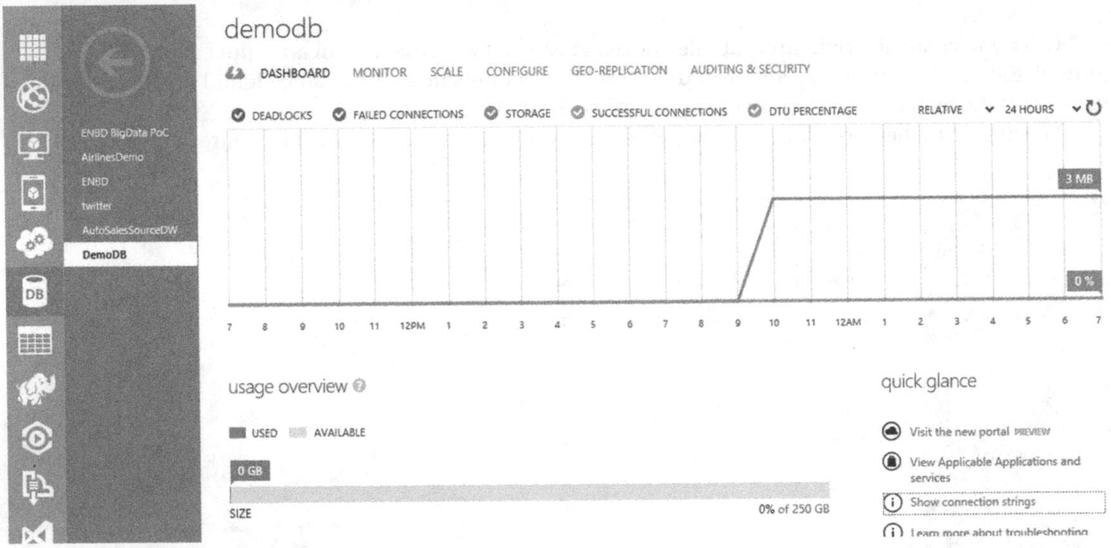

Figure 7-2. Database dashboard screen

As shown in Figure 7-3, click **Show connection strings**, which shows all the available connection strings. Hence, you get the parameters for connecting to the server.

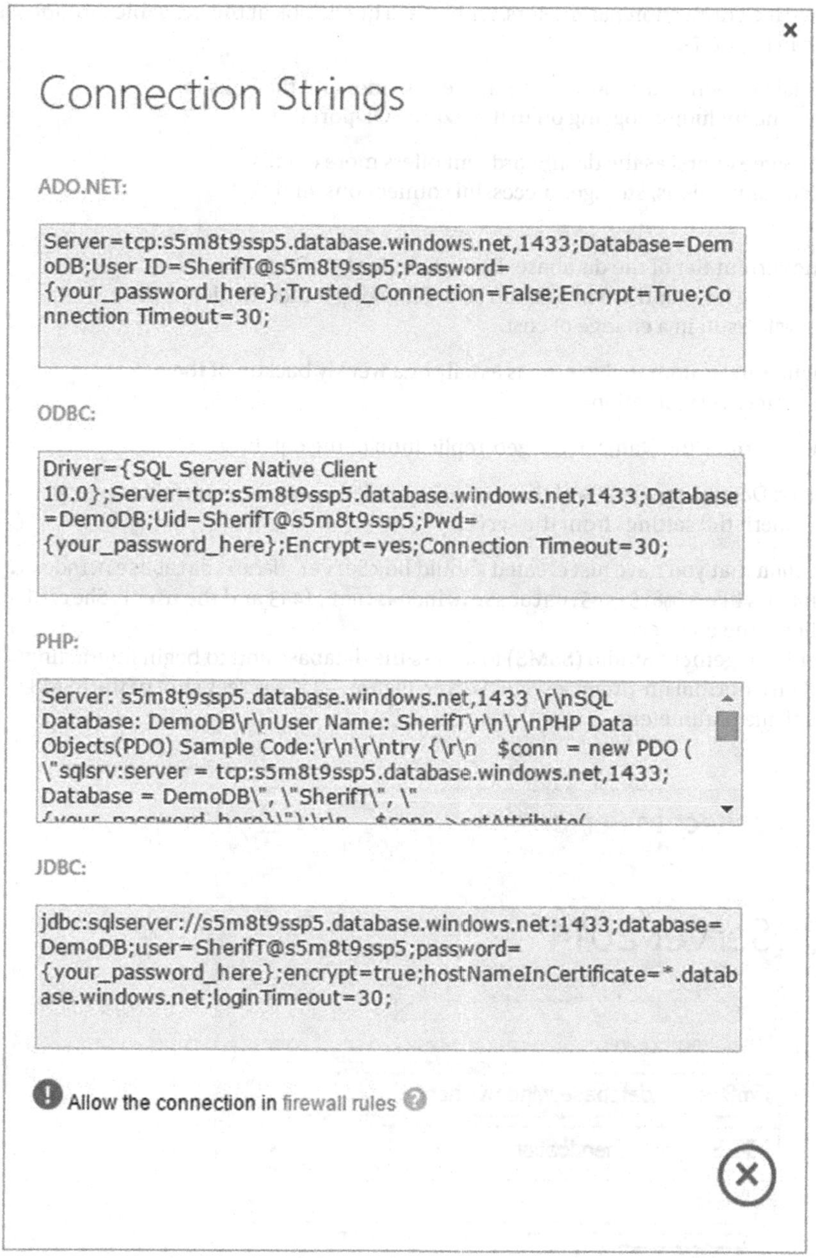

Figure 7-3. *Azure SQL Database connections string pop-up*

But before continuing on to the connection parameters, let's have a quick look at the available tabs for the DemoDB database (shown in Figure 7-2).

- **Dashboard**: The main screen that shows the database activities and the links for database management, including logging on to the Azure SQL portal.
- **Monitor**: It has the same charts as the dashboard, but offers more details on deadlocks, failed connections, storage, successful connections, and DTU percentages.
- **Scale**: Changes the current tier of the database: Basic, Standard, or Premium. Defines the performance level and the maximum size. Changing either the tier or the performance level will result in a change of cost.
- **Configure**: Configures the automated export as a daily or a weekly backup of the database for disaster recovery situations.
- **Geo-Replication**: Describes the status of the geo-replication of the database.
- **Auditing & Security**: Defines the details of the security-enabled access to determine whether or not to inherit the settings from the server.

The current server connection that you have just created should be <Server_Name>.database.windows.net,1433. So in the example it looks like `s5m8t9ssp5.database.windows.net,1433` and the user is `SherifT` with the password added earlier in the chapter.

Let's try to use SQL Server Management Studio (SSMS) to access the database and to begin interacting on it as if it's a database stored on a normal on-premises SQL Server. Figure 7-4 is a screenshot of the SSMS connection form populated with the parameters.

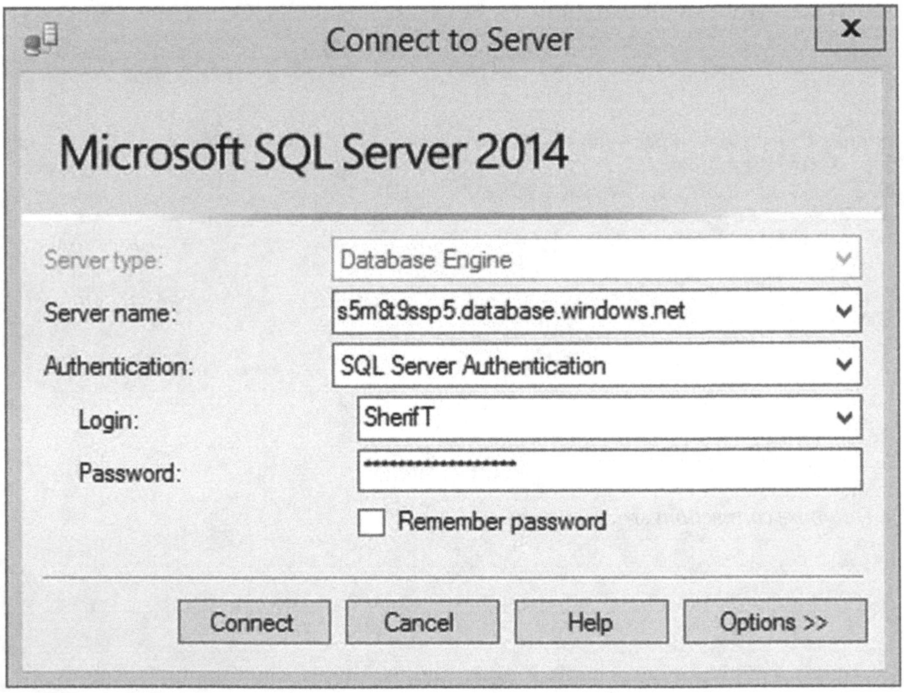

Figure 7-4. SQL Server connection wizard

After clicking the **Connect** button, SQL Server connects to the server and shows all the available databases that you can easily interact with. You can write queries, create tables, and even optimize the index if needed. Figure 7-5 shows a query to create a table called Names with three columns: id, FirstName, and LastName.

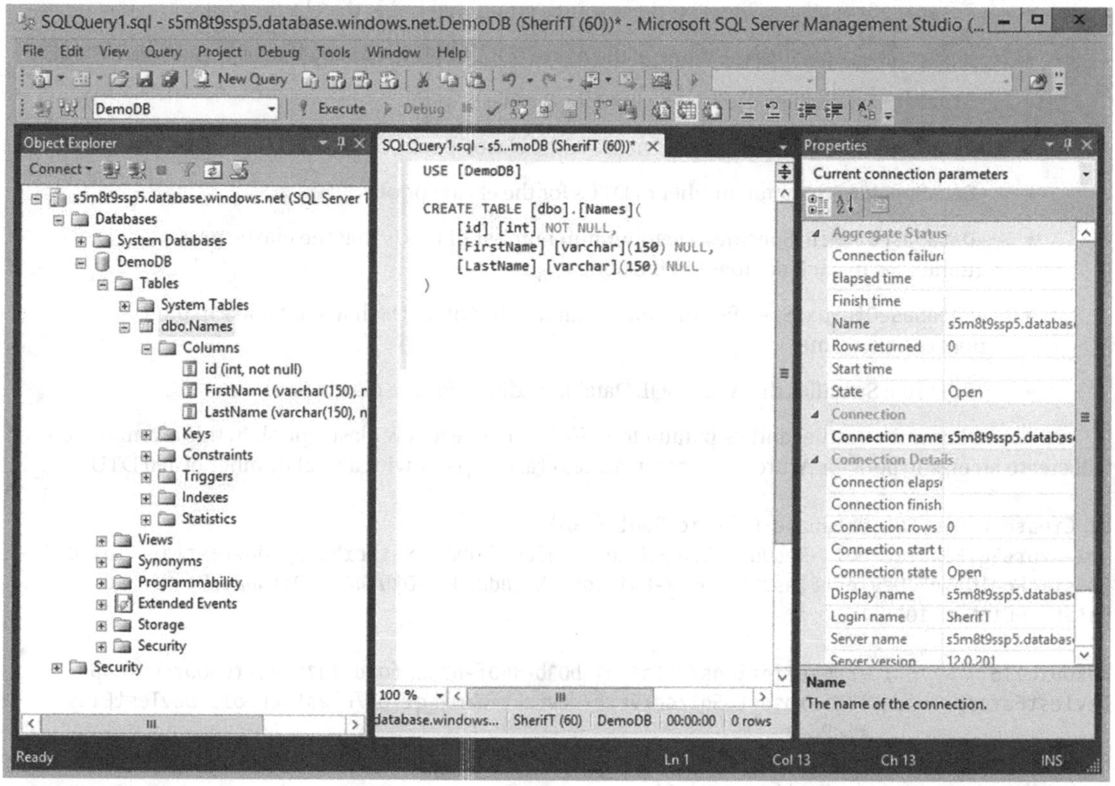

Figure 7-5. *Creating a table on the Azure SQL Database*

The connection string that you acquired from the Azure portal helps you to connect to it through PowerShell and to start executing queries for creating tables or retrieving data from the server.

■ **Caution** Any table created on an Azure database has to have a primary key or a unique index. You cannot create heap tables on an Azure database, because this is not supported.

Creating Elastic Pools and Databases

When creating the first Azure SQL Database using the ARM module, I mentioned the `-ElasticPoolName` parameter to specify the name of the pool in which to put the new database in.

An Azure SQL Database *elastic pool* is simply a pool (collection) of resources that are shared by multiple databases. The resources in the elastic pools are the database throughput unit (DTU) and storage.

Azure SQL Databases that are members of an elastic pool are called *elastic databases*. The elastic databases in the pool utilize only the resources that they require from the pool, freeing up available resources for only the active databases that need them.

To create an Azure SQL Database elastic pool, you use the `New-AzureSqlElasticPool` cmdlet along with the following parameters:

- `-ResourceGroupName`: Specifies the resource group that holds the elastic pool.
- `-ServerName`: Specifies the name of the Azure SQL Server to create the elastic pool on.
- `-StorageMB`: Specifies the storage limit for the elastic pool.
- `-ElasticPoolName`: Specifies the name of the elastic pool.
- `-Dtu`: Specifies the total number of DTUs for the elastic pool.
- `-DatabaseDtuMin`: Specifies the minimum number of DTUs that the elastic pool guarantees to each database in the pool.
- `-DatabaseDtuMax`: Specifies the maximum number of DTUs that a database in the pool can consume.
- `-Edition`: Specifies the Azure SQL Database edition for the elastic pool.

Now you know the cmdlet and its parameters. So, let's create a new elastic pool. In this example, you will create an elastic pool for Azure SQL Server `devtestfarm-sql-01` with a total number of 400 DTUs.

```
## Create Azure SQL Database Elastic Pool (ARM)
New-AzureSqlElasticPool -ResourceGroupName "DevTestFarm" -ServerName "devtestfarm-sql-01" -
ElasticPoolName "DevTestElasticPool" -Edition "Standard" -Dtu 400 -DatabaseDtuMin 10 -
DatabaseDtuMax 100

ResourceId        : /subscriptions/7d2a1de7-b03b-460f-b752-fdeda1d7144c/resourceGroups/
DevTestFarm/providers/Microsoft.Sql/servers/devtestfarm-sql-01/elasticPools/DevTestElas
                    ticPool
ResourceGroupName : DevTestFarm
ServerName        : devtestfarm-sql-01
ElasticPoolName   : DevTestElasticPool
Location          : West US
CreationDate      : 8/21/2015 3:47:43 AM
State             : Ready
Edition           : Standard
Dtu               : 400
DatabaseDtuMax    : 100
DatabaseDtuMin    : 10
StorageMB         : 409600
Tags              :
```

The total number of DTUs, minimum DTUs, maximum DTUs, and storage in the previous example are not randomly selected values. These values are based according to the eDTUs (elastic database throughput units) and storage limits for the elastic pool. You can read more about these limits at `https://azure.microsoft.com/en-us/documentation/articles/sql-database-elastic-pool-reference/`.

If you want to change any of the DTU values or the storage limit for an elastic pool after creating it, you can use the `Set-AzureSqlElasticPool` cmdlet with the same parameters as the `New-AzureSqlElasticPool` cmdlet.

Now that you have created an Azure SQL elastic pool, it's time to utilize it by creating elastic databases. To create an elastic database, you use the -ElasticPoolName parameter with either the New-AzureSqlDatabase cmdlet, if it's a new database, or the Set-AzureSqlDatabase cmdlet, if you are moving an existing database to the elastic pool.

```
## Moving Database to Elastic Pool (ARM)
Set-AzureSqlDatabase -ResourceGroupName "DevTestFarm" -ServerName " devtestfarm-sql-01"
-DatabaseName "DemoDB" -ElasticPoolName "DevTestElasticPool"
```

You can track the status of moving an elastic database in and out of an elastic pool by using the Get-AzureSqlElasticPoolDatabaseActivity cmdlet.

```
## Get Status of All Database to Elastic Pool (ARM)
Get-AzureSqlElasticPoolDatabaseActivity -ResourceGroupName "DevTestFarm" -ServerName
" devtestfarm-sql-01" -ElasticPoolName "DevTestElasticPool"
```

■ **Note** The elastic pool is still a feature in preview; it is available only on version 12.0 Azure SQL Database servers. Keep in mind that many changes take place while a product is still in preview, so please keep following the reference links for updates.

Importing and Exporting an Azure Database

Let's work with more operations using PowerShell on the database that you have just created. First get the database operations by using the Get-AzureSqlDatabaseOperation cmdlet. One of the required parameters for the Get-AzureSqlDatabaseOperation cmdlet is -ConnectionContext, which can be created using the New-AzureSqlDatabaseServerContext cmdlet.

```
# Creating PSCredential Object
$Username = "SherifT"
$Password = "pass@word1" | ConvertTo-SecureString -AsPlainText -Force
$Cred = New-Object System.Management.Automation.PSCredential($Username,$Password)
```

The preceding code creates a credential object using the administrator credential for provisioning the Azure SQL Database server. Now you create the connection context, as shown in the following code.

```
# Creating Connection Context (ASM)
$sqlContext = New-AzureSqlDatabaseServerContext -ServerName $AzureDatabaseServer.ServerName
-Credential $Cred
```

With the credentials object, you add the server name as a parameter as well. $sqlContext now holds the connection context that you need. Printing to the screen shows that the object holds identifiers for the session activity, client activity, client request, server name, and the credentials.

```
$sqlContext

SessionActivityId : 2bbed30b-522e-4fd5-8846-9e7110c114a3
ClientSessionId   : c2b04eb6-79fb-4dc7-b6f7-f46adebdb8d8-2015-08-23 04:14:54Z
ClientRequestId   : 59acc30c-3fc9-48e0-88a9-32a604caa585-2015-08-24 12:19:21Z
```

```
ServerName       : s5m8t9ssp5
SqlCredentials   : Microsoft.WindowsAzure.Commands.SqlDatabase.Services.Common.
                   SqlAuthenticationCredentials
```

One of the most important jobs that an administrator needs to handle is backup and restore. In the Azure SQL Database service, it is known as *import and export*. Now that you have an Azure database context, let's do a backup or an export of the database. You need to have an Azure storage account to store the backup file on. The creation of a storage context was discussed in Chapter 3, but it's good to refresh your memory.

```
# Create Azure Storage Context (ASM)
$StorageName = "mylabstroageaccount"

$StorageAccessKey = Get-AzureStorageKey -StorageAccountName $StorageAccountName | Select
-ExpandProperty Primary

$StorageCtx = New-AzureStorageContext -StorageAccountName $StorageName -StorageAccountKey
$StorageAccessKey
```

Now let's identify the container. Through the portal, you created a storage container named `demodbbackup`, which is the one that you'll use.

```
# Get Storage Container Information (ASM)
$Container = Get-AzureStorageContainer -Name "demodbbackup" -Context $StorageCtx
```

Now everything is ready to export the database using all the variables that you prepared in the preceding cmdlets. For the purpose of this task, use the `Start-AzureSqlDatabaseExport` cmdlet.

```
# Exporting Azure SQL Database (ASM)
$dbexport = Start-AzureSqlDatabaseExport -SqlConnectionContext $sqlContext -DatabaseName
"DemoDB" -StorageContainer $Container -BlobName "demodbexport"
```

Finally, you have a backup of the database that you can use on another Azure database or whenever something goes wrong with this database. The new backup file will appear on the portal under the backup container as shown in Figure 7-6.

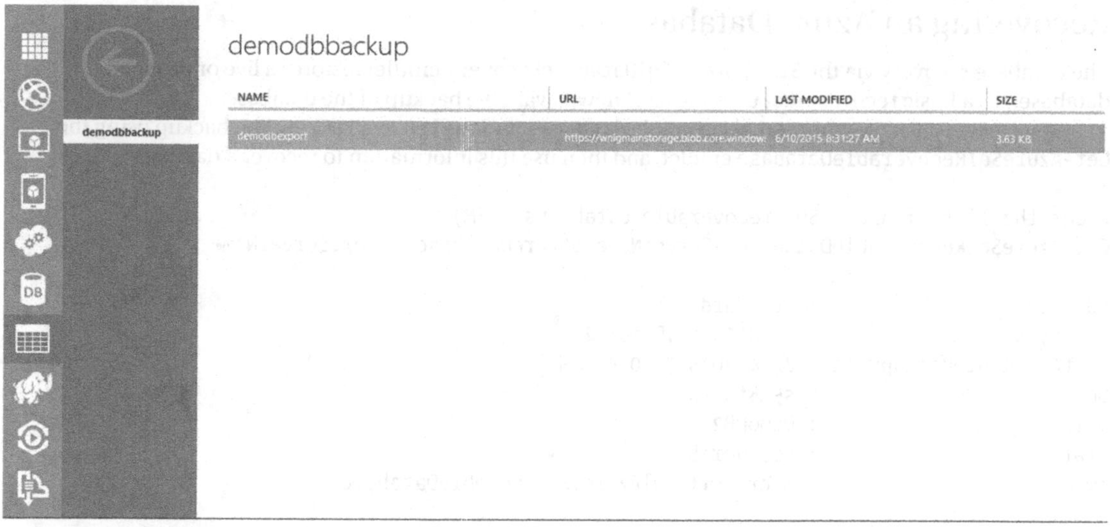

Figure 7-6. Azure SQL Database backup file

Importing this backup is a fairly easy job using the `Start-AzureSqlDatabaseImport` cmdlet, which has the same parameters as the export cmdlet.

```
# Importing Azure SQL Database (ASM)
$importRequest = Start-AzureSqlDatabaseImport -SqlConnectionContext $sqlContext
-StorageContainer $Container -DatabaseName "demodb" -BlobName "demodbexport"
```

You can keep track of the import and export status using the `Get-AzureSqlDatabaseImportExportStatus` cmdlet along with the `-Request` parameter to specify which request to track.

```
# Tracking Azure Database Export Status (ASM)
Get-AzureSqlDatabaseImportExportStatus -Request $exportRequest
```

Recovering and Restoring an Azure Database

The previous section discussed how to back up your Azure SQL Database using the import and export operation, which is a manual process. On the other hand, an Azure SQL Database automatically retains a backup of your database so that you can restore it later. One way that it does this is with a point-in-time restore.

This section discusses a couple of cmdlets that allow you to perform a point-in-time restore and to restore a dropped database.

Recovering an Azure Database

The database recovery via the `Start-AzureSqlDatabaseRecovery` cmdlet restores a live or dropped database. It's a basic recovery that uses the last known available backup of the database.

You can get a list of Azure SQL recoverable databases and the last available online backup using the `Get-AzureSqlRecoverableDatabase` cmdlet, and then use this information to recover a database.

```
# Get the list of Azure SQL recoverable databases (ASM)
Get-AzureSqlRecoverableDatabase -ServerName $AzureDatabaseServer.ServerName

Edition                   : Standard
EntityId                  : s5m8t9ssp5,DemoDB2
LastAvailableBackupDate   : 8/24/2015 5:40:45 AM
ServerName                : s5m8t9ssp5
Name                      : DemoDB2
State                     : Recoverable
Type                      : Microsoft.SqlAzure.RecoverableDatabase

Edition                   : Standard
EntityId                  : s5m8t9ssp5,DemoDB
LastAvailableBackupDate   : 8/24/2015 2:54:49 PM
ServerName                : s5m8t9ssp5
Name                      : DemoDB
State                     : Recoverable
Type                      : Microsoft.SqlAzure.RecoverableDatabase

# Recover Azure SQL Database (ASM)
$Database = Get-AzureSqlRecoverableDatabase -ServerName $AzureDatabaseServer.ServerName -
DatabaseName "DemoDB"

Start-AzureSqlDatabaseRecovery -SourceDatabase $Database -TargetDatabaseName
"DemoDB-Restored"
```

The recovery operation creates a new database, so make sure to specify a different name if you recover a live database on the same server. To restore the database with the same name but on a different server, use the preceding code and replace the `-TargetDatabaseName` parameter with the `-TargetServerName` parameter.

```
# Recover Azure SQL Database on different server (ASM)
$Database = Get-AzureSqlRecoverableDatabase -ServerName $AzureDatabaseServer.ServerName -
DatabaseName "DemoDB"

Start-AzureSqlDatabaseRecovery -SourceDatabase $Database -TargetServerName "br0psdx14"

Id                 : 51a315ab-e5e3-4af7-832d-95b907751d91
SourceDatabaseName : DemoDB
TargetDatabaseName : DemoDB
TargetServerName   : br0pvcsf14
Name               :
State              : Created
Type               : Microsoft.SqlAzure.RecoverDatabaseOperation
```

Restoring an Azure Database

The restore operation is a little different from the recovery operation. While the recovery operation uses the last available backup, the point-in-time restore gives you the flexibility to choose from different restore points.

As mentioned earlier, a point-in-time restore retains basic database backup for a number of days, based on the database tier: 7 days for Basic, 14 days for Standard, and 35 days for Premium.

To perform a point-in-time restore, you use the `Start-AzureSqlDatabaseRestore` cmdlet. First, you need to get the database you want to restore, and then pass it to the `Start-AzureSqlDatabaseRestore` cmdlet along with the point in time that you need.

```
## Azure SQL Database - Live DB - Point In Time (ASM)
# Get Database Information
$Database = Get-AzureSqlDatabase -ServerName $AzureDatabaseServer.ServerName -DatabaseName
"DemoDB"

# Start Restore Operation
$RestoreOperation = Start-AzureSqlDatabaseRestore -SourceDatabase $Database -TargetDatabaseName
"PITDB"  -PointInTime "8/24/2015 01:23:43 PM"
```

In the previous line of code, you defined the `$RestoreOperation` variable to store the restore operation information so that later on you can use it to track the operation status using the `Get-AzureSqlDatabaseOperation` cmdlet.

```
# Track Point-in-Time Restore Operation Status (ASM)
Get-AzureSqlDatabaseOperation -ServerName $AzureDatabaseServer.ServerName -OperationGuid
$RestoreOperation.RequestID
```

To restore a dropped database, you add the `-RestorableDropped` flag to the `Get-AzureSqlDatabase` cmdlet.

Azure SQL Database Geo-Replication

Geo-replication is another way to protect an Azure SQL Database against failure, loss, and downtime. With it, you have a copy of one or more databases stored on a different server in a different region; it can be used whenever needed.

The geo-replication could be a one-time copy operation or a continuous copy operation. To configure geo-replication via PowerShell, you use the `Start-AzureSqlDatabaseCopy` cmdlet.

This cmdlet allows creating a one-time copy of the database, an online continuous copy (a.k.a. Active Geo-Replication), and an offline continuous copy (a.k.a. Standard Geo-Replication).

■ **Tip** Read more about Standard Geo-Replication for the Azure SQL Database at `https://msdn.microsoft.com/en-us/library/dn758204` and Active Geo-Replication for the Azure SQL Database at `https://msdn.microsoft.com/en-us/library/dn741339`.

The following code samples show how to create the three types of replication for an Azure SQL Database.

```
## Creating One-Time Copy (ASM)
Start-AzureSqlDatabaseCopy -ServerName "s5m8t9ssp5" -DatabaseName "DemoDB" -PartnerServer
"br0pvcsf14" -PartnerDatabase "DemoDBCopy"

EntityId                         : f4acce06-98ce-4e10-a642-6918c4a80976
SourceServerName                 : s5m8t9ssp5
SourceDatabaseName               : DemoDB
DestinationServerName            : br0pvcsf14
DestinationDatabaseName          : DemoDBCopy
IsContinuous                     : False
ReplicationState                 : 0
ReplicationStateDescription      : PENDING
LocalDatabaseId                  : 5
IsLocalDatabaseReplicationTarget : False
IsInterlinkConnected             : True
StartDate                        : 8/22/2015 7:27:44 PM
ModifyDate                       : 8/22/2015 7:27:44 PM
PercentComplete                  : 0
IsOfflineSecondary               : False
IsTerminationAllowed             : True

## Creating Online Continuous Copy (ASM)
Start-AzureSqlDatabaseCopy -ServerName "s5m8t9ssp5" -DatabaseName "DemoDB" -PartnerServer
"br0pvcsf14" -ContinuousCopy

## Creating Offline Continuous Copy (ASM)
Start-AzureSqlDatabaseCopy -ServerName "s5m8t9ssp5" -DatabaseName "DemoDB" -PartnerServer
"br0pvcsf14" -ContinuousCopy -OfflineSecondary
```

You can monitor the operation by using the `Get-AzureSqlDatabaseCopy` or the `Get-AzureSqlDatabaseOperation` cmdlet.

■ **Caution** To configure geo-replication for an Azure SQL Database, both servers must be under the same Azure subscription; otherwise, the cmdlet execution will fail.

The continuous replication builds a copy relationship between the source server and the partner server. If you want to terminate this relationship, which means no more replicating between the servers, then use the `Stop-AzureSqlDatabaseCopy` cmdlet. Once you terminate the relationship, the secondary database state becomes a stand-alone online database.

```
## Stop Azure SQL Database Copy (ASM)
Stop-AzureSqlDatabaseCopy -ServerName "s5m8t9ssp5" -DatabaseName "DemoDB" -PartnerServer
" br0pvcsf14"
```

The previous code initiates a planned termination, which means that termination process is pending until all transactions are replicated from the source database to the secondary database. To force the termination process without waiting, or to stop termination from the secondary server, you use the `-ForcedTermination` parameter.

Querying an Azure SQL Database

To query an Azure SQL Database, you must realize that it doesn't differ from any normal SQL Server database. You create a connection and fire the queries the same way that you create a connection to a local SQL. Let's look at how you can do this.

First, you need to prepare some variables to use in the connection that you'll open to execute the query. You need to identify the connection string as shown earlier.

```
# Azure SQL Database Connectin String
$ConStr = "Server=tcp:s5m8t9ssp5.database.windows.net,1433;Database=DemoDB;User ID=SherifT@
s5m8t9ssp5;Password=pass@word1;Trusted_Connection=False;"
```

The variable `$ConStr` now contains the connection information to the Azure SQL Database. The next step is to create a connection and open it.

```
# Create and open SQL Connection
$SQLConnection =  New-Object System.Data.SqlClient.SqlConnection;
$SQLConnection.ConnectionString = $ConStr;
$SQLConnection.Open();
```

After you create the connection object, assign the connection string to it, and successfully open the connection, you are ready to start querying the database. This database is new, so you need to create a new table. Call it `Services` and give it two columns; then enter some data and query it.

```
# Create New Table using T-SQL Query
$Query = "Create table Services ( id int not null primary key, servicename varchar(50) )"
$command = $SQLConnection.CreateCommand()
$command.CommandText = $Query
$command.ExecuteNonQuery()
```

In the preceding code, you created a string variable that holds the table creation SQL command. Next, you created a command object from the connection that was previously created and opened. Then, you assigned the query.

Now you can use the `ExecuteNonQuery()` function because the table created is a DDL statement that doesn't return a result set.

■ **Note** The commands used in querying the database are ADO.NET commands, which are the same as those used when writing a .NET application connecting to a database. PowerShell utilizes the .NET objects to facilitate the database connection.

After creating the table, you write some insert commands to fill the table with data, as shown in the following code.

```
# Insert data to SQL Database Table
$InsertSQL = "insert into Services values(1, 'Database');
insert into Services values(2, 'Storage');
insert into Services values(3, 'Compute'); insert into Services values(4, 'HDInisght');
insert into Services values(5, 'Stream analytics');"
```

```
$command = $SQLConnection.CreateCommand()
$command.CommandText = $InsertSQL
$command.ExecuteNonQuery()
```

You prepared the insertion command with five insert statements. After preparing the command object, you executed it and the PowerShell screen printed 5, which is the number of affected rows.

After the table is created and you have a table with data, try to run a select statement on the table to get the results.

```
# Query Data from Azure SQL Database Table
$SelectSQL = "Select id, servicename from Services;"
$SelectCommand = $SQLConnection.CreateCommand()
$SelectCommand.CommandText = $SelectSQL
$results = $SelectCommand.ExecuteReader()
```

Running the preceding commands prepares a select statement; the results return in the `$results` object. However, printing this object results in showing the number of fields, not the data output, so you need to reformat the output to see the exact results. In the next command, you see how to reformat this output to show the actual data inserted, instead of the dump from the data reader object.

```
PS C:\Users\Sherif> # Query Data from Azure SQL Database Table
$SelectSQL = "Select id, servicename from Services;"
$SelectCommand = $SQLConnection.CreateCommand()
$SelectCommand.CommandText = $SelectSQL
$results = $SelectCommand.ExecuteReader()

PS C:\Users\Sherif> $results

  FieldCount
  ----------
           2
           2
           2
           2
           2
```

To reformat the output, use the following commands in a very simple `For` loop to loop on the items in the reader collection. And then print it out.

```
# Reformatting Quert output
$results = $SelectCommand.ExecuteReader()

For($i = 0; $i -le 9 ; $i = $i+2)
{
        $indic = $results.Read()
        $results[0].ToString() + " " + $results[1]
}
```

The For loop iterates through the collection. For each row, a Read() function should be called to read the next row. The array of the $results reader contains the values of the columns in this row. After executing this loop, the data will print correctly.

```
PS C:\Users\Sherif> for($i = 0; $i -le 9 ; $i = $i+2)
{
    $indic = $results.Read()
    $results[0].ToString() + " " + $results[1]
}

1 Database
2 Storage
3 Compute
4 HDInisght
5 Stream analytics
```

Alternatively, you can use the Adapter object to load the data using a dataset, as shown in the following commands.

```
# Using Adapter Object to Query Table
$adapter = New-Object System.Data.SqlClient.SqlDataAdapter $SelectCommand
$dataset = New-Object System.Data.DataSet
$adapter.Fill($dataSet)
$dataSet.Tables[0]
```

The Adapter object fills the dataset. As the select statement is returning a data table, it'll find the object with index 0.

■ **Note** The command cannot have two open connections to the database. When you create the dataset, you may receive an error because this command is associated with an open reader. You have to call the $results.Close() function to close the reader and fill the dataset.

A wrapper function to call the database and execute queries can be created to ease the process and save lines of code. But any type of Data Definition Language (DDL) or Data Manipulation Language (DML) can be executed through PowerShell to the Azure database.

Summary

PowerShell can be used to manage Azure SQL databases and servers to create, access, and modify a database. The commands are fairly simple. They go around the database server name, the database name, or the connection context. A database on Azure can be used like any normal database and it can be accessed by any of the common tools, like SQL Server Management Studio, or with an ADO.NET connection string.

In the next chapter, you learn about using PowerShell along with the Azure Automation service to build advanced automation runbooks for Azure services and workloads. You'll also learn about Automation workflows, checkpoints, and assets. Turning Azure VMs on and off at specific times is an example of an Azure Automation service.

CHAPTER 8

Azure Automation

Since the beginning of the book, we have talked about using PowerShell to automate different Azure services, such as virtual machines, virtual networks, SQL databases, and so many others. The focus, so far, has been mainly on learning how to perform certain tasks in PowerShell so that you can use it for automation purposes. For instance, how to provision a virtual machine via PowerShell so that you can later put this code inside a loop to provision a hundred virtual machines at a time. The same concept applies to other services, like creating Azure web sites, Azure AD users, uploading files to Azure storage, and so on.

In this chapter, you are going to learn about Azure Automation but in a different style. This time, it's not about using PowerShell cmdlets to automate an Azure service but about an Azure service that uses PowerShell as a platform to automate other Azure components. This is the Azure Automation service.

What's Azure Automation?

Azure Automation service is Microsoft's answer to Automation as a Service. The reason it's called Automation as a Service is that in order to automate components in a traditional on-premises scenario, you need an automation tool or software that needs underlying hardware and network requirements. Then, you can start building your automation workflows and scripts. However, in Azure Automation, everything is already set: you just log in to the console to build the workflows and scripts.

Azure Automation is the IT automation process for Azure. If you've had the chance to work with System Center Orchestrator, then you might say that Azure Automation is the "Orchestrator" for Azure services.

Azure Automation allows you to automate the creation, deployment, maintenance, and monitoring of Azure services and resources in your environment. It also allows you to take proper actions proactively based on some specific attributes and values.

The great thing about Azure Automation is that it's based on Windows PowerShell and the Windows PowerShell Workflows engine. This means that your existing Azure scripts can work with Azure Automation with only minor modifications. You don't have to learn something new. The knowledge you gain from this book applies to Azure Automation.

I know that this sounds a little confusing, and you are probably wondering why you need the Azure PowerShell module if you have Azure Automation services.

To make things clear, Azure Automation is not a replacement for Azure PowerShell. Actually, it uses the Azure PowerShell cmdlets to automate Azure services and resources. The point is that Azure Automation provides you with a reliable automation platform that you can use to automate your Azure services, instead of using local PowerShell consoles on a local computer.

For instance, if you want to shut down some Azure virtual machines, you can simply open your PowerShell console, use the respective cmdlets to perform that task, and everything is set. But with Azure Automation, you build a runbook using the same PowerShell cmdlets, save it, and configure a scheduler to run this script automatically at a specific time.

You don't have to run anything manually. You don't have to keep your machine up and running. You don't have to do anything else. Just do it once, and enjoy it forever. That's why I like to use the term "unattended automation" to describe the Azure Automation service.

Getting Started with Azure Automation

Chapter 3 talked about Azure storage. There I mentioned that to get access to Azure storage, you need to create an Azure storage account.

The same happens with Azure Automation. To start using it, you need to first create an Azure Automation account. The automation account contains automation resources such as runbooks, credentials, variables, and connections.

The resources held by one automation account are totally isolated and cannot be shared with another automation account. This means that you can have more than one account, each with its own resources. For instance, think of having one automation account for the test/dev environment and another automation account for the production environment.

To create an Azure Automation account, you use the `New-AzureAutomationAccount` cmdlet. This cmdlet requires the `-Name` parameter to specify the name of the automation account, and `-Location` to specify the region of the automation account.

■ **Note** As of this writing, the Azure Automation service is available only in the following Azure regions: East US 2, Japan East, South Central US, Southeast Asia, and West Europe. However, an Azure Automation account can manage resources in different regions.

```
#Create New Azure Automation Account
New-AzureAutomationAccount -Name DevTestAA -Location "West Europe"

AutomationAccountName        Location        State        Plan
---------------------        --------        -----        ----
DevTestAA                    West Europe     Ready        Free
```

So, you create your first Azure Automation account, DevTestAA, for the test/dev environment; it's located in the West Europe region. You also find another property called *plan* and its value is free.

The plan property reflects the Azure Automation account's pricing plan. There are two pricing offerings for Azure Automation: Free and Basic.

The difference between the two offerings is the amount of time that the automation job runs (CPU time). The free offering gives you up to 500 minutes of CPU time per subscription, while basic gives unlimited minutes of CPU time per automation account. The basic offering costs $0.02 per 10 minutes.

To change the offering from free to basic, or vice versa, go to the Azure portal. In Automation, select the automation account that you want to change. Click the **Scale** tab and choose either **Free** or **Basic**. Finally, click **Save**, as shown in Figure 8-1.

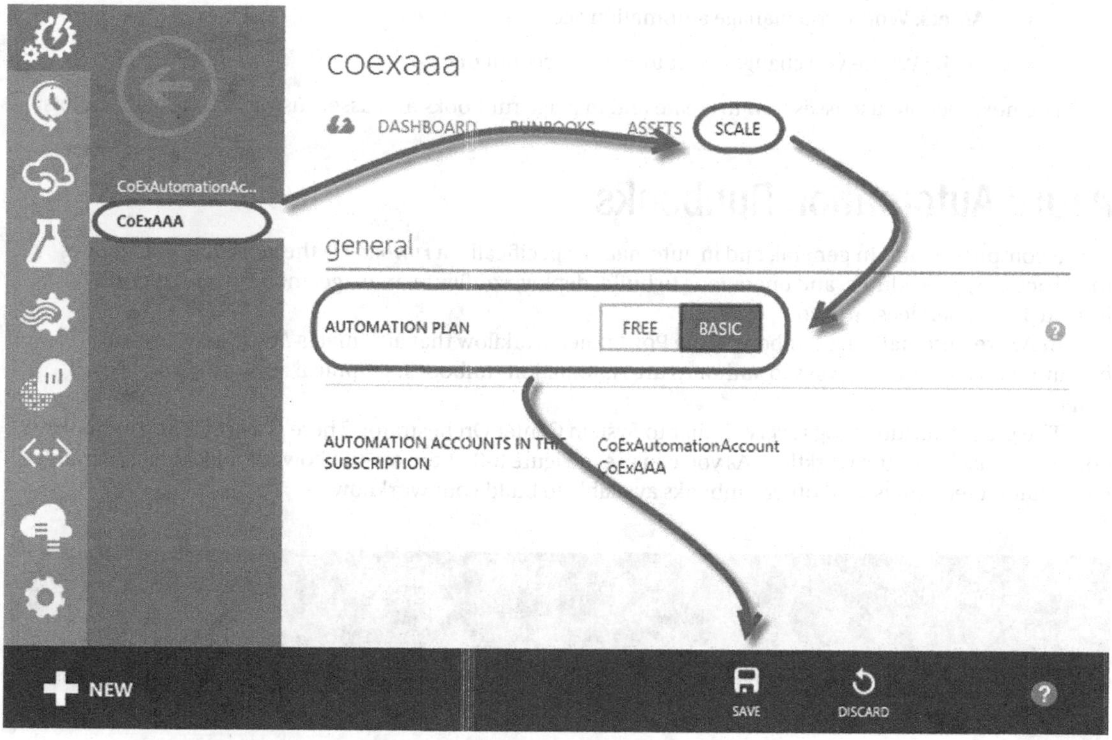

Figure 8-1. *Change the Azure Automation account offering*

There is no cmdlet to modify the settings of an Azure Automation account, but you still have the `Get-AzureAutomationAccount` cmdlet that lists all the automation accounts, and the `Remove-AzureAutomationAccount` cmdlet to remove an automation account.

```
#Remove Azure Automation Account
Remove-AzureAutomationAccount -Name "DevTestAAA" -Force
```

Under each automation account, there are four tabs that represent the properties and resources of the account, as shown in Figure 8-2.

Figure 8-2. *Azure Automation account tabs*

The account tabs can be described as follows.

- **Dashboard**: Shows diagnostic information, jobs status history, runbooks, usage statistics, and assets.
- **Runbook**: Shows the list of available runbooks and the status of each runbook. Also allows you to create, start, import, and export runbooks.

- **Assets**: Where you manage automation account resources.
- **Scale**: Where you change the automation account offering.

The next section discusses how to create and manage runbooks and assets using PowerShell cmdlets.

Azure Automation Runbooks

In the computer world in general, and in automation specifically, a *runbook* is the workflow that defines the processes, procedures, and operations to build, deploy, configure, manage, monitor, and report IT infrastructure, services, and components.

In Azure Automation, a runbook is the PowerShell workflow that automates Azure services and operations. There are two ways to author Azure Automation runbooks: graphical authoring and textual authoring.

The graphical authoring is very similar to System Center Orchestrator. There is a graphical runbook editor that visualizes the workflow. As you can see in Figure 8-3, there are the PowerShell cmdlets, variables, certificates, credentials, and other runbooks available to build your workflow.

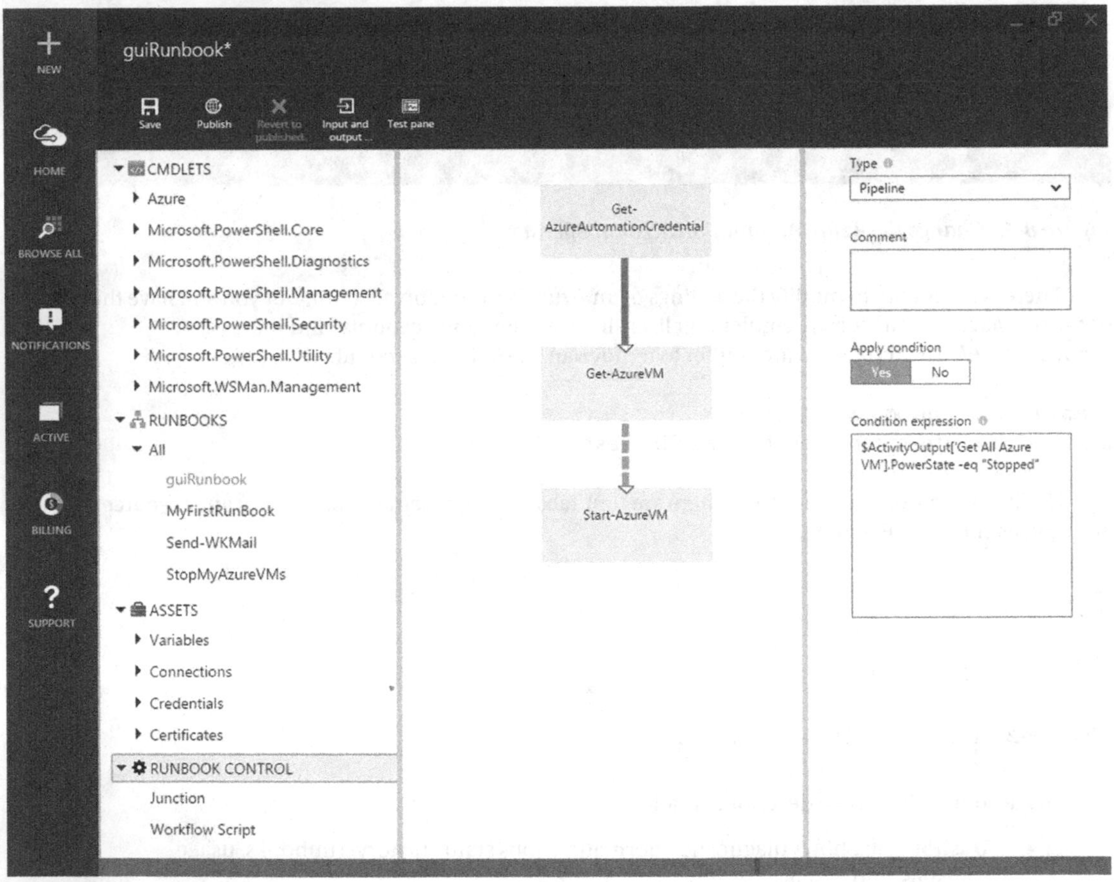

***Figure 8-3.** Azure Automation graphical runbook editor*

■ **Note** The graphical runbook editor is available only on the new Azure portal.

Although it's a graphical editor, the runbook still uses PowerShell in the background. Also, the customization for the workflow is entirely via PowerShell. For instance, if you want to make an action based on a condition, you define this condition using PowerShell code, not the graphical editor.

The textual authoring is simply an online PowerShell editor where you can build a runbook from scratch using purely PowerShell code, as shown in Figure 8-4.

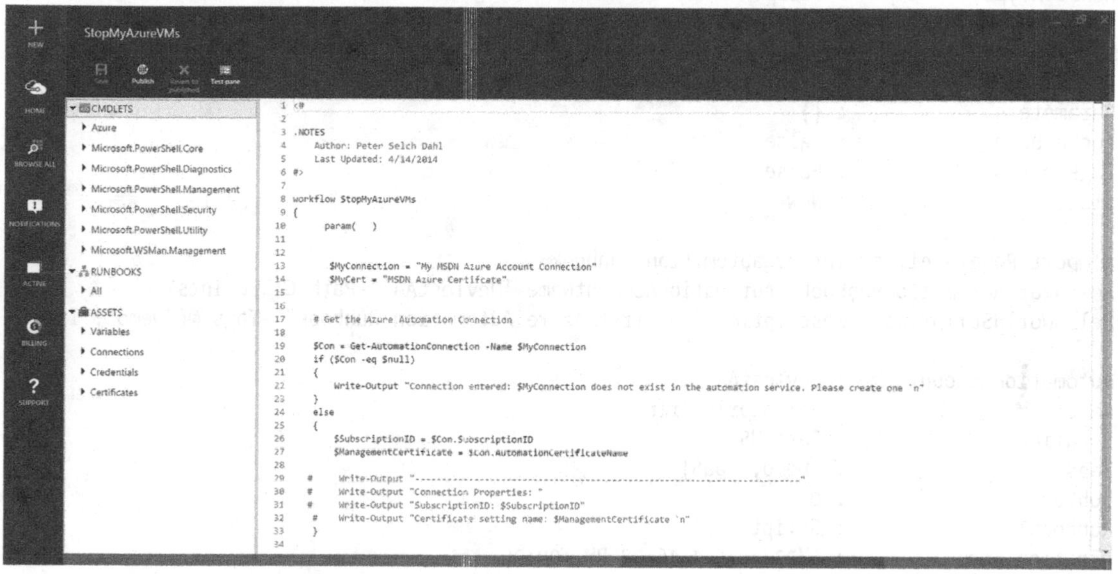

***Figure 8-4.** Azure Automation textual runbook editor*

Now that you understand runbooks, let's learn how to create them.

Creating Runbooks

There are different ways to create Azure Automation runbooks. You can create a new empty runbook or a runbook from a template in the runbooks gallery, and you can import existing PowerShell scripts.

The options to create an empty runbook or import an existing PowerShell script as a runbook are available in both the Azure portal and via Azure PowerShell cmdlets. In contrast, the option to create runbooks from the gallery is available only on the Azure portal, but not via Azure PowerShell cmdlets. You can still download the scripts from the script center repository, however, at `https://gallery.technet.microsoft.com/scriptcenter` and import as runbooks.

To create an Azure Automation runbook using PowerShell, you use the `New-AzureAutomationRunbook` cmdlet. This cmdlet has two parameter sets: the `ByRunbookName` parameter set to create a new empty runbook and the `ByPath` parameter set to import a PowerShell script or workflow as a runbook.

The main difference between these two parameter sets is that `ByRunbookName` uses the `-Name` parameter to specify a name for the runbook, and `ByPath` uses the `-Path` parameter to specify the path of the PowerShell script to import. But the rest of parameters, such as `-Description`, `-AutomationAccountName`, and `-Tags`, remain the same.

```
#Create a new empty Runbook
New-AzureAutomationRunbook -AutomationAccountName 'DevTestAA' -Name HelloWorldRunbook
-Description "My first Azure Automation Runbook" -Tags @("Demo","IaaS")

AutomationAccountName : DevTestAA
Name                  : HelloWorldRunbook
Location              : East US
Tags                  : {Demo, IaaS}
JobCount              : 0
RunbookType           : Script
CreationTime          : 6/23/2015 1:16:08 PM +00:00
LastModifiedTime      : 6/23/2015 1:16:08 PM +00:00
Description           : My first Azure Automation Runbook
Parameters            : {}
LogVerbose            : False
LogProgress           : False
State                 : New

#Import PowerShell script as automation runbook
New-AzureAutomationRunbook -AutomationAccountName 'DevTestAA' -Path C:\Scripts\
HelloWorldScript.ps1 -Description "My first Azure Automation Runbook" -Tags @("Demo","IaaS")

AutomationAccountName : DevTestAA
Name                  : HelloWorldScript
Location              : East US
Tags                  : {Demo, IaaS}
JobCount              : 0
RunbookType           : Script
CreationTime          : 6/23/2015 1:16:08 PM +00:00
LastModifiedTime      : 6/23/2015 1:16:08 PM +00:00
Description           : My first Azure Automation Runbook
Parameters            : {}
LogVerbose            : False
LogProgress           : False
State                 : New
```

In addition to the previous cmdlets, you have the `Set-AzureAutomationRunbook` cmdlet that allows you to modify the properties of an existing runbook, including name, description, and tags. It also allows you to enable and disable runbook logging.

There are two types of logging available for Azure Automation runbook: verbose logging and progress logging. To enable these logging capabilities, you use the `-Logverbose` parameter for verbose logging and the `-LogProgress` parameter for progress logging.

```
#Enable Runbook Logging
Set-AzureAutomationRunbook -AutomationAccountName 'DevTestAA' -Name HelloWorldRunbook
-LogProgress $true -LogVerbose $true

AutomationAccountName : DevTestAA
Name                  : HelloWorldRunbook
Location              : East US 2
Tags                  : {}
JobCount              : 0
```

```
RunbookType          : Script
CreationTime         : 6/23/2015 1:31:25 PM +00:00
LastModifiedTime     : 6/23/2015 2:31:54 PM +00:00
Description          : My first Azure Automation Runbook
Parameters           : {}
LogVerbose           : True
LogProgress          : True
State                : Edit
```

In order to query the list of runbooks under a specific automation account, you use the `Get-AzureAutomationRunbook` cmdlet, which is very similar to all the other cmdlets that query items, such VMs, vNETs, and so forth. But this is not everything; there is also the `Get-AzureAutomationRunbookDefinition` cmdlet that shows the definition and the contents of the runbook itself.

```
#Get Runbook Definition
Get-AzureAutomationRunbookDefinition -AutomationAccountName DevTestAA -Name
HelloWorldRunbook

AutomationAccountName : DevTestAA
Name                  : HelloWorldRunbook
Slot                  : Draft
RunbookType           : Script
CreationTime          : 6/23/2015 1:31:48 PM +00:00
LastModifiedTime      : 6/23/2015 1:31:48 PM +00:00
Content               : <#
                            This PowerShell script was automatically converted to PowerShell
Workflow so it can be run as a runbook.
                            Specific changes that have been made are marked with a comment
starting with "Converter:"
                        #>
                        workflow HellowWorldRunbook {
                            inlineScript {
                                Get-Service
                            }
                        }
```

On the other side, if you want to update a draft definition of a runbook, you can use the `Set-AzureAutomationRunbookDefinition` cmdlet to achieve this task. As usual, you use the `-AutomationAccountName` and `-Name` parameters to select the required runbook. Then, you use the `-Path` parameter to specify the path of the PowerShell file containing the updated definition. Finally, you use the `-overwrite` parameter to overwrite the existing draft definition.

```
#Update Runbook Definition
Set-AzureAutomationRunbookDefinition -AutomationAccountName 'DevTestAA' -Name
HelloWorldRunbook -Path "C:\Scripts\HelloWorldv2.ps1" -Overwrite $true
```

When you create or import an automation runbook, it is in `draft` state, which means that you cannot use it or start it until the state is changed from `draft` to `published`. To publish a runbook, you use the `Publish-AzureAutomationRunbook` cmdlet. You use the `-AutomationAccountName` and `-Name` parameters to specify which runbook to publish.

```
#Publish Runbook
Publish-AzureAutomationRunbook -AutomationAccountName 'DevTestAA' -Name HelloWorldRunbook

AutomationAccountName : DevTestAA
Name                  : HelloWorldRunbook
Location              : East US
Tags                  : {Demo, IaaS}
JobCount              : 0
RunbookType           : Script
CreationTime          : 6/08/2015 1:16:08 PM +00:00
LastModifiedTime      : 6/08/2015 1:16:08 PM +00:00
Description           : My first Azure Automation Runbook
Parameters            : {}
LogVerbose            : False
LogProgress           : False
State                 : Published
```

Once you publish a runbook, you will be able to start it from either the Azure portal or Azure PowerShell. To start a runbook via PowerShell, you use the `Start-AzureAutomationRunbook` cmdlet along with the `-AutomationAccountName` and `-Name` parameters.

```
#Start Automation Runbook
Start-AzureAutomationRunbook -AutomationAccountName 'DevTestAA' -Name HelloWorldRunbook
```

The moment the runbook starts—either manually using the cmdlet or automatically via a predefined schedule, a runbook job is created for that runbook. Each runbook job has an id that can be used to get the job information and output, and to control the job execution with commands like suspend, stop, and resume.

If you start a runbook via PowerShell, then you get the job information, including the id. Otherwise, you can still get the runbook job information using the `Get-AzureAutomationJob` cmdlet. You can query runbook jobs by job id, runbook name, and job status.

```
#Get list of runbook jobs
Get-AzureAutomationJob -AutomationAccountName DevTestAA -RunbookName HelloWorldRunbook

AutomationAccountName     : DevTestAA
Id                        : a9747c86-e901-4272-bc29-96d48543faf7
CreationTime              : 6/08/2015 1:40:32 PM +00:00
Status                    : Completed
StatusDetails             :
StartTime                 : 6/08/2015 1:40:42 PM +00:00
EndTime                   : 6/08/2015 1:40:44 PM +00:00
Exception                 :
LastModifiedTime          : 6/08/2015 1:40:44 PM +00:00
LastStatusModifiedTime    : 1/1/0001 12:00:00 AM +00:00
JobParameters             : {}
RunbookName               : HelloWorldRunbook
HybridWorker              :
```

You can get the output of a specific runbook job by using the `Get-AzureAutomationJobOutput` cmdlet along with the `-Id` parameter to specify the job, and the `-Stream` parameter to specify the type of output. The stream parameter accepts the following values: `Any`, `Debug`, `Error`, `Progress`, `Verbose`, `Warning`, and `Output`.

```
#Query runbook job output
Get-AzureAutomationJobOutput -AutomationAccountName DevTestAA -Id a9747c86-e901-4272-bc29-96d48543faf7 -Stream Any
```

There are also the `Suspend-AzureAutomationJob`, `Resume-AzureAutomationJob`, and `Stop-AzureAutomationJob` cmdlets that allow you to control the execution of a runbook job.

I've mentioned a few times that the Azure Automation service is built on top of the Windows PowerShell Workflow engine. This means that you use the normal Windows PowerShell Workflows mechanism with Azure Automation. The next section explains why PowerShell workflows are important to Azure Automation.

PowerShell Workflows and Checkpoints

One powerful feature of Windows PowerShell Workflows is checkpoints. A checkpoint is like a snapshot of generated outputs, serialized state information, or variables, along with their values, at the moment the checkpoint was taken. So, you can say that checkpoints for a workflow are similar to snapshots for a virtual machine.

Checkpoints make workflows more persistent and reliable. For instance, let's say you have a complex workflow that does multiple tasks on multiple environments. This long and complex workflow might trigger an error and an execution failure for a variety of reasons—it could be a syntax error, a resource that is unreachable or no longer available, or something else. It might be OK to restart the workflow if you get the error at an early stage. But what if the error happens in the middle of execution? You definitely don't want to go back to square one and start everything from scratch.

Therefore, checkpoints allow you to divide the workflow into multiple stages and capture the output of each successful stage. So, if an error occurs and the workflow is suspended, checkpoints let you resume from the latest checkpoint (stage) rather than starting from the beginning.

You use the `Checkpoint-Workflow` activity within the PowerShell workflow to immediately persist a checkpoint.

■ **Note** The term *cmdlet* refers to commands in Windows PowerShell scripts, but you use the term *activity* to refer to commands in Windows PowerShell Workflows. That's why we say `Checkpoint-Workflow` activity, not cmdlet.

■ **Caution** When a checkpoint is invoked, a serialization state of data persists to the storage. The more checkpoints you add, the more data to add to the storage. This affects the performance of the running workflow. So, make sure to use checkpoints wisely and when really needed. Also, sometimes it's much faster to restart a workflow from the beginning than to use checkpoints.

By design, the Azure Automation service limits the amount of runbook execution time to 30 minutes. The Azure Automation service automatically unloads any runbook taking more than 30 minutes, assuming that either something went wrong or that the runbook is monopolizing the service.

Therefore, if you have a long runbook that might take more than 30 minutes to execute, make sure to use checkpoints at intervals under 30 minutes so that you can complete it later.

In some cases, the workflow depends on manual tasks, so you have to suspend the execution until you complete those manual steps and then resume it again. To suspend a workflow, you use the `Suspend-Workflow` activity, and you use the `Resume-Workflow` activity to resume it again.

Azure Automation Assets

Azure Automation assets are a set of predefined and reusable global resources that are shared across runbooks under the same Azure Automation account. These resources are used to make the process of building and editing runbooks easier and consistent.

For example, one of the assets is called a *credentials asset*, which allows you to define an object that stores your credentials securely; later on you can call this credential asset directly within the runbook rather than hard-coding it. This means that if you have multiple runbooks, use this credential the next time you change the password; you will have to update the credential asset instead of manually updating the credential in each and every runbook that you have.

There are different types of Azure Automation assets. The following sections describe and explain them, including how to create and use them.

Automation Credential

In Chapter 2, you learned how to prepare Azure PowerShell to connect to an Azure subscription. One of the steps was authenticating PowerShell against Azure in order to reach out to the Azure subscription(s). The authentication options you had were certificates and Azure AD accounts.

In this chapter, you have a very similar scenario. You still want to use PowerShell to manage and automate Azure, but this time from the Azure Automation console, not the PowerShell console on a local machine.

That's why there are the automation credential settings that securely store the credential information used within the automation runbook. The automation credential assets could be used for Azure itself and the services running on it. For instance, you can use the credential to connect to Azure and to deploy Azure web apps.

The automation credential can store certificates and accounts as well, as shown in Figure 8-5.

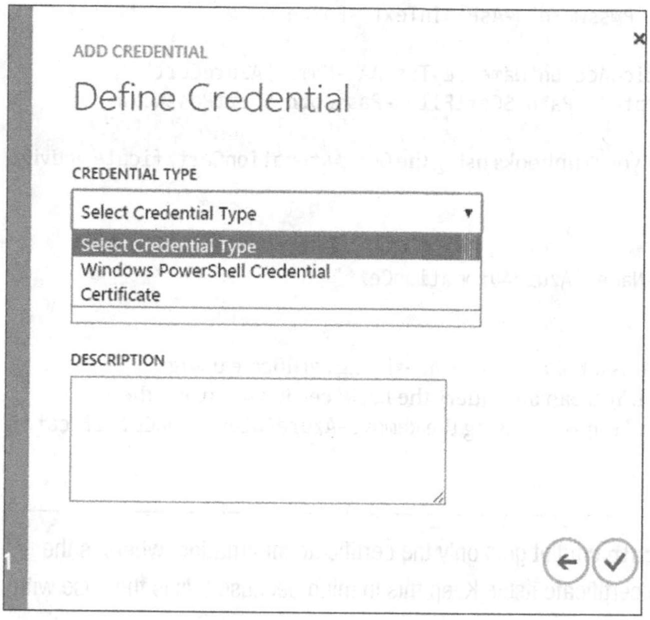

Figure 8-5. *Azure Automation credential types*

The next two sections explain how to create each of the types.

Credential Asset: Certificate

This example assumes that you already have an Azure management certificate. If you don't have one, then please refer to the tutorial at `https://msdn.microsoft.com/en-us/library/azure/gg551722.aspx` to create a new one.

After creating and uploading the Azure management certificate, return to the same machine that you created the certificate, and then export it with private keys so that you have a `.pfx` certificate file that can be used by the automation service.

You can use the following PowerShell code to export the certificate with a private key.

```
#Export Certificate with Private Keys (PFX)
$CertPassword = ConvertTo-SecureString -String "P@sswOrd" -Force -AsPlainText

$AzureMgmtCert = Get-ChildItem -Path Cert:\CurrentUser\My | where {$_.Subject -match
"AzureCert"}

Export-PfxCertificate -FilePath "C:\Certs\AzureCert.pfx" -Password $CertPassword -Cert
$AzureMgmtCert
```

Now that you have the `*.pfx` file, let's use it to create a new automation certificate asset. To do so, you use the `New-AzureAutomationCertificate` cmdlet.

```
#Create Azure Automation Certificate
$CertFile = "C:\Certs\AzureMgmtCert.pfx"
```

```
$CertPassword = ConvertTo-SecureString "P@ssw0rd" -AsPlainText -Force

New-AzureAutomationCertificate -AutomationAccountName DevTestAA -Name "AzureCert"
-Description "Azure Automation Certificate" -Path $CertFile -Password $CertPassword
```

Once you create the certificate, you call in your runbooks using the `Get-AutomationCertificate` activity.

```
#Using Automation Certificate
workflow HelloWorldRunbook {
    $Cert = Get-AutomationCertificate -Name 'AzureAutomationCert'
}
```

You can update the automation certificate asset or overwrite an existing certificate using the `Set-AzureAutomationCertificate` cmdlet. You can also query the list of certificates using the `Get-AzureAutomationCertificate` cmdlet, and remove it using the `Remove-AzureAutomationCertificate` cmdlet.

■ **Note** The `Get-AzureAutomationCertificate` cmdlet gets only the certificate information, whereas the `Get-AutomationCertificate` activity gets the certificate itself. Keep this in mind because this is the case with most of the automation assets.

Credential Asset: PowerShell Credential

The second type of automation credential asset is the PowerShell account. This asset stores security credentials (username and password) in a form of a `PSCrdential` object. Later on, this credential asset can be used for authentication purposes.

You create an automation credential asset using the `New-AzureAutomationCredential` cmdlet.

```
#Create Azure Automation Credential (Get-Credential)
New-AzureAutomationCredential -AutomationAccountName "DevTestAA" -Name "MyCredential" -Value
(Get-Credential admin@Company123.com) -Description "Azure Automation Credential"
```

In the previous code, you used the `Get-Credential` cmdlet to provide the credential (username and password) in `PSCredential` object format. The `Get-Credential` cmdlet prompts a credential box for you to manually enter the username and password.

If you want to do this silently without any prompts, then you can explicitly create `PSCredential` using the `New-Object` cmdlet and provide the username and password (in clear text) as arguments, as shown in the following code.

```
#Create Azure Automation Credential (New-Object)
$Username = Yahia.Sherif@meacoex.com

$Password = ConvertTo-SecureString "Master@123" -AsPlainText -Force

$Cred = New-Object -TypeName System.Management.Automation.PSCredential -ArgumentList
$Username, $Password

New-AzureAutomationCredential -AutomationAccountName "DevTestAA" -Name "MyCredential" -Value
$Cred -Description "Azure Automation Credential"
```

To use the automation credential within a runbook, you use the `Get-AutomationPSCredential` activity.

```
#Using Automation Credential
workflow HelloWorldRunbook {
    $Cred = Get-AutomationPSCredential -Name 'MyCredential'
    $Username = $Cred.UserName
    $securePassword = $Cred.Password
    $Password = $Cred.GetNetworkCredential().Password
}
```

You can update an automation credential asset or overwrite an existing credential using the `Set-AzureAutomationCredential` cmdlet. You can also query the list of certificates using the `Get-AzureAutomationCredential` cmdlet, and remove it using the `Remove-AzureAutomationCredential` cmdlet.

Variable Assets

Automation variable assets allow the creation of persistent variables and share their values across runbooks. You can retrieve and set the value of these variable assets during execution time. The variable asset value can be set by a runbook and retrieved by another runbook. Even if the runbook fails, the value remains because it's persistent.

To create a new variable asset, you use the `New-AzureAutomationVariable` cmdlet along with the `-Name` parameter to specify the variable's name, and the `-Value` parameter to specify its value. You can also use the `-Encrypted` parameter to specify whether the value of this variable is viewable from the portal or via the `Get-AzureAutomationVariable` cmdlet. The `-Encrypted` parameter is very important when storing confidential values such as passwords.

```
#Create Azure Automation Variable
New-AzureAutomationVariable -AutomationAccountName 'DevTestAA' -Name "myPassword" -Encrypted
$true -Value "P@ssw0rd"
```

The variable asset can store any kind of value of type `<System.Object>`; it could be regular data types (strings, int, double, etc.) like in the previous example, or it could be any PowerShell object. For example, you can store a VM or vNET object in a variable asset, as shown in the following code.

```
#Store VM object in Automation Variable
$VM = Get-AzureVM -ServiceName 'WebFarm' -Name 'WebSrv01'

New-AzureAutomationVariable -AutomationAccountName 'DevTestAA' -Name 'WebFarmVM' -Encrypted
$false -Value $VM
```

Unlike the `Get-AzureAutomationCertificate` and `Get-AzureAutomationCredential` cmdlets that return only information about the asset, the `Get-AzureAutomationVariable` cmdlet returns the variable and its value as long as the variable is not encrypted. If the variable asset is encrypted, then you get it only within your runbook using the `Get-AutomationVariable` activity.

```
#Using Automation Variable - Cmdlet
Get-AzureAutomationVariable -AutomationAccountName 'DevTestAA' -Name varX

Name                : varX
CreationTime        : 6/8/2015 12:03:32 AM +00:00
LastModifiedTime    : 6/8/2015 12:14:51 AM +00:00
```

```
Value                 : Hellow World
Description           :
Encrypted             : False
AutomationAccountName : DevTestAA

#Using Automation Variable - Runbook Activity
workflow HelloWorldRunbook {
    Get-AutomationVariable -Name 'varX'
}
```

Also, you can update the value of an existing variable asset using either the `Set-AzureAutomationVariable` cmdlet or from a runbook using the `Set-AutomationVariable` activity.

```
#Set Automation Variable Value - Cmdlet
Set-AzureAutomationVariable -AutomationAccountName 'DevTestAA' -Name varX -Value
'Hello World' -Encrypted $false

#Set Automation Variable Value - Activity
workflow HelloWorldRunbook {
    Set-AutomationVariable -Name 'varY' -Value <System.Object>
}
```

Last but not least, you can remove a variable asset using the `Remove-AzureAutomationVariable` cmdlet.

Connection Assets

An automation connection asset stores the information required to connect to an external system, service, or application. Connection information includes IP addresses, ports, protocols, credentials, tokens, and so on. The connection information varies from one service to another. That's why the connection asset is not specific to a strict format.

To create an automation connection asset, you use the `New-AzureAutomationConnection` cmdlet along with the `-ConnectionTypeName` parameter to specify the type of connection, and the `-ConnectionFieldValues` parameter to specify the PowerShell hash table that contains the connection information.

```
#New Azure Automation Connection
$CertName = "AUTOMATION_CERTIFICATE_NAME"
$SubID  = "SUBSCRIPTION_ID"
$FieldValues = @{"AUTOMATIONCERTIFICATENAME" = $CertName;"SUBSCRIPTIONID"=$SubID}

New-AzureAutomationConnection -AutomationConnectionName 'DevTestAA' -Name 'AzureConn'
-Description "Connection to Azure Subscription XYZ" -ConnectionTypeName 'Azure'
-ConnectionFieldValues $FieldValues
```

The field values must match; they are identified in the connection type settings. For example, an Azure connection type requires an automation certificate name and a subscription ID. So, the field values hash table must contain these keys and values or it will trigger a "Field: <Field_Value_Name> not found" error.

There is no cmdlet to modify the settings of a connection asset. To be more specific, there is no cmdlet to change the connection type of a connection asset. However, there is a cmdlet to change the field values of an existing connection asset. This is the `Set-AzureAutomationConnectionFieldValue` cmdlet.

You use the Set-AzureAutomationConnectionFieldValue cmdlet along with the -ConnectionFieldName parameter to specify the name of the field to change, and the -Value parameter to specify its value.

```
#Set Connection asset Field Value
Set-AzureAutomationConnectionFieldValue -AutomationAccountName DevTestAA -Name AzureConn
-ConnectionFieldName AutomationCertificateName -Value AzureCert2
```

■ **Caution** The -ConnectionFieldName parameter is case sensitive. So make sure that you get the exact name of the field by using (Get-AzureAutomationConnection -AutomationAccountName 'DevTestAA' -Name AzureConn).FieldDefinitionValues.

You might have noticed that in the preceding examples, you have used only connection type Azure. And this is because it is the only available connection type. If you want to manage a different system or service, then you have to make the following modifications to the PowerShell integration module of that service before uploading.

Let's assume that you have a PowerShell module for external service XYZ. You will upload that module to be able to automate XYZ service using an automation runbook.

To create a custom connection for XYZ service, open the XYZ PowerShell module folder on your local computer, and then create a JSON file with the naming convention <Module-Name>-Automation.json, which in this case should be XYZ-Automation.json, and copy the following code to it.

```
//JSON code for automation file
{
    "ConnectionFields":  [
                            {
                                "IsEncrypted"  :  false,
                                "IsOptional"   :  false,
                                "Name"         :  "WebServiceURL",
                                "TypeName"     :  "System.String"
                            },
                            {
                                "IsEncrypted"  :  true,
                                "IsOptional"   :  false,
                                "Name"         :  "WebServiceAuthToken",
                                "TypeName"     :  "System.String"
                            }

                        ],
    "ConnectionTypeName":  "XYZ",
    "IntegrationModuleName":  "XYZ"
}
```

In the previous code, you defined the connection asset settings for the XYZ external service. You used ConnectionField to define the field values. Each field value has the following properties: IsEncrypted, IsOptional, Name, and TypeName. Also, you used ConnectionTypeName to specify the name of the connection type. Finally, you used IntegrationModuleName to specify the name of the PowerShell integration module.

Now, the module is ready—just zip and upload it. And feel free to use XYZ as a connection type the next time that you use the New-AzureAutomationConnection cmdlet.

Integration Module Assets

The integration module asset is a PowerShell module that you upload to an Azure Automation account in order to add new activities to an Azure Automation service.

You want to automate the XYZ external service using your runbooks, so you upload the respective PowerShell module as an asset in order to use its activities. While uploading the module, Azure Automation extracts the cmdlets of this module and converts them to activities, as shown in Figure 8-6, so that it can be embedded and used by runbooks later.

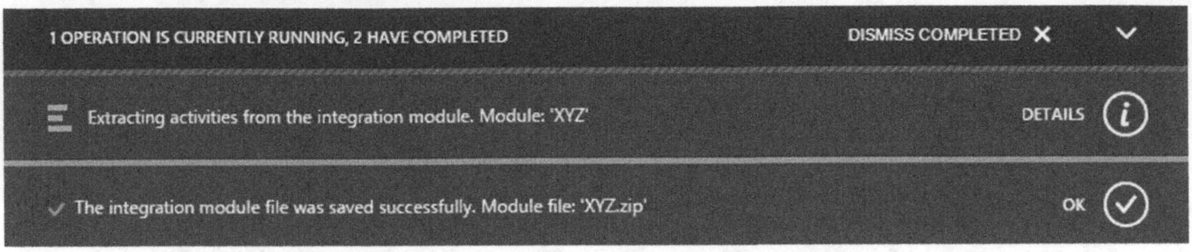

Figure 8-6. *Importing an integration module to an Azure Automation account*

By default, the Azure Automation service comes with the following modules:

- Azure
- Microsoft.PowerShell.Core
- Microsoft.PowerShell.Diagnostics
- Microsoft.PowerShell.Management
- Microsoft.PowerShell.Security
- Microsoft.PowerShell.Utility
- Microsoft.WSMan.Management

The integration module must be compressed with a `*.zip` file extension and have a maximum size of 40 MB. Also, the module file must contain one of the following files:

- A Windows PowerShell module (psm1 file).
- A Windows PowerShell module manifest (psd1 file).
- An assembly (dll file)

Once the module zip file is ready, upload it to any public storage, such Azure blob, or even FTP. After that, you can use the `New-AzureAutomationModule` cmdlet to import it.

```
#Import Integration Module
New-AzureAutomationModule -AutomationAccountName 'DevTestAA' -Name XYZ -ContentLink
http://mylabstorage.blob.core.windows.net/modules/XYZ.zip
```

You can modify the settings of the module or upload a newer version of the module by using the `Set-AzureAutomationModule` cmdlet. To upload a newer version, you use the `-ContentLinkUri` parameter to specify the location of the updated version, and the `-ContentLinkVersion` parameter to specify the version of that update.

```
#Updating Integration Module
New-AzureAutomationModule -AutomationAccountName 'DevTestAA' -Name XYZ -ContentLink
http://mylabstorage.blob.core.windows.net/modules/XYZ.zip -ContentLinkVersion "1.1"
```

Besides this, you have the `Get-AzureAutomationModule` and `Remove-AzureAutomationModule` cmdlets.

Schedule Assets

The Automation Schedules asset is used to enable runbooks to automatically run at specific times. It's like a task scheduler, but for the cloud. The schedule asset could be configured to run runbooks hourly, daily, or one time.

You use the `New-AzureAutomationSchedule` cmdlet to define a new schedule asset. This cmdlet has three parameter sets, each reflecting a specific schedule type: `ByHourly`, `ByDaily`, and `ByOneTime`. The next examples explain how each parameter set works.

In the first example, you create a one-time schedule asset to run the next day at 6:30 PM.

```
#Create Automation Schedule - ByOneTime
$StartTime = (Get-Date "18:30:00").AddDays(1)

New-AzureAutomationSchedule -AutomationAccountName DevTestAA -Name OneTimeSchedule
-StartTime $StartTime -OneTime
```

In the second example, you create a recurring schedule asset to run every eight hours, starting the next day at 6:30 PM for a period of one month.

```
#Create Automation Schedule - ByHourly
$StartTime = (Get-Date "18:30:00")

$EndTime = $StartTime.AddMonths(1)

New-AzureAutomationSchedule -AutomationAccountName DevTestAA -Name HourlySchedule -StartTime
$StartTime -ExpiryTime $EndTime -HourInterval 8
```

In the third example, you create a recurring schedule asset to run every two days, starting the next day at 6:30 PM for a period of one month.

```
#Create Automation Schedule - ByDaily
$StartTime = (Get-Date "18:30:00")

$EndTime = $StartTime.AddMonths(1)

New-AzureAutomationSchedule -AutomationAccountName DevTestAA -Name DailySchedule -StartTime
$StartTime -ExpiryTime $EndTime -DayInterval 2
```

After creating the schedule asset, you can disable or enable it as needed using the `Set-AzureAutomationSchedule` cmdlet along with the `-IsEnabled` parameter.

```
#Disable Automation Schedule
Set-AzureAutomationSchedule -AutomationAccountName DevTestAA -Name HourlySchedule -IsEnabled
$false
```

Once you create the automation asset, you have to link it to one of the runbooks. To do so, you use the `Register-AzureAutomationScheduledRunbook` cmdlet to link a specific schedule to a runbook, and the `Unregister-AzureAutomationScheduledRunbook` cmdlet to unlink it.

```
#Register Schedule to Runbook
Register-AzureAutomationScheduledRunbook -AutomationAccountName DevTestAA -RunbookName
HelloWorldRunbook -ScheduleName HourlySchedule

#Unregister Schedule to Runbook
Unregister-AzureAutomationScheduledRunbook -AutomationAccountName DevTestAA -RunbookName
HelloWorldRunbook -ScheduleName HourlySchedule
```

You can query the list of scheduled runbooks and get information on which runbook is linked to which schedule by using the `Get-AzureAutomationScheduledRunbook` cmdlet. You can also get the list of schedule assets and their properties using the `Get-AzureAutomationSchedule` cmdlet. Finally, you can remove any of the schedule assets using the `Remove-AzureAutomationSchedule` cmdlet.

Summary

This chapter focused on the Azure Automation service. You learned how the automation service is built on top of the PowerShell workflow engine. You also learned about automation runbooks—how they work, how to create them, and how to control them using checkpoints. The chapter also discussed how to use what you know about Azure PowerShell to build runbooks.

The chapter also covered automation assets, including credential, connection, variable, certificate, and schedule, as well as how to create and configure them using PowerShell.

CHAPTER 9

Azure RemoteApp

Cloud computing offers individuals access to data and applications from nearly any point of access to the Internet, offers businesses a whole new way to cut costs for technical infrastructure, and offers big computer companies a potentially giant market for hardware and services.

—Jamais Cascio

Nowadays, in an increasingly mobile world where sitting in the office in front of your desktop is no longer needed to do your tasks, 52% of information workers across 17 countries report using three or more devices for work.[1] It's very important for corporations to ensure that their employees are experiencing the core line-of-business (LOB) applications across these devices, keeping in mind that most devices are not Windows.

One of the strategies for enabling these mobile users is to build a phone app for each platform—Windows Phone, iOS, and Android. But sometimes (actually, most of time in specific industries) users get custom-made software from an independent software vendor (ISV), and unfortunately, this software doesn't support smart operating systems.

Thus, you find yourself stuck with a native Windows application, which you cannot install on iOS or Android, of course, and due to some critical business needs, you want give some users (if not all of them) remote access to it. The remote access could be provided via a technology such as a virtual private network (VPN) or DirectAccess, thus allowing users to connect via remote desktop to the office's computer to do their work.

Another solution for such a problem is to use application virtualization software such as Microsoft RemoteApp, which delivers Windows applications to users on any device, anywhere.

This chapter discusses creating and configuring an Azure RemoteApp environment via RemoteApp PowerShell cmdlets.

What's Azure RemoteApp?

RemoteApp started a long time ago in Windows Server as Remote Desktop Services (RDS) (formerly known as Terminal Services). Recently, it became one of Azure's hosted services, rather than building infrastructure, firewalls, load-balancers, and so forth, on-premise. Now, with less effort, you can get your RemoteApp environment up and running while Microsoft takes care of the storage, user density, high availability, and other operational and administrative tasks, as is the case with other Azure services.

[1]Forrester Research, "BT Futures Report: Info workers will erase boundary between enterprise & consumer technologies," `https://www.forrester.com/Info+Workers+Will+Erase+The+Boundary+Between+Enterprise+And+Consumer+Technologies/fulltext/-/E-res77881`, February 21, 2013.

RemoteApp delivers virtual applications, which means that you don't have to install anything on your device—whether it's Windows, iOS, or Android. The RemoteApp application is integrated with the device's desktop and it appears as if it is running locally.

Actually, the moment you click the app's shortcut, an RDP session (because it runs on top of RDS) is initiated; the RemoteApp application runs in its own resizable window, which can be dragged between multiple monitors and has its own entry in the taskbar.

Azure RemoteApp and PowerShell

The Azure PowerShell module comes with 34 cmdlets (as of this writing) that allow automating a variety of tasks, such creating templates, building collections, assigning users, and more.

Building Your First Azure RemoteApp Environment

In the next sections, you learn about RemoteApp-related cmdlets by building a complete RemoteApp scenario from scratch.

Step 1: Building an Azure RemoteApp Custom Image

Microsoft RemoteApp is about having a Windows Server machine running a Remote Desktop Session Host (RDSH) role service; it has one or more applications installed and configured on it. These applications are published and delivered to users via RemoteApp, which is backed by RDSH.

The first step is to build the Windows Server machine. You create a Windows Server 2012 R2 virtual machine (VM), install an RDSH role, install the applications to be published, and finally generalize the machine using the SysPrep tool to make an image. These steps sound easy and smooth, but are a little long.

What if you don't want to go through all of these steps? Are there any other options? Yes, there are.

The first option is to use one of the default template images that come with Azure RemoteApp. You use the `Get-AzureRemoteAppTemplateImage` cmdlet to list the available images, both default and custom.

```
# List Azure RemoteApp Template Images
Get-AzureRemoteAppTemplateImage | Select Name

Name
----
Office 365 ProPlus (Subscription required)
Office Professional Plus 2013 (30-day trial)
Windows Server 2012 R2
```

The default template images are Windows Server 2012 R2 and Microsoft Office 365 Office ProPlus. The template names describe what each template contains. You have a template for Windows Server 2012 R2, Windows Server 2012 with Office Professional Plus 2012, and a template for Windows Server 2012 R2 with Office 365 ProPlus.

You can read more information about each template at `https://azure.microsoft.com/en-us/documentation/articles/remoteapp-images/`.

The second option is to build the template using the Azure VM image that is preconfigured with RDSH and ready to be used with RemoteApp. This VM image has Windows Server 2012 R2 with an RDSH role installed, and it has a PowerShell script to validate the RemoteApp image requirements and generalize them. What does that mean? It means that all you have to do is simply install the applications.

To build an Azure VM using the RDSH image, from the Azure portal, create a virtual machine from the gallery and search for the **Windows Server Remote Desktop Session Host** image (see Figure 9-1).

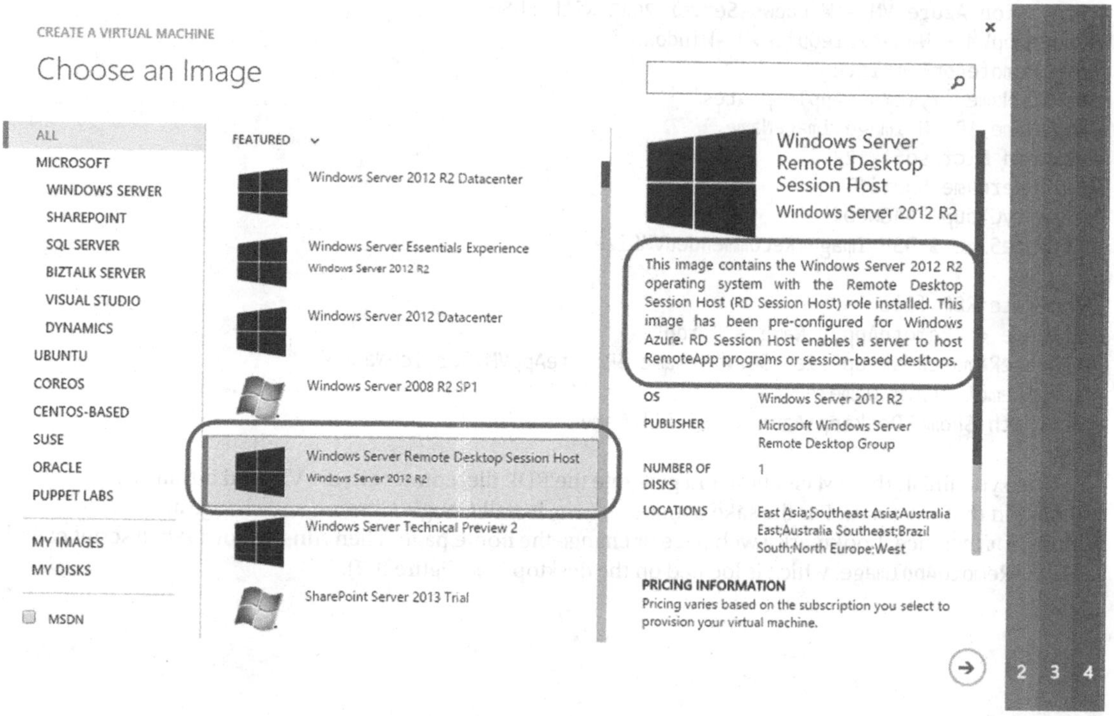

Figure 9-1. *Windows Server Remote Desktop Session Host—VM image*

You can refresh your memory here with PowerShell. Let's recall Chapter 4. Remember the VM cmdlets? First, let's get the list of available VM images by using the `Get-AzureVMImage` cmdlet, and then filter the result to get only the images with RDSH. Unlike the Azure portal, which shows only the latest image, the `Get-AzureVMImage` cmdlet retrieves all versions of the RDSH images, so you have to sort the output by the `PublishedDate` property in descending order and then select the most recent one.

```
# List Azure VM Image for Remote Desktop Session Host (RDSH)
$RDSH_Image = Get-AzureVMImage | `
Where Label -like "Windows Server Remote Desktop Session Host*" | `
Select Label, ImageName, PublishedDate, RecommendedVMSize | `
Sort PublishedDate -Descending | `
Select -First 1 | fl

$RDSH_Image

Label         : Windows Server Remote Desktop Session Host on Windows Server 2012 R2
ImageName     : ad072bd3082149369c449ba5832401ae__Windows-Server-Remote-Desktop-Session-
Host-on-Windows-Server-2012-R2-20150513-0525
PublishedDate : 5/13/2015 6:00:19 AM
RecommendedVMSize: Large
```

Now that you have the RDSH VM image name, the next step is to create a VM with that name using the `New-AzureQuickVM` cmdlet. It generates an RDP file using the `Get-AzureRemoteDesktopFile` cmdlet and saves it on the desktop so that you can use it to connect to the template to finalize the configuration.

```
# Provision Azure VM - Windows Server 2012 with RDSH
$RemoteAppVM = New-AzureQuickVM -Windows `
-Name RemoteAppTemplate `
-ServiceName 'myRemoteAppTemplates' `
-ImageName $RDSH_Image.ImageName `
-Password Microsoft@123 `
-AdminUsername SherifT `
-AffinityGroup "AAGWE01" `
-InstanceSize $RDSH_Image.RecommendedVMSize

# Generate RDP file
$FileName = $RemoteAppVM.Name + ".rdp"
Get-AzureRemoteDesktopFile -ServiceName $RemoteAppVM.ServiceName `
-Name $RemoteAppVM.Name `
-LocalPath $home\Desktop\AzureRDPs\$FileName
```

Once you finish the VM creation and generate the RDP file, connect to the VM and install any application that you want. For the sake of this scenario, install Google Chrome and change any of the settings; for instance, bookmark a web page or change the home page. Then run the PowerShell script called `ValidateRemoteAppImage`, which is located on the desktop (see Figure 9-2).

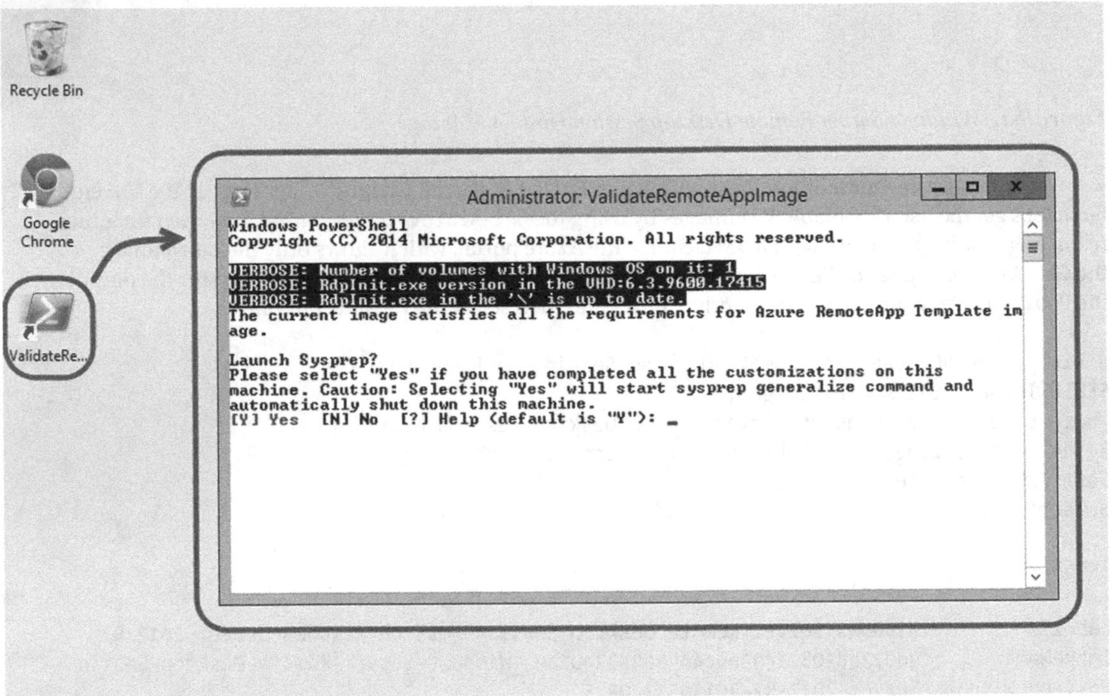

Figure 9-2. *ValidateRemoteAppImage script*

■ **Note** For the Azure RemoteApp to automatically detect the installed app on the custom image, make sure to add the application shortcut to the Start menu. Otherwise, it won't be detected and you will have to publish the application using its full path, such as C:\Program Files (x86)\Google\Chrome\Application\chrome.exe.

The script shown in Figure 9-2 validates the image configuration against the RemoteApp requirements; it lets you know whether you need to fix something or if you are good to go.

If the current image configuration satisfies all the requirements for Azure RemoteApp, then it asks you to launch SysPrep to generalize the machine and shut it down.

So far, you have an Azure VM configured to be an Azure RemoteApp template image, but it's not an image yet. To do that, you need to first add this VM as an image in the Azure VM library. To achieve this task, you need to capture the VM using the Save-AzureVMImage cmdlet.

```
# Capture Azure VM Image
Save-AzureVMImage -ServiceName 'myRemoteAppTemplates' `
-Name 'RemoteAppTemplate' `
-ImageName "RemoteAppTemplatev1" `
-ImageLabel "my Azure RemoteApp Template" `
-OSState Generalized
```

You are almost there. The last step in creating a RemoteApp template image is to import the VM template from the Azure VM library. It's a little confusing, but it is very important to differentiate between the Azure VM image and the Azure RemoteApp template image. The former is stored under the Azure VM library and used to create an Azure VM (see Figure 9-3), whereas the latter is stored under RemoteApp and is used to create Azure RemoteApp collections (see Figure 9-4).

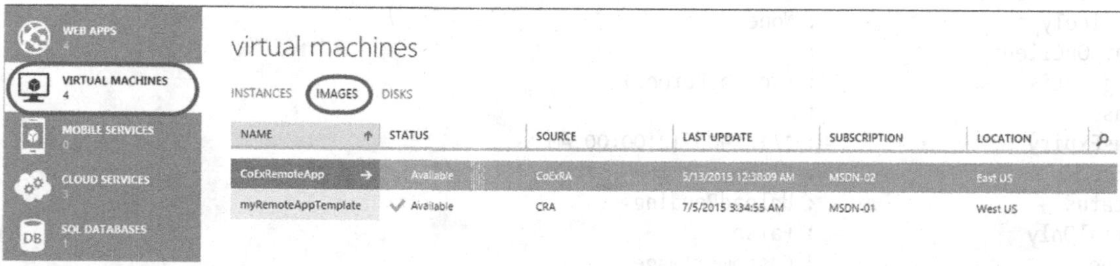

Figure 9-3. *Azure VM image library*

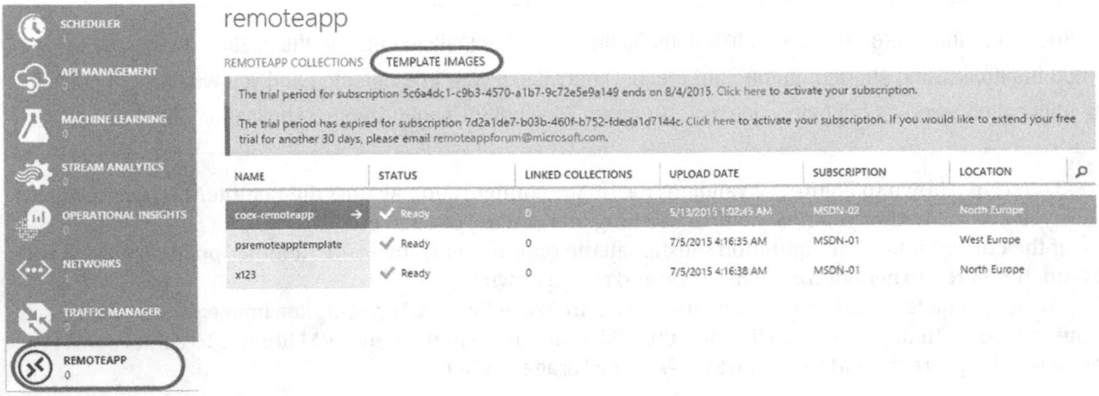

Figure 9-4. *Azure RemoteApp template images*

To create an Azure RemoteApp template image using the Azure VM image stored in the VM library, you use the New-AzureRemoteAppTemplateImage cmdlet.

```
# Create Azure RemoteApp Template Image
New-AzureRemoteAppTemplateImage -ImageName RemoteAppwithChrome `
-Location 'North Europe' `
-AzureVmImageName ' RemoteAppTemplatev1'

Id                        : 4074fc94-1bf3-4cff-9898-309c179d4649
Name                      : RemoteAppwithChrome
NumberOfLinkedCollections : 0
OfficeType                : None
PathOnClient              :
RegionList                : {North Europe}
Sas                       :
SasExpiry                 : 1/1/1900 12:00:00 AM
Size                      : 0
Status                    : UploadPending
TrialOnly                 : False
Type                      : CustomerImage
UploadCompleteTime        : 1/1/0001 12:00:00 AM
UploadSetupTime           : 7/5/2015 9:17:50 PM
UploadStartTime           : 1/1/0001 12:00:00 AM
Uri                       :
```

Once you execute the New-AzureRemoteAppTemplateImage cmdlet, the template status appears on the portal as **Upload Pending** and it remains for a minute or two; it changes to **Import in progress** and finally changes to **Ready** once the process is complete. The Ready status means that you are ready for the next step.

Before moving on to the next step, however, it's important that I mention two more cmdlets related to RemoteApp template images. The first is the Rename-AzureRemoteAppTemplateImage cmdlet, which is used to rename the existing RemoteApp template image.

```
# Rename RemoteApp Template Image
Rename-AzureRemoteAppTemplateImage -ImageName RemoteAppTemplateWithChrome `
-NewName RemoteAppTemplateWithLOBs
```

```
Id                        : 178d7946-28a7-494f-b701-0db730b86271
Name                      : RemoteAppTemplateWithLOBs
NumberOfLinkedCollections : 0
OfficeType                : None
PathOnClient              :
RegionList                : {West Europe}
Sas                       :
SasExpiry                 : 1/1/1900 12:00:00 AM
Size                      : 136365212160
Status                    : Ready
TrialOnly                 : False
Type                      : CustomerImage
UploadCompleteTime        : 7/5/2015 2:16:35 AM
UploadSetupTime           : 7/5/2015 1:45:58 AM
UploadStartTime           : 7/5/2015 2:14:37 AM
Uri                       : https://cdvwe014626977rdcm.blob.core.windows.net/
goldimages/178d7946-28a7-494f-b701-0db730b86271.vhd
```

The second cmdlet is the `Remove-AzureRemoteAppTemplateImage` cmdlet, which is used to remove the RemoteApp template image.

```
# Remove RemoteApp Template Image
Remove-AzureRemoteAppTemplateImage -ImageName RemoteAppTemplateWithLOBs
```

Now, let's the move to the next step.

Step 2: Creating an Azure RemoteApp Collection

After creating the Azure RemoteApp template image, the next step is to create your first RemoteApp collection. A RemoteApp collection is basically where you configure applications, data stores, user assignments, and so on. When you create a collection, Azure creates a VM using the RemoteApp template image that you selected.

You won't have access to this machine, but you have access to its configuration or Azure portal. It's very similar to the idea of web site hosting. A web site is hosted on a web server; and although you don't have access to the server, you can manage it via a control panel.

Azure RemoteApp has two types of collections: a *cloud collection* and *a hybrid collection*. Both collections are hosted on and store data on Azure. Users can access an application using their Active Directory credentials, whether synchronized using Azure Active Directory Connect or federated via Active Directory Federation Services (ADFS).

The only difference between cloud and hybrid collections is that the latter allows access to data and resources stored on the local network. This means that you need to integrate the Azure RemoteApp collection with the Azure virtual network connected to the local network via either ExpressRoute or site-to-site VPN.

To create an Azure RemoteApp collection, you use the `New-AzureRemoteAppCollection` cmdlet. This cmdlet works for both cloud and hybrid collections, but the parameters differ.

The following parameters are used to create a cloud collection:

- `-CollectionName`: Specifies a name for the new RemoteApp collection.
- `-ImageName`: Specifies the name of the RemoteApp template image that will be used to create the collection.

- `-Plan`: Specifies which pricing plan will be used for the collection. The available plans are Basic and Standard. You can get the RemoteApp plans using the `Get-AzureRemoteAppPlan` cmdlet. You can read more about these plans at `http://azure.microsoft.com/en-us/pricing/details/remoteapp/`.
- `-Location`: Specifies the Azure region that will host the collection. You can get the RemoteApp locations by using the `Get-AzureRemoteAppLocation` cmdlet.
- `-Description`: Describes the collection.

So by putting the previous parameters in action, the final command should look like the following.

```
# Create Azure RemoteApp Cloud Collection
New-AzureRemoteAppCollection -CollectionName 'col1' `
-ImageName 'RemoteAppTemplateWithChrome' `
-Plan Basic `
-Location 'North Europe' `
-Description 'Chrome Application'

TrackingId
----------
71a3dc4c-9818-494c-aa11-2f4a03e01e00
```

The collection-provisioning process takes time, usually 30 minutes or more. The cmdlet returns a tracking id that can be used with the `Get-AzureRemoteAppOperationResult` cmdlet to get the current status of the process.

```
# Track Status of Collection Provisioning Process
Get-AzureRemoteAppOperationResult -TrackingId 71a3dc4c-9818-494c-aa11-2f4a03e01e00 | fl

Description  : CreateFreshDeployment_Domain
ErrorDetails :
Status       : InProgress
```

If you want to create a hybrid collection, first you need to ensure that you have Azure virtual network created and connected to your on-premises network. Then, run the `New-AzureRemoteAppCollection` cmdlet with the same parameters that you use to provision a cloud collection (except the `-Location` parameter), in addition to the following parameters.

- `-VNetName`: Specifies the Azure virtual network that the collection will be linked to.
- `-SubnetName`: Specifies which subnet in the virtual network will be used to assign addresses to the RemoteApp collection.
- `-DnsServers`: Specifies the DNS server configuration for the collection if the DNS Server is not configured for the virtual network.
- `-Domain`: Specifies the local domain that the RDSH servers will join.
- `-Credentials`: Specifies the credentials of the service account that will be used to join the RDSH servers to the domain.
- `-OrganizationalUnit`: Specifies which organizational unit that the RDSH server computer object will be stored.

■ **Note** You don't use the `-Location` parameter because you use the same location configured in the virtual network.

```
# Create Azure RemoteApp Hybrid Collection
New-AzureRemoteAppCollection -CollectionName 'col1' `
-ImageName 'RemoteAppTemplateWithChrome' `
-Plan Basic `
-Description 'Chrome Application'
-VNetName 'S2SvNET' `
-SubnetName 'ARAsubnet' `
-Domain 'Company123.com' `
-Credentials (Get-Credential ServiceAccount@Company123.com'

TrackingId
----------
34u2e016-9818-494c-xx78-2f4a03e01e35
```

You can modify the settings of the collections that you have just created by using the `Set-AzureRemoteAppCollection` cmdlet. This cmdlet allows you to modify the collection plan from Basic to Standard, and vice versa, via the `-Plan` parameter. You can update the credentials of hybrid collections via the `-Credential` parameter. And you can set the RDP redirection options via the `-CustomRdpProperty` parameter.

Table 9-1 shows the available redirection options and their PowerShell value.

Table 9-1. *Azure RemoteApp Redirection Options*

Redirection Option	Setting Value	Enabled
Play sounds on the local computer (Play on this computer)	audiomode:i:0	Yes
Captures audio from the local computer and sends it to the remote computer (Record from this computer)	audiocapturemode:i:1	Yes
Print to local printers	redirectprinters:i:1	Yes
COM ports	redirectcomports:i:1	Yes
Smart card devices	redirectsmartcards:i:1	Yes
Clipboard (ability to copy and paste)	redirectclipboard:i:1	Yes
ClearType font smoothing	allowfontsmoothing:i:1	Yes
Redirect all supported Plug and Play devices	devicestoredirect:s:*	Yes
Drive redirection (drive mapping)	drivestoredirect:s:*	No
USB redirection	usbdevicestoredirect:s:*	No

Thus, to enable the drive and USB redirection for the Azure RemoteApp collection, the code should look like the following.

```
# Setting Azure RemoteApp Collection CutomRdpProperty
Set-AzureRemoteAppCollection -CollectionName col1 `
-CustomRdpProperty "drivestoredirect:s:*`nusbdevicestoredirect:s:*"
```

If you want to disable one of the default redirection settings, then make sure to replace the number 1 (at the end of the settings value) with 0; for example, if you want to disable smart card redirection, then replace the `redirectsmartcards:i:1` with `redirectsmartcards:i:0`.

```
# Disable Smartcard Redirection
Set-AzureRemoteAppCollection -CollectionName col1 `
-CustomRdpProperty "redirectsmartcards:i:0"
```

■ **Note** Make sure to log out all users before applying the redirection settings changes.

As part of collection maintenance, it might happen that you need to update, install, or even remove an application. So, instead of rebuilding the collection from scratch, republishing the applications, and reassigning the users, you can use the RemoteApp collection update capability, which allows you to in-place update the existing collection using a new RemoteApp template image while keeping the existing configuration.

To update an Azure RemoteApp collection via PowerShell, you use the `Update-AzureRemoteAppCollection` cmdlet along with the `-CollectionName` parameter to specify the collection to update and `-ImageName` to specify the name of the Azure RemoteApp template image used to update the collection. You can also use the `-ForceLogoffWhenUpdateComplete` parameter to log out all connected users and force them to reconnect to the updated collection. Otherwise, users are alerted that they must log out within 60 minutes, so that they have enough time to save their work.

```
# Update Azure RemoteApp Collection
Update-AzureRemoteAppCollection -CollectionName col1 `
-ImageName RATemplateWithBrowsers `
-ForceLogoffWhenUpdateComplete

TrackingId
----------
cc6a72bc-b408-42d4-8586-b5ee9c9d5dbd
```

You must do the update process manually for RemoteApp custom template images. However, if you are using a default RemoteApp template image, then you don't have to worry about it because Microsoft takes care of it.

Once the RemoteApp collection is ready (whether a new collection or an updated collection), you are ready to publish the programs.

Step 3: Publishing Azure RemoteApp Programs

Now that you have the RemoteApp collection ready, it is time to publish the programs you installed on the RemoteApp template image. To publish a RemoteApp program, you use the `Publish-AzureRemoteAppProgram` cmdlet along with the `-FileVirtualPath` parameter to specify the file path of the program executable file, and the `-DisplayName` parameter to specify the name of the application. Also, you can use the `-CommandLine` parameter to specify any additional parameter for that program. For instance, if you want to run Microsoft Word in safe mode, you use the `-CommandLine` parameter with value `'/s'`.

You installed Google Chrome while preparing the RemoteApp custom template image. The following code shows how to publish it.

```
# Publish RemoteApp Program - Google Chrome
Publish-AzureRemoteAppProgram -CollectionName col1 `
-FileVirtualPath "C:\Program Files (x86)\Google\Chrome\Application\chrome.exe" `
-DisplayName 'Google Chrome'
```

If the program you are trying to publish is a Start menu program, then you can replace the `-FileVirtualPath` parameter with the `-StartMenuAppId` parameter. You can get the Start menu programs by using the `Get-AzureRemoteAppStartMenuProgram` cmdlet.

```
# Get RemoteApp Start Menu Programs
Get-AzureRemoteAppStartMenuProgram -CollectionName col1

CommandLineArguments :
IconPngUris          : {[32, https://cdvne015027925rdcm.blob.core.windows.net/
icons/1a67d7cd-5311-47b7-81b1-3a6354763e0f.png?sv=2012-02-12&se=2015-07-06T22%3A49%3A05Z&sr=
b&sp=r&sig=VHoBYt45qScPrTXxt6koF%2FhzZKLMRDU3UNkfNVQ32Do%3D]}
IconUri              : https://cdvne015027925rdcm.blob.core.windows.net/icons/c55176df-506d-
4cc4-8885-d6402cd93b3a.ico?sv=2012-02-12&se=2015-07-06T22%3A49%3A05Z&sr=b&sp=r&sig=s6grcLbqb
7%2BKmHYckdQqmff1BTSeROUzagbUFPotzvM%3D
Name                 : Calculator
StartMenuAppId       : acc5f0f8-9f08-4fd6-aa61-3297fea5886b
VirtualPath          : %SYSTEMDRIVE%\Windows\System32\calc.exe

CommandLineArguments :
IconPngUris          : {[32, https://cdvne015027925rdcm.blob.core.windows.net/
icons/4d92d0a3-996b-46cd-a8ea-9987888b8c30.png?sv=2012-02-12&se=2015-07-06T22%3A49%3A05Z&sr=
b&sp=r&sig=lmCGUaSrwsc7zdLFrPwWyFqicRa69PbmgZVLbIdtipw%3D]}
IconUri              : https://cdvne015027925rdcm.blob.core.windows.net/icons/783c9d15-133f-
43bd-83b2-251dcc693e9d.ico?sv=2012-02-12&se=2015-07-06T22%3A49%3A05Z&sr=b&sp=r&sig=NtWG9pcUX
K2%2B5qTebOLqdODmMd22MXahCmn2ikzxgtI%3D
Name                 : cmd
StartMenuAppId       : b2a864fd-8959-4177-b692-f47ca22dbda7
VirtualPath          : %SYSTEMDRIVE%\Windows\System32\cmd.exe

CommandLineArguments :
IconPngUris          : {[32, https://cdvne015027925rdcm.blob.core.windows.net/icons/
dadb6671-9558-4141-8e44-2ced7ba0ae37.png?sv=2012-02-12&se=2015-07-06T22%3A49%3A05Z&sr=b&sp=r
&sig=RyJcEoSYBnb1uJh%2BwvKxd1JzWFfGOOvLeO9Erh8GQGk%3D]}
```

```
IconUri              : https://cdvne015027925rdcm.blob.core.windows.net/icons/cd9171b2-38c9-
4b94-8c92-0ad23266c5dc.ico?sv=2012-02-12&se=2015-07-06T22%3A49%3A05Z&sr=b&sp=r&sig=TrQITpeOg
4aXlHcfKTP%2Fqk6OuiIEZ%2BGOgi8yLmX%2BeCO%3D
Name                 : InternetExplorer
StartMenuAppId       : 0fdf8ce9-429a-44e9-9add-f3afccac3fce
VirtualPath          : %SYSTEMDRIVE%\Program Files\Internet Explorer\iexplore.exe
```

To unpublish a program, you use the `Unpublish-AzureRemoteAppProgram` cmdlet along with the `-Alias` parameter to specify the alias of the program to unpublish. You can get the aliases by using the `Get-AzureRemoteAppProgram` cmdlet.

```
# Get RemoteApp Program Alias
$Prog  = Get-AzureRemoteAppProgram -CollectionName col1 | `
Where Name -eq 'Google Chrome' |`
Select Alias

# Unpublish RemoteApp Program
Unpublish-AzureRemoteAppProgram -CollectionName col1 -Alias $Prog.Alias
```

At this stage, you are just one step away from getting everything done and ready to work.

Step 4: User Assignment

The final configuration step is the user assignments, in which you define which users have access to the RemoteApp collection. The users you add could be from Microsoft accounts or Azure AD accounts.

You use the `Add-AzureRemoteAppUser` cmdlet along with the `-Type` parameter to specify the user account type, whether **MicrosoftAccount** or **OrgId**, and you use the `-UserUpn` parameter to specify the user's UPN.

```
# Add Azure RemoteApp User
Add-AzureRemoteAppUser -CollectionName col1 `
-Type OrgId `
-UserUpn admin@Company123.com
```

To remove user access, you use the `Remove-AzureRemoteAppUser` cmdlet with the same parameters, like the `Add-AzureRemoteAppUser` cmdlet.

```
# Remove Azure RemoteApp User
Remove-AzureRemoteAppUser -CollectionName col1 `
-Type OrgId `
-UserUpn admin@Company123.com
```

Once you finish the user assignment process, go to the web site at `http://remoteapp.windowsazure.com`. Go to the Download page and select the client for your operating system. There is one available for Windows, Windows Phone, Android, iOS, and Mac OS X.

Install the application and log in using your corporate credentials (or Microsoft account) to go to the RemoteApp workspace and get to your applications (see Figure 9-5).

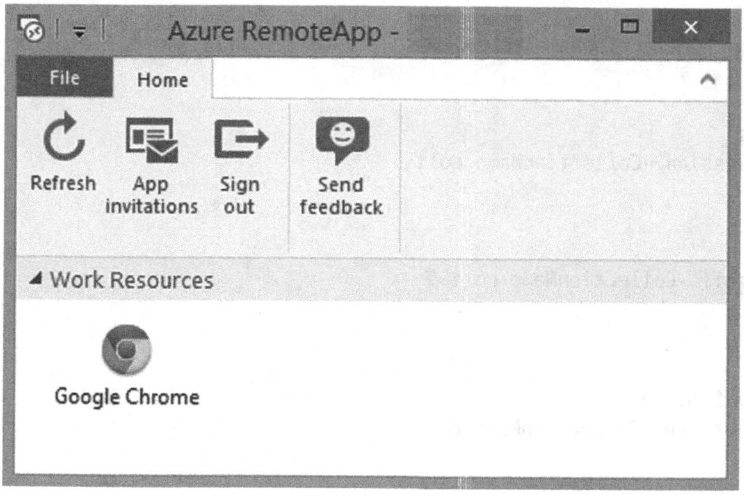

Figure 9-5. *Azure RemoteApp workspace—Windows OS*

In Figure 9-5, the workspace name appears to the user as **Work Resources**. You can change this name to whatever you want by using the Set-AzureRemoteAppWorkspace cmdlet.

```
# Set RemoteApp Workspace Name
Set-AzureRemoteAppWorkspace -WorkspaceName 'Company123 Workspace'
```

This code changes the workspace name from Work Resources to **Company123 Workspace**.

Finally, you can congratulate yourself. You built the RemoteApp template image, created the RemoteApp collection, published a program, and assigned access to users. Now you have users connected to the Azure RemoteApp environment, which means that you have a session.

The next section explains how to manage RemoteApp sessions.

Managing Azure RemoteApp Sessions

First off, to manage a session, you need to know which session you have, the state of the session (whether active or idle), the connected users, and their logon times. For the purpose of this task, you'll use the Get-AzureRemoteAppSession cmdlet to query all RemoteApp sessions for a specific collection.

```
# List RemoteApp Sessions
Get-AzureRemoteAppSession -CollectionName col1

LogonTimeUtc                          State       UserUpn
------------                          -----       -------
6/25/2015 11:15:10 PM                 Connected   admin@Company123.com
6/25/2015 10:19:34 PM                 Connected   Sherif@Company123.com
```

Once you know who is connected, you can decide the next action. You can disconnect these sessions by using the Disconnect-AzureRemoteAppSession cmdlet, log out of a session by using the Invoke-AzureRemoteAppSessionLogoff cmdlet, or send a message to all connected sessions by using the Send-AzureRemoteAppSessionMessage cmdlet.

```
# Disconnect RemoteApp Session
Disconnect-AzureRemoteAppSession -CollectionName col1 `
-UserUpn admin@meacoex.com

# Logoff All RemoteApp Sessions
$Sessions = Get-AzureRemoteAppSession -CollectionName col1

ForEach ( $s in $Sessions )
{
Invoke-AzureRemoteAppSessionLogoff -CollectionName col1 `
-UserUpn $s.UserUpn
}

# Send Message to All RemoteApp Sessions
$Sessions = Get-AzureRemoteAppSession -CollectionName col1

ForEach ( $s in $Sessions )
{
Send-AzureRemoteAppSessionMessage -CollectionName col1 `
-UserUpn $s.UserUpn `
-Message "You Session will be terminated in 60 minutes. Please, save you what you doing
now."
}
```

Sending a message to connected users is very important, especially if you just updated the collections. All users are forced to log out, so, you might want to warn them to save their work.

When we talk about sessions and active users, it means that there is a service being consumed; it's important to have an idea about the usage of this service.

The RemoteApp PowerShell has two cmdlets that get usage information for an Azure RemoteApp collection. The `Get-AzureRemoteAppCollectionUsageSummary` and the `Get-AzureRemoteAppCollectionUsageDetails` cmdlets are responsible for getting this kind of usage information. These cmdlets show you what you can get from the RemoteApp collection dashboard on the Azure portal.

Summary

In this chapter, you learned about the Azure RemoteApp service and its PowerShell cmdlets via a full end-to-end RemoteApp scenario. You started by building an Azure RemoteApp custom template with a Google Chrome application, and then you used the RemoteApp template image to create a RemoteApp collection.

While creating the RemoteApp collection, you built another custom image that had some changes and you used it to update the existing RemoteApp collection. Finally, you published the application inside the collection and assigned access to these applications to corporate users.

Also, you learned how to manage the connected session and take actions such as disconnecting a session, logging off a session, and sending a message to the active sessions.

Finally, you finished the chapter with getting RemoteApp usage information using PowerShell cmdlets.

CHAPTER 10

Azure Identity and Access

Identity is one of those things that you cannot live without, whether virtually in the electronic world or physically in your daily life. Identity is what tells us who we are and helps us interact with others.

For years, Active Directory has been one of the most important and popular directory services for handling user and computer identities, and for managing authorized access to corporate resources such as servers, e-mail, printers, and so on.

Today, with both vendors and consumers adopting cloud computing, it is important to have an identity management component for workloads, applications, and services. Therefore, Microsoft brought Active Directory to the cloud as Azure Active Directory (AD), with entirely new features and capabilities to match the nature and requirements of the cloud.

This chapter discusses configuring and managing Azure Active Directory with PowerShell.

What's Azure Active Directory?

Azure AD is an identity and access solution for both cloud and on-premises services. It integrates with Windows Server Active Directory to provide a single sign-on (SSO) for on-premises resources and applications, as well as Software as a Service (SaaS) apps.

Azure AD is the backbone for Microsoft Online Services like Office 365, Microsoft Intune, Azure RMS, and CRM Online. That's why if you are using any of these services, you can still use your domain credentials without noticing any difference.

Single Sign-On (SSO) for SaaS Apps

Azure AD offers out-of-the-box integration with more than 2,480 SaaS apps (Microsoft and third parties). For instance, you can integrate Azure AD with apps like Salesforce, Google Apps, Oracle CRM, Facebook, Twitter, and so many more. It's not only single sign-on but also account provisioning and de-provisioning.

Provisioning means that the next time that you create an account for a user, Azure AD automatically provisions a mailbox on Google Apps and an account on Salesforce. It is the same when you remove a user; Azure automatically de-provisions and removes the mailbox and Salesforce account.

A list of SaaS apps that Azure AD can integrate with is at `http://azure.microsoft.com/en-us/marketplace/active-directory/all`.

Group Management

Azure AD provides a Group Management feature in which you allow users to create their own AD security groups and Office 365 groups.

Also, you can enable group self-service to delegate the approval or rejection of membership requests. So, you can allow groups to manage their own user access without relying on the IT department.

Self-Service Password Reset (SSPR)

Another interesting component in Azure AD is self-service password reset (SSPR). Azure AD users can reset their passwords from a web portal that can be accessed from anywhere and at any time. It works very similarly to when you forget your Hotmail or Facebook password. You just log in to the web site and choose Forgot My Password, and then follow the procedure.

SSPR comes with password write-back capabilities that resets a password and syncs it back to the on-premises Active Directory.

Multi-Factor Authentication (MFA)

Multi-factor authentication (MFA) is a component that allows organizations to add a second security layer for people accessing sensitive business resources or data, such as accessing e-mail, connecting via a remote desktop session on a server, or even initiating a VPN session.

For a very long time, usernames and passwords have been used to protect information, accounts, computers, and so forth. Today, with a lot of security challenges and advanced security attacks, usernames and passwords are no longer enough. There are different reasons for this. For example, some people don't seem to regard their passwords as confidential information. (I think that most of us have a friend who, perhaps due to forgetfulness, writes down his password on a sheet of paper or writes his PIN on the back of his credit card.) Another reason is when the service provider doesn't maintain the right security standards; so if the service gets hacked, the users' information is exposed (this has happened with big-name companies such as LinkedIn[1]). For these reasons, organizations and service providers started to apply and enforce multi-factor authentication (a.k.a. dual-factor authentication) to protect their employees and customers.

Typically in multi-factor authentication implementation, credential-based authentication with username and password is first used; if the user succeeds, a second authentication is required. This could be via a phone call (to the user's number listed in the contact information stored in AD) asking for a personal PIN, or via an SMS containing a code, or via a randomly generated token, either a hard token or a soft-token app on the user's smartphone, such as Azure Authenticator or Google Authenticator. Azure MFA SDK has a library to implement voiceprint authentication, so the next time my phone rings, the MFA server can analyze my voice to verify my identity.

Devices Registration

In Windows Server Active Directory, desktops and servers are joined to the domain so that you can manage and control them by applying the right security policies via Group Policy. The same concept applies to Azure AD; it allows Microsoft, as well as non-Microsoft operating systems, to be registered under your tenant so that you can force policies on devices via Microsoft Intune, the Mobile Device Management solution. It also lets you keep track of the devices' activities (see Figure 10-1 and Figure 10-2).

---

[1]http://www.pcworld.com/article/257045/6_5m_linkedin_passwords_posted_online_after_apparent_hack.html.

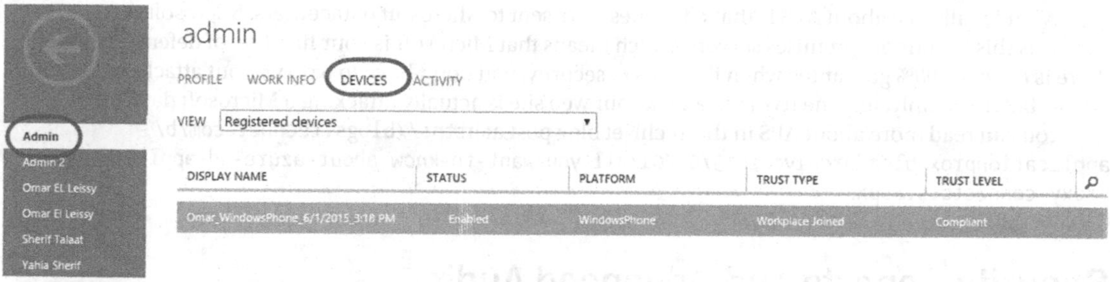

***Figure 10-1.** User's registered devices*

***Figure 10-2.** Devices and applications from which the user has signed in*

Devices Registration is also known as Workplace Join and Cloud Domain-Join (CDJ).

Application Proxy Service

Application Proxy Service (APS) allows secure publishing of internal web apps to remote and external users. The application proxy encrypts the traffic between Azure and the local web servers, defines a pre-authentication method (Azure AD or pass-through), applies multi-factor authentication, and also uses conditional access to identify which users are eligible to access which published applications from which IP addresses. You can consider APS as a reverse proxy as a service component; it is pretty much similar to Web Application Proxy (WAP), but on the cloud.

What I really like about APS is that all requests are sent to Microsoft datacenters. Microsoft then forwards this to your on-premises servers, which means that Microsoft is your first line of defense. Although there is never a 100% guarantee when it comes to security, you don't have to worry about attacks in the same way as before. Simply, anyone trying to attack your web site is actually attacking a Microsoft datacenter.

You can read more about APS in the TechNet blog post at `http://blogs.technet.com/b/applicationproxyblog/archive/2015/06/01/all-you-want-to-know-about-azure-ad-application-proxy-connectors.aspx`.

Security Reports and Advanced Audit

With all of these capabilities in Azure AD, it's very important to track and audit the services and applications. Azure AD provides a set of comprehensive and rich machine-learning-based security reports that allow you to audit every single access attempt to corporate resources. Table 10-1 describes these reports.

Table 10-1. *Azure AD Security Reports*

Report Name	Report Description
Sign-ins from unknown sources	May indicate an attempt to sign in without being traced.
Sign-ins after multiple failures	May indicate a successful brute-force attack.
Sign-ins from multiple geographies	May indicate that multiple users are signing in with the same account.
Sign-ins from IP addresses with suspicious activity	May indicate a successful sign-in after a sustained intrusion attempt.
Sign-ins from possibly infected devices	May indicate an attempt to sign in from possibly infected devices.
Irregular sign-in activity	May indicate events anomalous to users' sign-in patterns.
Users with anomalous sign-in activity	Indicates users whose accounts may have been compromised.
Audit report	Audited events in your directory.
Password reset activity	Provides a detailed view of password resets that occur in your organization.
Password reset registration activity	Provides a detailed view of password reset registrations that occur in your organization.
Self-service groups activity	Provides an activity log to all group self-service activity in your directory.
Application usage	Provides a usage summary for all SaaS applications integrated with your directory.
Account provisioning activity	Provides a history of attempts to provision accounts to external applications.
Password rollover status	Provides a detailed overview of automatic password rollover status of SaaS applications.
Account provisioning errors	Indicates an impact to users' access to external applications.

Azure AD has main three editions: Free, Basic, and Premium. Each edition has different capabilities and features. The list of available features per edition is available at `https://msdn.microsoft.com/en-us/library/azure/dn532272.aspx`.

Azure AD and PowerShell

Like most of the services of Azure, and even like Windows Server Active Directory, Azure AD can be managed by Windows PowerShell. Yet it's not using the same Azure PowerShell module, but a separate module known as the Windows Azure AD module for PowerShell.

You can download the Azure AD module for PowerShell from `http://go.microsoft.com/fwlink/p/?linkid=236297`. This module requires the Microsoft Online Services Sign-In Assistant for IT Professionals RTW component, which you can download from `http://go.microsoft.com/fwlink/?LinkID=286152`.

The Azure AD module doesn't cover all the features and capabilities of Azure AD, but it has powerful uses, especially when configuring users, groups, assigning licenses, and SSO configuration.

Once you download the module package and install it, you get a new module, MSOnline, added to your PowerShell modules store. You also get a desktop shortcut that you can use to launch it directly. Anyway, you don't need that shortcut because PowerShell version 3.0 (and newer) has module autoloading capability.

Before managing your Azure AD tenant, the first step is to connect to this tenant using the `Connect-MSOLService` cmdlet along with the `-Credential` parameter. The credential you pass should be one of the tenant administrators.

```
#Connecting to Azure AD Tenant
Connect-MSOLService -Credential (Get-Credential admin@<YOUR_TENANT>.onmicrosoft.com)
```

Once you connect, you are able to run the rest of the cmdlets to manage the different Azure AD services.

Managing Azure AD Users

There are two ways to get users onto Azure AD. The first one is to synchronize the local Windows Server AD with Azure AD using the Azure Active Directory Connect (the new DirSync), or to manually create users.

For the first option, Directory Synchronization, you have to enable it on the Azure AD tenant using the `Set-MsolDirSyncEnabled` cmdlet along with the `-EnableDirSync` parameter (used to enable or disable it).

```
#Enable Directory Synchronization
Set-MsolDirSyncEnabled -EnableDirSync $true
```

Once you turn on DirSync features, follow the step-by-step article on how to set up and configure the Azure AD Connect tool at `http://blogs.technet.com/b/ad/archive/2014/08/04/connecting-ad-and-azure-ad-only-4-clicks-with-azure-ad-connect.aspx`.

For the second method, which is to create users manually, you use the `New-MSOLUser` cmdlet. This cmdlet has a set of parameters that reflect all the users' information.

```
#New-MsolUser cmdlet Parameters
New-MsolUser -DisplayName -UserPrincipalName -AlternateEmailAddresses -BlockCredential
-City -Country -Department -Fax -FirstName -ForceChangePassword -ImmutableId
-LastName -LicenseAssignment -LicenseOptions -MobilePhone -Office -Password
-PasswordNeverExpires -PhoneNumber -PostalCode -PreferredLanguage -State -StreetAddress
-StrongPasswordRequired <Boolean> -TenantId -Title -UsageLocation
```

Although, there are a number of parameters, you still create an Azure AD user using only the -FirstName, -LastName, -DisplayName, and -UserPrincipalName parameters. Later on, you can update user accounts and add more information using the Set-MSOLUser cmdlet.

```
#create User Account with minimal parameters
New-MsolUser -FirstName 'Yahia' -LastName 'Sherif' -DisplayName "Yahia Sherif"-
UserPrincipalName Yahia.Sherif@Company123.com

Password        UserPrincipalName              DisplayName      isLicensed
--------        -----------------              -----------      ----------
Zaxu3578        Yahia.Sherif@Company123.com    Yahia Sherif     False
```

In the previous example, you didn't assign a password to the user, so the New-MSOLUser cmdlet generated a random password for that user account. You can reset the password later using the Set-MSOLUserPassword cmdlet.

```
#Reset Azure AD User Password
Set-MSOLUserPassword UserPrincipalName Yahia.Sherif@Company123.com -NewPassword
Microsoft@123 -ForceChangePassword $true
```

If you want to remove a user account from Azure AD, use the Remove-MSOLUser cmdlet. By the way, this cmdlet is the only way to remove an Azure AD user synced using Azure AD connect; there is no GUI for it.

By default, the Remove-MSOLUser cmdlet sends removed user accounts to the Azure AD recycle bin; so you can restore any users that have been accidentally removed. A removed user account remains in the recycle bin for 30 days, after which it is automatically deleted. If you want to permanently remove a user in one shot, then use the -RemoveFromRecycleBin parameter.

```
#Remove Azure AD User
Remove-MSOLUser -UserPrincipalName Yahia.Sherif@Company123.com -RemoveFromRecycleBin
```

To retrieve a user from the recycle bin, use the Get-MSOLUser cmdlet with -ReturnDeletedUsers. Then, use the Restore-MSOLUser cmdlet to restore the account.

```
#Restore Azure AD Deleted User
Get-MSOLUser -ReturnDeletedUsers | Restore-MSOLUser
```

So far, you have created an Azure AD user account, reset its password, removed an account, and then restored it. The next step is to assign a subscription license to this user account.

Managing Azure AD Licenses and Subscriptions

Earlier in the chapter, I mentioned that Azure AD is the backbone directory service for Microsoft Online Services like Azure, Intune, Office 365, and CRM. Azure AD stores these services' information, including services subscription, licenses, users, groups, devices, and so forth. And because you have this information, you can manage it.

You can get a list of all Microsoft Online Services subscriptions purchased by your company by using the Get-MSOLSubscription cmdlet. It tells you which subscriptions you have, as well as the purchase dates, the expiry/renewal dates, and the number of licenses.

Also, you use the Get-MSOLAccountSku cmdlet to get the license SKU (you need this information when assigning a license to a user), active licenses, consumed licenses, and warning licenses (mostly expired licenses).

The following code gets the available SKUs for Company123 tenants.

```
#Retriving Account SKUs
Get-MsolAccountSku

AccountSkuId                         ActiveUnits    WarningUnits    ConsumedUnits
------------                         -----------    ------------    -------------
Company123:CRMSTANDARD               0              25              3
Company123:INTUNE_A                  25             0               2
Company123:AAD_PREMIUM               100            0               4
Company123:RIGHTSMANAGEMENT_ADHOC    1000           1
```

The results of the Get-MsolAccountSku cmdlet shows that Company123 has

- 2 assigned Intune licenses (out of 25)
- 25 expired CRM licenses
- 4 assigned Azure AD Premium (out of 100)
- 1 assigned Azure RMS (out of 100)

For license assignments, you use the Set-MSOLUserLicense cmdlet. You use the -AddLicenses parameter to assign licenses, and the -RemoveLicenses to remove them. In the following example, you assign Intune and Azure AD Premium licenses to a user and remove the expired CRM license.

```
#Assign License to User
Set-MsolUserLicense -UserPrincipalName Yahia.Sherif@Company123.com `
-AddLicenses @("Company123:INTUNE_A","Company123:AAD_PREMIUM") `
-RemoveLicenses "Company123:CRMSTANDARD"
```

License assignment for PowerShell sounds a like geek showing off his PowerShell skills, but trust me, this is not the case. License assignment from the portal is not a smooth process (or let's say it's not that smooth yet). For instance, if you have an Intune or an Office 365 subscription, you have to assign the Intune license from the Intune portal, and then jump to the Office 365 portal to assign the Office 365 license. PowerShell provides a single place to manage both licenses and users.

Managing Azure AD Groups Membership

Windows Server Active Directory and Azure AD have groups. Actually, this makes sense because you have users and you need to categorize and filter them based on specific criteria or common property.

To create a new Azure AD security group, you use the New-MSOLGroup cmdlet along with the -DisplayName, -Description, and -ManagedBy parameters.

```
#Getting ManagedBy User information
$User = Get-MSOLUser -UserPrincipalName admin@Company123.com

#Create Azure AD Security Group
New-MSOLGroup -DisplayName 'Finance' -Description 'Finance Department Employees' -ManagedBy
$User.ObjectID
```

To update the information of the group that you just created, or even another existing group, you use the Set-MSOLGroup cmdlet with the same parameter as the New-MSOLGroup cmdlet. And to remove it, you use the Remove-MSOLGroup cmdlet.

```
#Get Group Object
$Group = Get-MsolGroup | Where DisplayName -eq "Finance"

#Remove Azure AD Security Group
Remove-MsolGroup -ObjectID $Group.ObjectID -Force
```

Now, that you have the group, let's add members to it. For the purpose of this task, you use the Add-MSOLGroupMember cmdlet along with the -GroupMemberObjectID parameter to specify the objectID of the member to add; the -GroupObjectID parameter to specify the objectID of the group to add members to; and the -GroupMemberType parameter to specify whether the member is User or Group. You can also add other security groups as members.

In the following example, you add user Yahia Sherif to the Finance group.

```
#Get Group Object
$Group = Get-MsolGroup | Where DisplayName -eq "Finance"

#Get Member Object
$Member = Get-MsolUser -UserPrincipalName Yahia.Sherif@Company123.com

#Add Member to Group
Add-MsolGroupMember -GroupObjectid $Group.ObjectId -GroupMemberObjectId
$Member.ObjectId-GroupMemberType "User"
```

To remove a member from a group, you use the previous code as is, but you replace the Add-MsolGroupMember cmdlet with the Remove-MsolGroupMember cmdlet.

```
#Get Group Object
$Group = Get-MsolGroup | Where DisplayName -eq "Finance"

#Get Member Object
$Member = Get-MsolUser -UserPrincipalName Yahia.Sherif@Company123.com

#Remove Member from Group
Remove-MsolGroupMember -GroupObjectid $Group.ObjectId -GroupMemberObjectId
$Member.ObjectId -GroupMemberType "User"
```

To get the list of members of a specific group, use the Get-MSOLGroupMember cmdlet.

```
#Get Group Object
$Group = Get-MsolGroup | Where DisplayName -eq "Finance"
```

Azure AD groups are similar to Azure AD users; they can be synchronized from the on-premises Windows Server Active Directory, or manually created from the portal or by using PowerShell. Also, like synced users, PowerShell is the only one you can use to remove synced groups.

Managing Azure AD Roles Membership

Azure AD has different user roles, including User, Global Administrator, Services Administrator, and so on. The more Microsoft Online Services that you have, the more roles you get. For example, in addition to the built-in roles, when you subscribe to Office 365, you get roles like Exchange Service Administrator, Lync Service Administrator, and SharePoint Service Administrator. With Intune, you get roles such as Devices Manager and Devices Administrators. And so on with other cloud services.

To get the list of available roles under your Azure AD tenant, use the `Get-MSOLRole` cmdlet (also see Figure 10-3).

```
#Get Azure AD Roles
Get-MsolRole | Select Name,Description | Out-GridView
```

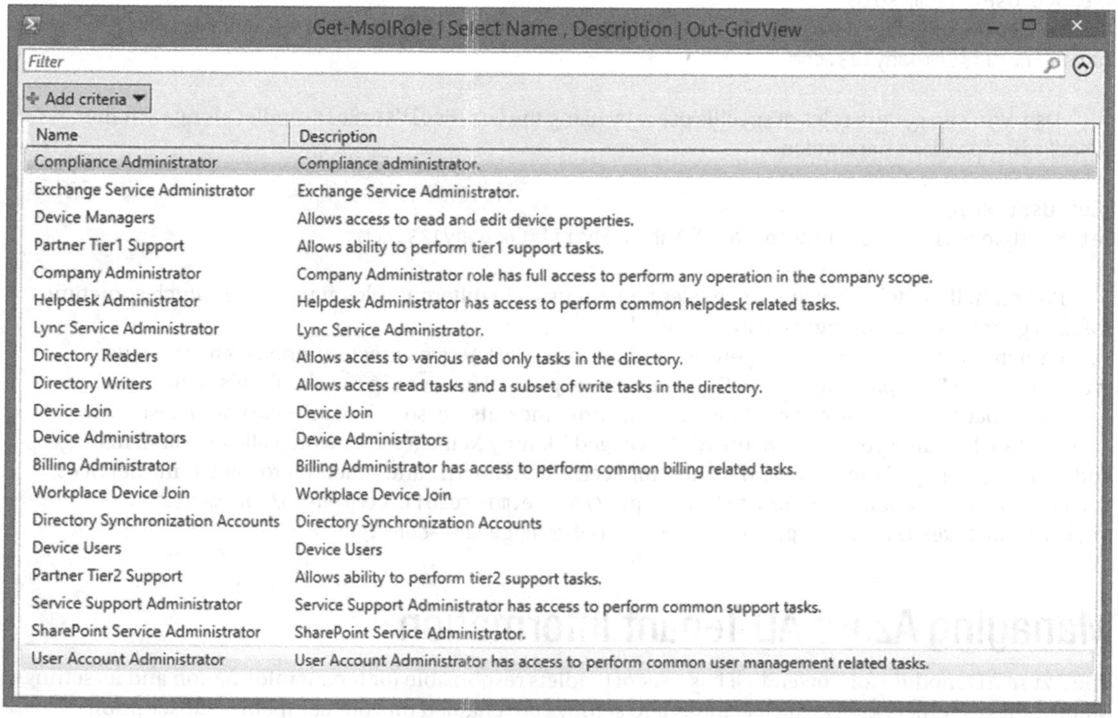

Get-MsolRole | Select Name , Description | Out-GridView

Name	Description
Compliance Administrator	Compliance administrator.
Exchange Service Administrator	Exchange Service Administrator.
Device Managers	Allows access to read and edit device properties.
Partner Tier1 Support	Allows ability to perform tier1 support tasks.
Company Administrator	Company Administrator role has full access to perform any operation in the company scope.
Helpdesk Administrator	Helpdesk Administrator has access to perform common helpdesk related tasks.
Lync Service Administrator	Lync Service Administrator.
Directory Readers	Allows access to various read only tasks in the directory.
Directory Writers	Allows access read tasks and a subset of write tasks in the directory.
Device Join	Device Join
Device Administrators	Device Administrators
Billing Administrator	Billing Administrator has access to perform common billing related tasks.
Workplace Device Join	Workplace Device Join
Directory Synchronization Accounts	Directory Synchronization Accounts
Device Users	Device Users
Partner Tier2 Support	Allows ability to perform tier2 support tasks.
Service Support Administrator	Service Support Administrator has access to perform common support tasks.
SharePoint Service Administrator	SharePoint Service Administrator.
User Account Administrator	User Account Administrator has access to perform common user management related tasks.

Figure 10-3. *Azure AD available roles*

You can retrieve the list of members of each role by using the `Get-MSOLRoleMember` cmdlet.

```
#Get all available roles
$Roles = Get-MsolRole

#Loop to Members of each Role
ForEach($Role in $Roles)
{
    Get-MsolRoleMember -RoleObjectId $Role.ObjectId
}
```

In order to add a user to a specific role, you use the `Add-MsolRoleMember` cmdlet along with the `-RoleName` parameter to specify the name of the role, and `-RolememberEmailAddress` to specify the e-mail address of the member to add to the role.

In the following example, you add Yahia Sherif to the Company Administrator, also known as Global Administrator if you are using the portal.

```
#Add User to Role
Add-MsolRoleMember -RoleName "Company Administrator" -RoleMemberEmailAddres
Yahia.Sherif@Company123.com
```

To remove a user from a role, you use the `Remove-MsolRoleMember` cmdlet with the same parameters as the `Add-MsolRoleMember` cmdlet.

```
#Remove User from Role
Remove-MsolRoleMember -RoleName "Company Administrator" -RoleMemberEmailAddres
Yahia.Sherif@Company123.com
```

Also, you can get the roles of specific users by using the `Get-MsolUserRole` cmdlet along with the `-UserPrincipalName` parameter.

```
#Get User Role
Get-MsolUserRole -UserPrincipalName Yahia.Sherif@Company123.com
```

PowerShell made it easy to change roles and put users in different roles at the same, which sometimes leads to giving users more rights than they need.

It's actually the same problem you face with on-premises Active Directory when someone puts everyone in the IT department in the Domain Admins group. However, in the cloud, this is far more dangerous because you have everything available from the outside, so a little mistake could cost a lot.

That's why I urge you to use Azure AD Privileged Identity Management, which allows you to manage and control privileged identities and to monitor access to Azure AD and other Microsoft Online Services. You can read more about it in the article at `https://azure.microsoft.com/en-gb/documentation/articles/active-directory-privileged-identity-management-configure/`.

Managing Azure AD Tenant Information

The Azure AD module for PowerShell has a set of cmdlets responsible for tenant information and its settings. Mainly, these cmdlets know which features and settings are enabled on your company's subscription, including the company contact information. For instance, the `Get-MsolCompanyInformation` cmdlet returns company information, as described in Table 10-2.

Table 10-2. Output Information for Get-MsolCompanyInformation

Property	Description
AuthorizedServiceInstances	A list of the company's services
City	The company's city
CompanyType	Type of company tenant (partner or regular tenant)
Country	The company's country
CountryLetterCode	The two-letter code for the company's country
DirectorySynchronizationEnabled	When true, this company has directory synchronization turned on
DisplayName	The display name of the company
InitialDomain	The initial domain of the company (companyname.onmicrosoft.com)
LastDirSyncTime	The last time that directory synchronization was run for the company
LastPasswordSyncTime	The last time that that password synchronization was run for the company
MarketingNotificationEmails	The e-mail address to send marketing notifications to
ObjectId	The unique id for the company
PasswordSynchronizationEnabled	When true, the company has password synchronization enabled
PostalCode	The company's postal location
PreferredLanguage	The default language for the company
SelfServePasswordResetEnabled	When true, the company has self-service password reset enabled
State	The company's state
Street	The company's street address
TechnicalNotificationEmails	The e-mail address to send important notifications to
TelephoneNumber	The company's telephone number
UsersPermissionToCreateGroupsEnabled	When true, users in the company are allowed to create groups
UsersPermissionToCreateLOBAppsEnabled	When true, users in the company are allowed to create new applications
UsersPermissionToReadOtherUsersEnabled	When true, users in the company are allowed to view the profile information of other users in the company
UsersPermissionToUserConsentToAppEnabled	When true, users in the company are allowed to consent to applications that require access to their cloud data

So, the information you just retrieved can be modified using a few `set-*` cmdlets. You already used the first cmdlet at the beginning of this chapter— `Set-MsolDirSyncEnabled` to turn DirSync on or off.

The second cmdlet is the `Set-MsolCompanyContactInformation` cmdlet that allows you to set the contact preferences for technical and marketing content. Thus, you use the `-MarketingNotificationEmails` and `-TechnicalNotificationEmails` parameters.

```
#Setting Company Contact Information
Set-MsolCompanyContactInformation -TechnicalNotificationEmails IT@Company123.com
-MarketingNotificationEmails info@Company123.com
```

The third cmdlet is the `Set-MsolCompanySecurityComplianceContactInformation` cmdlet that allows you to set the contact preferences for security and compliance content. For this cmdlet, you use the `-SecurityComplianceNotificationEmails` and `-SecurityComplianceNotificationPhones` parameters.

```
#Setting Security and Compliance Contact Information
Set-MsolCompanySecurityComplianceContactInformation -SecurityComplianceNotificationEmails
security@Company123.com -SecurityComplianceNotificationPhones "0123456789"
```

The fourth cmdlet is the `Set-MsolCompanySettings` cmdlet, which allows modification of the following settings:

- `-SelfServicePasswordResetEnabled`: Specifies whether to enable or disable the user self-service password reset.
- `-UsersPermissionToCreateGroupsEnabled`: Specifies whether to allow users to create groups or not.
- `-AllowAdHocSubscriptions`: Specifies to sign up for e-mail-based subscriptions as individuals, such as signing up RMS for individuals.
- `-DefaultUsageLocation`: Specifies the default usage location for company users instead of assigning it manually for each user.
- `-UsersPermissionToReadOtherUsersEnabled`: Specifies whether to allow users to read other users' information or not.
- `-AllowEmailVerifiedUsers`: Specifies whether the users with a verified domain can join the tenant or not.

All the previous parameters are used to enable or disable a setting, so they accept a Boolean value of either true or false. For example, if you want to enable self-service passwords along with allowing users to read others' information but not to create groups, then the code would look like the following.

```
#Modifying Company Settings
Set-MsolCompanySettings -SelfServePasswordResetEnabled $true
-UsersPermissionToReadOtherUsersEnabled $true -UsersPermissionToCreateGroupsEnabled $false
```

The company-wide settings are not something to change every day or even every week; however, it's important to keep aware of this information, especially user-related settings like group creation and self-service passwords.

Managing Azure AD Domains

If you have experience with any of the Microsoft Online Services, then you've noticed that first-time activation requires the creation of a tenant in the form of a *`company`*`.onmicrosoft.com` domain. Actually, because the Microsoft Online Services relies on Azure AD, it creates an Azure AD tenant for your organization.

This *company*.onmicrosoft.com UPN suffix is good, as long as you are using it for administration and configuration. However, it doesn't look good to use it for user accounts, especially e-mail (e.g., *User*@Company.onmicrosoft.com). So, Azure AD allows you to add your own custom domain and use it as a UPN suffix for users' accounts, which means that *Company*.com is somehow mapped to *Company*.onmicrosoft.com.

To add a domain to Azure AD tenant, you use the New-MsolDomain cmdlet along with the -Name parameter to specify the domain name, and the -Authentication parameter to specify whether this domain is managed or federated. If you didn't specify the -Authentication parameter, then the default value for domain authentication is managed.

The federate domains are those configured for single sign-on with on-premises Windows Server Active Directory via Active Directory Federation Services (ADFS), whereas managed domains are simply those stand-alone Azure AD tenants. You can change the domain later to federate or manage using the Convert-MsolDomainToFederated cmdlet and the Convert-MsolDomainToStandard cmdlet.

```
#Add New MSOL Domain
New-MsolDomain -Name CompanyDomain.com

Name                    Status          Authentication
----                    ------          --------------
CompanyDomain.com       Unverified      Managed
```

The domain has been successfully added; however, its status is showing that it's unverified. This is because adding a domain doesn't mean that you are the domain's owner, or even that your company owns it. So, to validate your ownership, Azure AD asks to create a unique DNS record on your domain's public DNS.

A DNS record could be a TXT or an MX record. To retrieve the information of the record to create, use the Get-MsolDomainVerificationDns cmdlet with the -DomainName parameter to specify the domain name, and the -Mode parameter to specify the type of record, whether DnsTXTRecord or DnsMXRecord.

```
#Get Domain Verification DNS
Get-MsolDomainVerificationDns -DomainName Company123.com -Mode DnsTXTRecord
Label : Company123.com
Text  : MS=ms89288253
Ttl   : 3600
```

Once you create the DNS record, use the Confirm-MsolDomain cmdlet to verify the domain. Keep in mind that there may be a delay in reflecting the new DNS record; it might take between 15 and 60 minutes.

```
#Verify Domain
Confirm-MsolDomain -DomainName Company123.com

#Validate Domain Verification
(Get-MsolDomain -DomainName Company123.com).Status
```

If you have more than one domain and you want to make a specific domain the default domain, then use the Set-MsolDomain cmdlet with the -IsDefault parameter.

```
#Set Default Domain
Set-MsolDomain -Name Company123.com -IsDefault $true
```

Once you add the domain and verify it, you can now assign it to the current users and change their UPN from *company*.onmicrosoft.com to *company*.com using the Set-MsolUserPrincipalName cmdlet.

```
#Change User UPN
Set-MsolUserPrincipalName -UserPrincipalName Yahia.Sherif@Company123.onmicrosoft.com
-NewUserPrincipalName Yahia.Sherif@Company123.com
```

You can also manage the password policy for the entire tenant or specific domain. The password policy has two settings: the *validity period* to specify the number of days in which the password remains valid before asking the user to change it, and the *notification days*, which is when to start prompting a user to change his password.

To get the password policy settings for the company, use the Get-MsolPasswordPolicy cmdlet.

```
#Getting Password Policy
Get-MsolPasswordPolicy -DomainName Company123.com

ExtensionData                          NotificationDays             ValidityPeriod
-------------                          ----------------             --------------
System.Runtime.Serializ...                            14                       730
```

And you can set the password policy settings using the Set-MsolPasswordPolicy cmdlet along with the -NotificationDays and -ValidityPeriod parameters.

```
#Setting Password Policy for Domain
Set-MsolPasswordPolicy -DomainName Company123.com -NotificationDays 10 -ValidityPeriod 72
```

You can read more about Azure password policies and requirements in the article at https://msdn.microsoft.com/en-us/library/azure/jj943764.aspx.

Summary

This chapter discussed an entirely new area in Azure: identity and access management. You learned about Azure Active Directory and its features, as well as the Azure AD module for PowerShell and how to get it.

Then, you moved on to managing Azure AD users, groups, memberships, security roles, and company information settings, as well as domain management.

The next chapter doesn't move far away from Azure Active Directory, but covers another service that relies on it. You will learn about information and content protection components in Azure, which is known as Azure Right Management Services (RMS). You will learn how to manage keys, how to configure users and templates, and how to analyze the logs.

CHAPTER 11

Azure Rights Management Services

In the mobile world that we live in today, everyone can use a personal device to access corporate data, e-mail, LOB apps, and other sensitive information—from any place and at any time. A huge amount of data can be exposed to and accessed by unauthorized people, whether from the loss or theft of a device, or even when a user doesn't follow the right procedures to protect a device and the data on it.

It is very important to have information and content protection solutions to make sure that data is always protected and only accessed by the right people. Usually, rights management solutions allow you to encrypt and protect files by simply defining the rights of each user (e.g., read-only, edit, copy, paste, print, forward, etc.).

This chapter discusses Microsoft Azure Rights Management Services (RMS) and how to configure, manage, and maintain it using PowerShell.

Azure Rights Management Services

You can think of Azure RMS as the second generation of Microsoft RMS. Actually, RMS is not something new to Microsoft. RMS has been available as Active Directory Rights Management Services (AD RMS) since Windows Server 2003; it is used to help protect sensitive corporate data and information.

AD RMS isn't popular for several reasons: it only works on the Windows operating system; it only protects Microsoft Office files; it requires third parties to protect PDF files; it is not possible to share protected content with people working in another organization unless there is federation trust between both organizations; and the most important reason is the implementation complexity.

The good news is that Microsoft has overcome all of AD RMS's limitations and has even added interesting capabilities in Azure RMS.

Azure RMS is a cross-platform solution; it works on Windows, Windows Phone, Mac OS, iOS, and Android. It can protect any file, not just Microsoft Office files. It's a cloud service that relies on Azure Active Directory (AD), which means that all encryption keys management and exchange are stored over there. It's reachable from any place and on any device, making it possible to share protected files with anyone, whether an internal employee or an external customer/partner, and without the need for AD federation.

You can read more about the differences between AD RMS and Azure RMS in the article at `https://technet.microsoft.com/en-us/library/jj739831.aspx`.

Azure RMS also allows features like document tracking, which keeps the file owner aware of who successfully accessed or failed to access a protected file. There is even a feature that permits immediate access revocation. You can read more about the Azure RMS document tracking portal in the article at `http://blogs.technet.com/b/rms/archive/2015/05/04/doctracking.aspx`.

Although Azure RMS is a cloud service, it can still integrate with on-premises servers such as Exchange Server, SharePoint Server, and file servers. This integration is done through an Azure RMS connector that allows these on-premises services to communicate with Azure RMS.

Before moving to the next section, make sure that you have a subscription to Azure RMS. If you don't have one, you can get it by subscribing to an Office 365 Enterprise E3 trial at `https://products.office.com/en/business/compare-more-office-365-for-business-plans`.

Azure RMS and PowerShell

Azure RMS has its own PowerShell module: Azure Active Directory Rights Management (AADRM). The AADRM PowerShell module comes as part of the Azure Rights Management Administration Tool that you download from `http://go.microsoft.com/fwlink/?LinkId=257721`.

AADRM PowerShell modules require at least PowerShell v2.0 and .NET Framework 4.5, so if you are running Windows 8.0 or Windows Server 2012, you are good to go without any extra steps. Also, it requires the Microsoft Online Services Sign-in Assistant, similar to the Azure AD module for PowerShell. Thus, if you followed the installation of the Azure AD module in the previous chapter, then nothing else is required from your side.

As of this writing, 2.2.0.0 is the current version of the AADRM module; you can always check your module's version by using the following command.

```
## Check AADRM Module Version
Import-Module AADRM

(Get-Module aadrm).Version

Major  Minor  Build  Revision
-----  -----  -----  --------
2      2      0      0
```

To begin managing Azure RMS via PowerShell, you need to connect to Azure RMS. It is similar to the Azure AD PowerShell module. Do you remember the `Connect-MsolService` cmdlet? The equivalent cmdlet in the AADRM module is the `Connect-AadrmService` cmdlet; it also has the `-Credential` parameter. The credential you pass should be one of the Azure RMS administrators.

```
#Connecting to Azure RMS Serivce
Connect-AadrmService -Credential (Get-Credential admin@<YOUR_TENANT>.onmicrosoft.com)
```

You can disconnect from the Azure RMS using the `Disconnect-AadrmService` cmdlet.

Now that you are connected to the Azure RMS, let's have a look at the configuration of the Azure RMS tenant. To achieve this task, use the `Get-AadrmConfiguration` cmdlet.

```
#Get Azure RMS Configuration
Get-AadrmConfiguration

BPOSId                                   : 7b0d20e9-f930-7777-8888-e8572a9caf93
RightsManagementServiceId                : 284fd103-dd93-3333-4444-bca2ba2e66c9
LicensingIntranetDistributionPointUrl    : https:// 284fd103-dd93-3333-4444-
                                           bca2ba2e66c9.rms.eu.aadrm.com/_wmcs/licensing
```

```
LicensingExtranetDistributionPointUrl      : https:// 284fd103-dd93-3333-4444-
                                             bca2ba2e66c9.rms.eu.aadrm.com/_wmcs/licensing

CertificationIntranetDistributionPointUrl : https:// 284fd103-dd93-3333-4444-bca2ba2e66c9
                                             .rms.eu.aadrm.com/_wmcs/certification

CertificationExtranetDistributionPointUrl : https:// 284fd103-dd93-3333-4444-bca2ba2e66c9
                                             .rms.eu.aadrm.com/_wmcs/certification

AdminConnectionUrl                         : https://admin.eu.aadrm.com/admin/admin.svc/
                                             Tenants/284fd103-dd93-3333-4444-bca2ba2e66c9

AdminV2ConnectionUrl                       : https://admin.eu.aadrm.com/adminV2/admin.svc/
                                             Tenants/284fd103-dd93-3333-4444-bca2ba2e66c9

OnPremiseDomainName                        :
Keys                                       : {284fd103-dd93-3333-4444-bca2ba2e66c9}
CurrentLicensorCertificateGuid             : 284fd103-dd93-3333-4444-bca2ba2e66c9
Templates                                  : {7ad4e974-e616-7777-88888-50583c202233,
                                             dba93e31-77dd-2222-9ea2-58cdbdb833e0,
                                             2fa3ddce-21ee-5555-8abd-1826cbe974ca,
                                             56ee69a5-40bb-42f2-bffa-54d4c855cfa2...}
FunctionalState                            : Enabled
SuperUsersEnabled                          : Disabled
SuperUsers                                 : {}
AdminRoleMembers                           : {}
KeyRolloverCount                           : 0
ProvisioningDate                           : 9/11/2014 3:32:23 PM
IPCv3ServiceFunctionalState                : Enabled
DevicePlatformState                        : {Windows -> True, WindowsStore -> True,
                                             WindowsPhone -> True, Mac -> True...}
FciEnabledForConnectorAuthorization        : True
```

As mentioned earlier, Azure RMS integrates with on-premises services such as Exchange Server and SharePoint Server. It also integrates with the Windows Server File Classification Infrastructure (FCI). This integration happens via a component called the *Azure RMS connector*; thus, the preceding configuration with the `FciEnabledForConnectorAuthorization` property indicates that the Azure RMS tenant is enabled for FCI integration.

Now you know the Azure RMS tenant configuration. Let's activate the RMS service. If you don't know whether the Azure RMS is already activated or not, use the `Get-Aadrm` cmdlet. To activate Azure RMS, use the `Enable-Aadrm` cmdlet; of course, you use the `Disable-Aadrm` cmdlet to deactivate it.

```
#Activating Azure RMS
If((Get-Aadrm) -eq 'Disabled')
{
        Enable-Aadrm
}
Else
{
        "Azure RMS is aleady enabled."
}
```

Azure RMS is cross platform and supports different operating systems. So, you can use PowerShell to limit Azure RMS's capabilities on those platforms.

First, for Azure RMS to work on mobile devices, you need to make sure that the MSIPCv3 platform is enabled. To achieve this task, you can use the `Get-AadrmIPCv3Service` cmdlet. This service should be enabled by default; but if you find it disabled for any reason, then use the `Enable-AadrmIPCv3Service` cmdlet to enable it again.

```
#Enable MS IPC v3 Platform
Enable-AadrmIPCv3Service
```

By design, Azure RMS is enabled for all device platforms. You can easily verify this by using the `Get-AadrmDevicePlatform` cmdlet along with the `-All` parameter to show the current status of all available platforms. You can also get the support status of a specific operating system by using right parameters, such as `-Windows` to get the status of Windows or `-Android` to get the status of Android, and so on.

```
#Get Azure RMS support status for Devices
Get-AadrmDevicePlatform -All

Key                                     Value
---                                     -----
Windows                                 True
WindowsStore                            True
WindowsPhone                            True
Mac                                     True
iOS                                     True
Android                                 True
Web                                     True
```

To enable or disable Azure RMS support for a specific platform, use the `Enable-AadrmDevicePlatform` and `Disable-AadrmDevicePlatform` cmdlets. Both cmdlets use the same parameters as the `Get-AadrmDevicePlatform` cmdlet. You can use `-All` to enable or disable all platforms at once, or you can specify the parameter of each platform that you want to control.

For example, to disable Azure RMS support for Android and Windows Store, you use the `Disable-AadrmDevicePlatform` cmdlet along with the `-Android` and `-WindowsStore` parameters.

```
#Disable Azure RMS for specific platform
Disable-AadrmDevicePlatform -WindowsStore -Android
Specified device platform for Rights management IPC v3 service has been successfully
disabled.

#Get Azure RMS support status for Devices
Get-AadrmDevicePlatform -All

Key                                     Value
---                                     -----
Windows                                 True
WindowsStore                            False
WindowsPhone                            True
Mac                                     True
iOS                                     True
Android                                 False
Web                                     True
```

So far, so good. You had Azure RMS activate and support all platforms. Now it's time to do some configuration and build a couple of templates.

Working with Rights Policy Templates

The RMS template defines how the documents are protected and which rights are assigned to which users. Figure 11-1 shows all the policy templates available for an Azure tenant on the Azure portal.

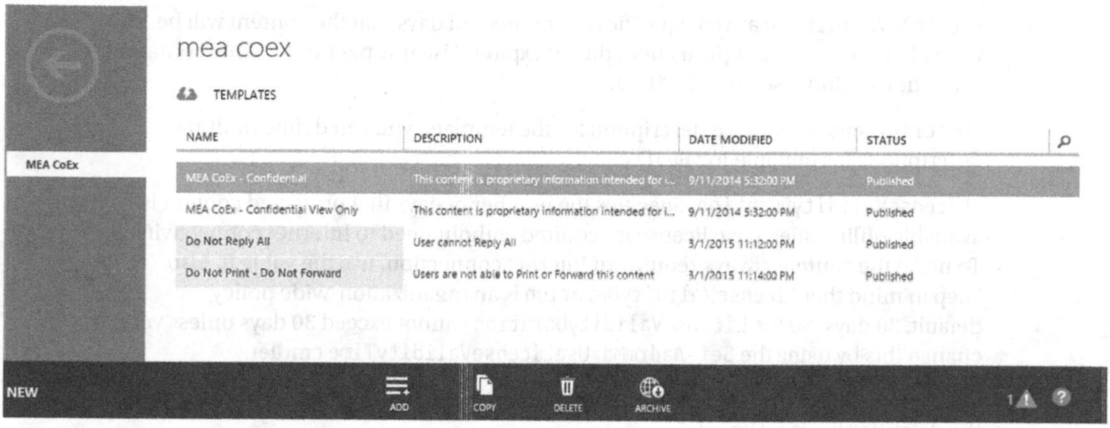

Figure 11-1. *Azure RMS rights policy templates*

To get the templates shown in Figure 11-1, log in to the Azure portal and follow these steps:

1. In the left pane, click ACTIVE DIRECTORY.
2. From the Active Directory page, click RIGHTS MANAGEMENT.
3. Select the directory to manage Rights Management.

The rights policy templates can be managed and configured from the Azure portal or from PowerShell. You can learn more about configuring custom templates for Azure RMS in the article at `https://technet.microsoft.com/library/dn642472.aspx`.

From PowerShell, the AADRM has a set of cmdlets for templates configuration and management. You can get the list of these cmdlets using the following command.

```
#Get AADRM Templates Cmdlets
Get-Command -Module AADRM -Noun *Template* | Select Name

Name
----
Add-AadrmTemplate
Export-AadrmTemplate
Get-AadrmTemplate
Get-AadrmTemplateProperty
Import-AadrmTemplate
Remove-AadrmTemplate
Set-AadrmTemplateProperty
```

For the purpose of creating a policy template using PowerShell, use the `Add-AadrmTemplate` cmdlet. The `Add-AadrmTemplate` cmdlet contains the following parameters:

- `-Names`: Specifies a name for the template; you can define multiple names for multiple locale IDs.
- `-ContentExpirationOption`: Specifies when the content protected by this template expires. The options are `Never`, `OnDate`, `AfterDays`.
- `-ContentExpirationDate`: Specifies the date on which the content will expire. Use this parameter if the Content Expiration option is set to `OnDate`.
- `-ContentValidityDuration`: Specifies the number of days that the content will be valid after the first day of protection; then it expires. Use this parameter if the contact expiration option is set to `AfterDays`.
- `-Descriptions`: Specifies a description for the template; you can define multiple descriptions for multiple locale IDs.
- `-LicenseValidityDuration`: Specifies the number of days that protected content is available offline after a use license is acquired without need to Internet connectivity. To make the content always require an Internet connection, use the value 0. Also keep in mind that `LicenseValidityDuration` is an organization-wide policy; by default, 30 days. So the `LicenseValidityDuration` cannot exceed 30 days unless you change this by using the `Set-AadrmMaxUseLicenseValidityTime` cmdlet.
- `-Status`: Specifies the status of the template: `Archived` or `Published`. If not specified, the default value is archived.
- `-RightsDefinitions`: Specifies the list of rights granted to users or groups to access the contents protected by this template. The rights definition object is created using the `New-AadrmRightsDefinition` cmdlet. Table 11-1 shows the list of available rights.

***Table 11-1.** Rights Definitions Value for the New-AadrmRightsDefinition Cmdlet*

Right	Description
VIEW	Interpreted by most applications as allowed to present the data on the screen.
EDIT	Interpreted by most applications as allowed to modify content in the document and save it.
DOCEDIT	Interpreted by most applications as allowed to modify the content of the document.
EXTRACT	Interpreted by most applications as allowed to copy the content to the clipboard or otherwise extract the content in unencrypted form.
VIEWRIGHTSDATA	Interpreted by applications as allowed to view the policy on the document.
EDITRIGHTSDATA	Interpreted by applications as allowed to modify the policy on the document.
OBJMODEL	Interpreted by most applications as allowed to access the document programmatically; for example, by using macros.
EXPORT	Interpreted by most applications as allowed to save the file in unencrypted form; for example, this right allows you to save in a different file format that does not support protection.
PRINT	Interpreted by most applications as allowed to print the document.
OWNER	User has all rights on the document, including the ability to remove protection.

- `-ScopedIdentities`: Specifies the users or groups that can see and select these templates. If you are using the Azure portal, these are known as *departmental templates*. To use `ScopedIdentities`, the applications must support departmental templates. Otherwise, you have to set the `-EnableInLegacyApps` parameter to true.
- `-EnableInLegacyApps`: Allows the departmental templates to be accessed by applications that don't support it. In that case, all users are able to see and select. If set to false, then no one is able to see or select the templates from these applications, even if they have rights.

Now you know the cmdlets and the parameters. Let's create the first template. The template that you are about to create allows read-only access to the content protected by it. This template will also have multiple locale IDs (English and French).

■ **Tip** You can get the list of locale IDs from `https://msdn.microsoft.com/en-us/goglobal/bb895996.aspx`).

```
#Create Read-Only Policy Template
#Define Policy Template Names (English & French)
$Names = @{}
$Names[1033] = "Company123 - Confidential Content"
$Names[1036] = "Company123 - Content Confedential"

#Define Policy Template Descriptions (English & French)
$Descriptions = @{}
$Descriptions[1033] = "The content protected by this template is read-only"
$Descriptions[1036] = "Le contenu protégé par ce modèle est en lecture seule"

#Rights Definitions
$RD1 = New-AadrmRightsDefinition -EmailAddress engineering@company123.com -Rights
"VIEW","EXPORT"

$RD2 = New-AadrmRightsDefinition -EmailAddress Sherif.Talaat@company123.com -Rights "OWNER"

#Creating Policy Template
Add-AadrmTemplate -Name $Names -Descriptions $Descriptions -RightsDefinitions $RD1,$RD2 -
ContentExpirationOption AfterDays -ContentValidityDuration 14 -LicenseValidityDuration 0

A template with ID 5d538fc3-95a6-4f69-88f0-551a64c35c48 was added to the list of templates
for the Rights management service.

TemplateId  : 5d538fc3-95a6-4f69-88f0-551a64c35c48
Name        : Company123 - Confedential Content
Description : The content protected by this template is read-only
```

The preceding code created a template and defined almost everything, but the template was not published, which means that the template is there but no one can use or see it.

To change any of the template's properties after creating it, you use the `Set-AadrmTemplateProperty` cmdlet along with the `-TemplateId` parameter (which the last command returned) to define the template to update, and the property that you want to change, which is `-Status` in this case.

```
#Update Template Property
Set-AadrmTemplateProperty -TemplateId 5d538fc3-95a6-4f69-88f0-551a64c35c48 -Status Published

Template with ID 5d538fc3-95a6-4f69-88f0-551a64c35c48 was successfully updated for the
Rights management service.

TemplateId  : 5d538fc3-95a6-4f69-88f0-551a64c35c48
Name        : Company123 - Confidential Content
Description : The content protected by this template is read-only
```

You can list all the templates under Azure RMS using the `Get-AadrmTemplate` cmdlet; you can remove a template using the `Remove-AadrmTemplate` cmdlet. Also, you can list the templates' properties using the `Get-AadrmTemplateProperty` cmdlet along with the `-TemplateId` parameter and the name of the property that you want to get. For example, to get the template names and status, you specify the `-Names` and `-Status` parameters.

```
#Get Template Property
Get-AadrmTemplateProperty -TemplateId 5d538fc3-95a6-4f69-88f0-551a64c35c48 -Status -Name

Key                        Value
---                        -----
Names                      {1033 -> Company123 - Confidential Content}
Status                           Published
```

Moreover, the policy templates can be exported and imported using the `Export-AadrmTemplate` and `Import-AadrmTemplate` cmdlets.

The following code exports all available Azure RMS policy templates to XML files; each file has a name that represents the English name of the template.

```
#Export All Azure RMS Templates
$Templates = Get-AadrmTemplate

ForEach($t in $Templates)
{
    Export-AadrmTemplate -TemplateId $t.TemplateId -Path ("C:\AzureRMS\Templates\" +
$t.Names[0].Value + ".xml")
}
```

Now, delete one of the templates that you have and then import it from the XML files that were exported in the previous code. If you didn't remove the template before executing the import cmdlet, then the existing template will be overwritten by the template that you are importing.

```
#Import Azure RMS Template
Import-AadrmTemplate -Path 'C:\AzureRMS\Templates\Company123 - Content Confedential.xml'
```

```
The template file was uploaded successfully to the Rights management service and a template
with ID 87145634-1bf9-4b71-8587-e71b9fe06be3 was created or updated.

TemplateId  : 87145634-1bf9-4b71-8587-e71b9fe06be3
Name        : Company123 - Confedential Content
Description : The content protected by this template is read-only
```

Ta-da! The template has been restored successfully. Notice that the imported template status is archived, so don't forget to change it to published if you want to keep users seeing it.

It's very important to use the export feature as a backup option so that you have a reference of the template in the event that is deleted by mistake.

Azure RMS Super User

The Azure RMS super-user features allow authorized persons and services to access and inspect protected contents, and to remove or change the applied protections.

Popular scenarios for using the super-user feature include when you have antimalware products that need to inspect files or when Exchange Server needs to index mailboxes for search operations. Another scenario is when you need to allow auditors or the legal department to have access to specific documents.

By default, the super-user feature is not enabled and no users are assigned this role. However, it is enabled automatically if you configure the rights management connector for Exchange Server.

To determine the status of the super-user feature for your organization, use the `Get-AadrmSuperUserFeature` cmdlet. You use the `Enable-AadrmSuperUserFeature` cmdlet to enable it and the `Disable-AadrmSuperUserFeature` cmdlet to disable it.

```
#Enable Azure RMS Super User Feature
Enable-AadrmSuperUserFeature

The super user feature is enabled for the Rights management service.
```

Once you enable the super-user feature, you need to add users to this role. You can only add a user to super-user list; groups are not supported. This makes perfect sense. Of course, you don't want to add a group that anyone could join and get super-user privileges.

To add a user to a super-user list, use the `Add-AadrmSuperUser` cmdlet along with the `-EmailAddress` parameter.

```
#Add Azure RMS Super User
Add-AadrmSuperUser -EmailAddress admin@company123.com

admin@company123.com was added to the list of super users for the Rights management service.
```

To remove a user from the super-user list, use the `Remove-AadrmSuperUser` cmdlet along with the same `-EmailAddress` parameter. Also, you can get the list of super users using the `Get-AadrmSuperUser` cmdlet.

The super-user feature is a double-edged sword. Please be careful when you deal with it and make sure to have as few users as possible.

Configuring Azure RMS Role-Based Admins

The Azure RMS allows you to delegate RMS component administration tasks. By default, Azure RMS has two role-based administration roles:

- **RMS Global Administrator**: The users and groups assigned to this role have full administrative privileges on the Azure RMS tenant.
- **RMS Connector Administrator**: The users and groups assigned to this role have the rights to install and administer the RMS connector for the organization.

To grant a user administrative rights on the Azure RMS tenant, you use the `Add-AadrmRoleBasedAdministrator` cmdlet. Use the `-Role` parameter to specify the role type, either `GlobalAdministrator` or `ConnectorAdministrator`. Use the `-EmailAddress` parameter to specify the e-mail address of the user. However, if you want to grant admin rights to a group, then you replace the `-EmailAddress` parameter with the `-SecurityGroupDisplayName` parameter.

The following example shows how to grant admin rights to a user.

```
#Grant Admin. Rights to User
Add-AadrmRoleBasedAdministrator -Role GlobalAdministrator -EmailAddress admin@company123.com

admin@company123.com was added to the list of administrators for the Rights management service.
```

Also, you can list all the role-based administrators using the `Get-AadrmRoleBasedAdministrator` cmdlet; you can remove them using the `Remove-AadrmRoleBasedAdministrator` cmdlet.

Azure RMS Usage Logging

When you grant users administrative or super-user rights, it's very important to keep track of how these rights are being used. Logging is one of the important ways to keep an eye on this in solutions such as Azure RMS. In this section, you learn how to enable, configure, and download Azure RMS usage logging.

Azure RMS uses Azure storage to save the log, so before you start, you need to make sure that you have an Azure storage account. Make sure to create the Azure storage account in the same location as your Azure RMS tenant.

Afterward, you use the `Set-AadrmUsageLogStorageAccount` cmdlet to define the log storage settings.

```
#Setting Log Storage Account
$AccessKey = ConvertTo-SecureString "<Storage_Account_Access_Key>" -AsPlainText -Force

Set-AadrmUsageLogStorageAccount -AccessKey $AccessKey -StorageAccount
"<Storage_Account_Name>"

<Storage_Account_Name> was set as the storage account for the usage log feature for the
Rights management service.
```

Once you set the log storage account, you can enable the usage log features. To do so, use the `Enable-AadrmUsageLogFeature` cmdlet.

```
#Enable Usage Log Feature
Enable-AadrmUsageLogFeature

The usage log feature is enabled for the Rights management service.
```

You can disable the usage log feature using the Disable-AadrmUsageLogFeature cmdlet. There are two logs that you can generate using PowerShell. The first log type is the admin log, which generates logs for all Azure RMS administrative commands. You can get this log using the Get-AadrmAdminLog cmdlet. You choose a specific period using the -FromTime and -ToTime parameters.

```
#Get Azure RMS Admin Log
Get-AadrmAdminLog -Path "C:\AzureRMS\Logs\Admin\AdminLog.log" -FromTime "06/01/2015
08:00:00" -ToTime "06/10/15 07:00:00"
```

The Get-AadrmAdminLog cmdlet is very important for monitoring the global administrators of the Azure RMS tenant. These global administrators can enable the super-user feature and assign themselves as super users, and potentially decrypt all the files that your organization protects.

The second log type is the usage log, which downloads logs about Azure RMS usage to the local storage. You get the usage log using the Get-AadrmUsageLog cmdlet.

```
#Get Azure RMS Usage Log
Get-AadrmUsageLog -Path "C:\AzureRMS\Logs\UsageLog"
```

The usage log can be used to monitor and track the activities of super users, including the decryption of files.

The previous two log cmdlets help you get the log files, but not read them. If you don't have experience with reading Azure RMS logs and parsing them, read the TechNet article at https://technet.microsoft.com/library/dn529121.aspx.

The RMS Protection Tool

The RMS protection tool is a set of PowerShell cmdlets designed to help script the bulk protect and unprotect processes of the files, whether using AD RMS or Azure RMS. It can be downloaded from https://www.microsoft.com/en-us/download/details.aspx?id=47256.

To use the RMS protection tool, you first need to use Service-to-Service (S2S) authentication. For this task, use the Set-RMSServerAuthentication cmdlet along with three identifiers: BposTenantId, AppPrincipalId, and SymmetricKey.

■ **Caution** As of this writing, the RMS Protection Tool cmdlets are not supported outside North America. As a workaround, you can edit the registry, as documented at https://msdn.microsoft.com/en-us/library/mt433202.aspx.

You can get the BposTenantId using the Get-AadrmConfiguration cmdlet, as shown in the following example.

```
# Get BPOS Tenant Id
(Get-AadrmConfiguration).BPOSId

Guid
-----
7b0d20e9-f930-7777-8888-e8572a9caf93
```

You can create the AppPrincipalId and SymmetricKey values by using the New-MsolServicePrincipal cmdlet in the Azure AD PowerShell module.

```
# Create Service Principal
$Cred = Get-Credential admin@Company123.com
Connect-MSOLService -Credential $Cred

New-MsolServicePrincipal -DisplayName 'AzureRMSPrincipal'

The following symmetric key was created as one was not supplied OfJmfLbu+kCytVwkN888JE5rwBP
XKC2qqBOsZxt4QgY=

DisplayName           : AzureRMSPrincipal
ServicePrincipalNames : {dbf65047-3df7-40bb-9be5-87c1fe51ada8}
ObjectId              : 0821e96e-32b3-4316-b0dc-1d40beb4fe43
AppPrincipalId        : dbf65047-3df7-40bb-9be5-87c1fe51ada8
TrustedForDelegation  : False
AccountEnabled        : True
Addresses             : {}
KeyType               : Symmetric
KeyId                 : 8596ed76-dafb-48d6-9f17-12f76a920f6f
StartDate             : 9/18/2015 5:04:08 AM
EndDate               : 9/18/2016 5:04:08 AM
Usage                 : Verify
```

■ **Caution** Please note that the symmetric key appears once and you won't be able to get it from anywhere else. So, make sure to store it safely.

Now you have the parameters needed for the Set-RMSServerAuthentication cmdlet. Let's connect to the server.

```
# Set RMS Server Authentication
$Key = 'OfJmfLbu+kCytVwkN888JE5rwBPXKC2qqBOsZxt4QgY='
$AppPrincipalId = 'dbf65047-3df7-40bb-9be5-87c1fe51ada8'
$TenantId = 7b0d20e9-f930-7777-8888-e8572a9caf93

Set-RMSServerAuthentication -Key $Key -AppPrincipalId $AppPrincipalId -BposTenantId
$TenantId

The RmsServerAuthentication is set to ON
```

Once the RMS server authentication is on, you are connected to the server hosting the RMS service. The next step is to protect the files.

Protecting and Unprotecting Files

To protect and unprotect files, there are three cmdlets: Protect-RMSFile to protect content, Unprotect-RMSFile to unprotect a protected file, and Get-RMSFileStatus to get the current protection status of a file.

Let's start with protecting files. To achieve this task, you use the Protect-RMSFile cmdlet along with the following parameters:

- -File: Specifies the path of the file to protect.
- -Folder: Specifies the path of a folder in which all stored files are protected in one shot.
- -Recurse: Use this parameter with the -Folder parameter to protect the files in subfolders.
- -OutputFolder: Specifies the folder in which you store the protected versions of your files without affecting the original files.
- -OwnerEmail: Specifies a different owner for the protected file instead of the user who is currently protecting the files. By default, if not used, your e-mail address identifies you as the owner.
- -TemplateId: Specifies the ID of template that is used to protect the files. You can get the templates and their IDs using the Get-RMSTemplate cmdlet.
- -License: Specifies an ad hoc rights policy rather than using one of the existing templates. The ad hoc rights policy is created using the New-RMSProtectionLicense cmdlet.
- -DoNotPresistEncryptionKey: Use this to prevent offline access to protected content. The user must be authenticated each time the file is accessed and the policy is checked for any changes. The available values are Disk, License, and All.

```
#Listing RMS Templates
Get-RMSTemplate

ID      Name
-----   ------------
10001   Company 123 - Confidential
10002   Company 123 - Confidential View only
10003   Company 123 - Do Not Forward or Print

#Protect RMS File
Protect-RMSFile -File C:\Documents\MyCompanySecret.docx -TemplateId 10003

InputFile                              EncryptedFile
---------                              -------------
C:\Documents\MyCompanySecret.docx      C:\Documents\MyCompanySecret.docx
```

To unprotect a protected file, you use the Unprotect-RMSFile cmdlet with the following parameters:

- -File: Specifies the path of the file to unprotect.
- -Folder: Specifies the path of a folder in which all stored files are unprotected in one shot.

- -Recurse: Use this parameter with the -Folder parameter to unprotect the files in subfolders.
- -OutputFolder: Specifies the folder in which you store the unprotected versions of your files without affecting the protected files.

```
#Unprotect RMS File
Unprotect-RMSFile -File C:\Documents\MyCompanySecret.docx

InputFile                                DecryptedFile
---------                                -------------
C:\Documents\MyCompanySecret.docx        C:\Documents\MyCompanySecret.docx
```

■ **Note** The cmdlets do not support e-mail messages; you can protect and unprotect files only. However, all file types are supported.

Ad Hoc Rights Policy

Sometimes you want to protect a document or file with different rights, and the rights you are looking for are not implemented in any of the templates you have. Also, you may need this customized policy for one-time use and there is no need to create a permanent policy for it. For that purpose and similar situations, the RMS protection tool allows you create an ad hoc rights policy using the New-RMSProtectionLicense cmdlet along with the following parameters:

- -OwnerEmail: Specifies the owner of the rights policy. It could be a user or a group (a distribution list or an e-mail-enabled security group).
- -UserEmail: Specifies the user(s) who have access to the files protected by the ad hoc rights policy.
- -Permission: Specifies the usage rights of the ad hoc rights policy. The available permissions are VIEW, EDIT, PRINT, EXPORT, COMMENT, VIEWRIGHTSDATA, EDITRIGHTSDATA, EXTRACT, and OWNER.
- -ValidForDays: Specifies the expiry period (in days) for the content protected by the ad hoc rights policy.

```
## Protect a File using Ad-Hoc Rights Policy

# Creating Ad-Hoc rights policy
$License = New-RMSProtectionLicense -OwnerEmail 'Sherif@Company123.com' -UserEmail
'Yahia@Company123.com' -Permission 'VIEW', 'COMMENT' -ValidForDays 10

# Protect File
Protect-RMSFile -File C:\Documents\MyCompanySecret.docx -License $License
```

The preceding example created an ad hoc rights policy that allows only view and comment rights with a validity of 10 days, starting when the policy is applied to the file(s). These rights are assigned only to `Yahia@Company123.com`, while the ownership is assigned to `Sherif@Company123.com`. The `Protect-RMSFile` cmdlet was used along with the `-License` parameter to protect the `MyCompanySecret.docx` Word document with the new ad hoc rights policy.

Summary

In this chapter, you learned about information and the content protection component in Azure, which is Azure Rights Management Services (RMS). You started with Azure RMS features and its advantages over AD RMS. You also learned about the Azure RMS module for PowerShell.

Next, you created RMS policy templates and you learned about rights definition, configuring super-user features, managing role-based administrators, and enabling and managing Azure RMS logging. Moreover, you learned how to bulk protect and unprotect content via the RMS protection tool.

The next chapter spotlights a fashionable IT trend known as *big data*. It covers a Microsoft implementation of big data: HDInsight. Using PowerShell, you will learn how to build and configure HDInsight clusters from A to Z.

CHAPTER 12

Building and Managing Azure HDInsight Clusters

Big data is at the foundation of all of the megatrends that are happening today, from social to mobile to the cloud to gaming.

—Chris Lynch, the ex-CEO of Vertica Systems

Data size has massively exploded, and with more and more terabytes generated every day, normal relational database systems cannot keep up. Now, we have what is called *big data*. It is a must to find faster solutions to process these massive volumes of data.

Big data processing solutions simply break the data into blocks, distributed across a cluster of nodes, which then process the data on each node in parallel, to finally combine it into an aggregated results set.

This chapter looks at Azure HDInsight as one of the big data solutions implemented by Microsoft, hosted on the Azure platform and delivered as Platform-as-a-Service. The chapter also discusses how developers and business users work with big data to get the most out of it in an easy and fast way.

What Is Big Data?

As a matter of fact, there are a lot of definitions out there for big data, so there is no need to focus on one or even come up with a new one. What's common among big data are its characteristics, or what's called the *3Vs*.

- **Volume**: Big data always comes with large volume, in terabytes, thus the origin of the name. Let's take YouTube as an example: every minute, more than 25 hours of videos are uploaded to YouTube. This gives you a quick perspective on the size of big data. Another example is the log data generated from machines creating the Internet of Things (IoT). Processing big volumes of date was a difficult issue in the past, but not anymore.
- **Velocity**: The speed at which big data is generated is very fast. And handling data that is received out of a fire hose is very challenging and requires special tools and skills. For example, the number of tweets generated every minute surpasses 98,000. Social media analytics solutions have to handle this frequency of received data.
- **Variety**: Big data is not just logs and records; it's also audio, videos, images, and binary files that need to be processed. Sometimes, it is a mix between these different types. Getting the most valuable information out of such a variety of data is no easy job.

A lot of enterprises now make use of the concept of the *data lake*. This is where all their data resides, from structured data solutions (like ERP and CRM) and normal database solutions, to unstructured types of data like server logs, PR materials, and even the social feed that's concerned with their products. Trying to marry both types is a key differentiator for an enterprise, and a challenging job as well.

Now you understand what big data is. Next, you need to understand what HDInsight is, but before then, it is very important to understand what Hadoop is since it's the core of HDInsight.

What Is Hadoop?

Hadoop is an Apache open source software library and framework that enables distributed storage and the processing of large data sets across clusters of computers.

The framework can handle high availability, detect and handle any issues of failures in the application layer, and is designed to scale from a single computer to thousands of machines. Storing data and processing it happens on each machine, which allows a parallel processing of data in an easier and faster way.

Hadoop was founded by Doug Cutting and Mike Cafarella in 2005. Cutting was a Yahoo! employee at the time. He named Hadoop after his son's toy elephant (that's why the elephant icon is always the representation for Hadoop, and many times for big data in general).

Currently, Hadoop has a very large ecosystem of libraries and a wide community of committers and contributors to its source. However, the framework basically consists of four main components:

- **Hadoop Common**: The common utilities that support other modules.
- **Hadoop Distributed File System (HDF)**: A distributed file system that provides high-throughput and performance access to application data across Hadoop clusters.
- **Hadoop YARN**: A framework for job scheduling and cluster resource management.
- **Hadoop MapReduce**: A YARN-based system for parallel processing of large data sets.

Remember that Hadoop is written in Java. In this chapter you are introduced to Hadoop components and usage, and you are shown how you can work with it.

Introduction to HDInsight

HDInsight is the result of a partnership between Hortonworks and Microsoft. It's the implementation of Hadoop in the cloud.

Using Microsoft Azure, developers and administrators can easily create, scale, and maintain a large cluster of nodes. So, you can imagine that Microsoft layered Apache Hadoop with a thin layer of .NET libraries and integrated it into Windows to facilitate working on the Azure infrastructure.

HDInsight can be found in three implementations:

- **Windows downloadable**: A single node for HDInsight on one machine; for testing and development purposes only, not for production use.
- **Microsoft APS**: The Analytical Platform System. HDInsight can be bought as a separate portion, mounted and connected to the platform.
- **Microsoft Azure**: The focus of this chapter. You can utilize the cloud computing capabilities and infrastructure to create and use any number of nodes per cluster.

■ **Note** Microsoft APS is the Analytical Platform system, formerly known as Parallel Data Warehouse (PDW). It's an implementation of shared-nothing parallel SQL Servers deployed on a number of machines with a master node that distributes tables between different servers, and queries and returns the results. It exists as a stand-alone appliance in which customers can add more servers for storage and processing power. Also, customers can choose either a SQL Server or HDInsight portion to be added to the appliance.

Creating an HDInsight cluster on Azure is an easy and straightforward task. Just enter the name of the cluster, which must be unique, give it a password for the admin user, and enter the number of data nodes required. Azure provisions and configures the cluster in minutes and it will be operational.

So, what actually happens in the background when you first create a new cluster request? As an example, let's assume you are creating a four-node cluster.

First, Azure validates the cluster requirements, and then creates two head nodes on *A3* or *A4* VM instances and two nodes for high-availability clusters; according to the requested number of data nodes, there is an *A3* VM instance for each node—in this case, four *A3* VM instances. These six machines (two head VMs and four data VMs) are billed from the user account. Head and data nodes are billed by the minute.

Next, Azure creates another two machines on *A2* VM instances for security and three Zookeeper nodes on *A1* VM instance for cluster management. These five machines are free—users don't get charged for them.

Keep in mind that there are other Azure-associated services that charge for use, such as storage and data transfer. However, compared to the cost of the VMs, these charges are considered minimal to some extent.

■ **Note** An HDInsight cluster is billed the moment the cluster is created. Clusters cannot be deallocated or put on hold. Therefore, the only way to stop billing is to delete the cluster itself.

Unlike typical Hadoop distribution installation that requires data to be stored on machines that contain data nodes, Microsoft implemented a seamless library for HDInsight to access Azure Storage blobs. So, no need to move the data inside the data nodes. Data can reside in normal Azure blob storage and HDInsight is able to access and process it. This is extremely useful for two reasons:

- The ease of uploading data to Azure, either from a running system or using PowerShell.
- When the cluster is deleted, data is preserved so that the cluster can be utilized for processing only, instead of maintaining data; this saves a lot of cost.

Still, you can use the internal storage of the data nodes, but it's always preferable to use the Azure blob storage for the previous two points. Figure 12-1 shows how the storage works in Azure HDInsight.

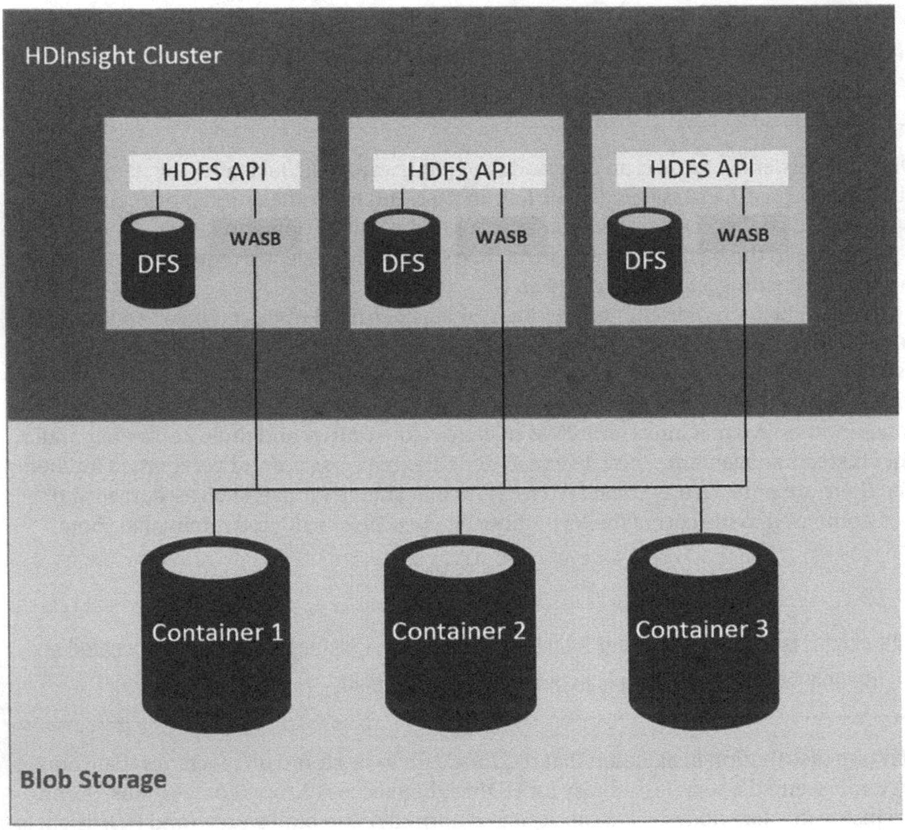

Figure 12-1. *HDInsight cluster storage mechanism*

Understanding how the storage for HDInsight works is crucial before proceeding, because all the examples utilize the Azure blob storage.

Creating Your First Cluster

Now, let's get started with creating your first HDInsight cluster. You can use either the Azure management portal or PowerShell.

Creating HDInsight Cluster Using PowerShell

Before you start building the HDInsight cluster, let's prepare the storage that will be used by your cluster. Actually, Azure storage was discussed in Chapter 3, but this is a good opportunity to refresh your memory.

To provision the cluster, you first need to add storage to be used for the cluster.

```
New-AzureStorageAccount -StorageAccountName "pshdclstrstorage" -Location "East US"
```

■ **Note** Remember that the storage location should in one of the data centers with available HDInsight service, which are Southeast Asia, North Europe, West Europe, East US, and West US.

After successfully creating a storage account, you need to create a container for the cluster data so that you can provision the cluster. Just remember that to create the container, you need the storage context object.

```
$StorageAccountName = "pshdclstrstorage"

$StorageAccountKey = Get-AzureStorageKey pshdclstrstorage | %{$_.Primary}

$storageContext = New-AzureStorageContext -StorageAccountName $StorageAccountName
-StorageAccountKey $StorageAccountKey

New-AzureStorageContainer -Name "storageforcluster" -Context $storageContext
```

Now you're ready to provision your cluster. For this purpose, you will use the `New-AzureHDInsightCluster` cmdlet. The following code sample creates a one node cluster named `pshdclstr` located in the East US region.

```
$ClusterName = "pshdclstr"

$ClusterStorageAccountName = "pshdclstrstorage.blob.core.windows.net"

$ClusterStorageContainer = "storageforcluster"

$ClusterSize = 1

New-AzureHDInsightCluster -Name $ClusterName -Location "East US" -DefaultStorageAccountName
$ClusterStorageAccountName -DefaultStorageAccountKey $StorageAccountKey
-DefaultStorageContainerName $ClusterStorageContainer -ClusterSizeInNodes $ClusterSize
```

After submitting the request, a pop-up for username and password appears. It asks you for the cluster's credentials. The credentials that you enter create a new account to start the Azure HDInsight cluster.

You may watch the progress in the upper bar of the PowerShell window or by logging in to the management portal and watching the updates. After the successful creation of the cluster, you receive the message shown in Figure 12-2.

```
ClusterSizeInNodes     : 1
ClusterType            : Hadoop
VirtualNetworkId       :
SubnetName             :
ConnectionUrl          : https://pshdclstr2.azurehdinsight.net
CreateDate             : 5/4/2015 1:41:40 PM
DefaultStorageAccount  : pshdclstrstorage2.blob.core.windows.net
HttpUserName           : hdadmin
Location               : West Europe
Name                   : pshdclstr2
State                  : Running
StorageAccounts        : {}
SubscriptionId         : 7d2a1de7-b03b-460f-b752-fdeda1d7144c
UserName               : hdadmin
Version                : 3.1.3.537
VersionStatus          : Compatible
```

Figure 12-2. *Created cluster information*

Congratulations, you have created your first cluster. Now list the details of your new cluster using the `Get-AzureHDInsightCluster` cmdlet. Specify the name of the cluster using the `-Name` parameter.

```
Get-AzureHDInsightCluster -Name pshdclstr
```

You can also destroy (delete) the cluster using the `Remove-AzureHDInsightCluster` cmdlet.

```
Remove-AzureHDInsightCluster -Name pshdclstr
```

Now that you've created your first Azure HDInsight cluster and learned how to destroy it, let's look at what you can achieve with it.

Working with HDInsight Clusters

The cluster is now ready to operate. You can start using it to submit the MapReduce jobs you need. But, first you need to understand the MapReduce concepts and methods of dealing with big data.

From the name, you may notice that MapReduce is divided into two actions: the Map job and the Reduce one. For mapping, code is written to run on the data nodes to do actions on the data, such as counting the number of occurrences of a specific word, or calculating the average of all numbers. The Reduce job is the code that happens on the master node that collects all the results from all the nodes and presents the result at the end.

MapReduce is a framework that is used by many other applications of the Hadoop ecosystem to carry out functions. Also, many MapReduce jobs can run simultaneously with the YARN framework (which separates the resource allocation from MapReduce).

Hadoop MapReduce job code is written in Java, and with HDInsight it can be written in C# as well. The following example shows how to submit a MapReduce job, receive the output, read the files, and print it to the screen.

Now you use the word count sample that's available with every newly created cluster. First, you have to define the MapReduce job using the `New-AzureHDInsightMapReduceJobDefinition` cmdlet. Also, you need to use the `-JarFile` parameter to specify that the jar file contains the code, the `-ClassName` parameter to define the name of the job class in the jar file, and the `-Arguments` parameter to select the file that you want to count the number of words and the location to store the output file.

```
#Specify the Jar file location
$JarFilePath = "/example/jars/hadoop-mapreduce-examples.jar"

#Define the Job class name within the JarFile
$ClassName = "wordcount"

#Define the MapReduce Job
$wordCountJob = New-AzureHDInsightMapReduceJobDefinition -JarFile $JarFilePath
-ClassName $ClassName -Arguments "/example/data/gutenberg/ulysses.txt", "/example/data/
WordCountOutput2"
```

Next, you use the `Start-AzureHDInsightJob` cmdlet to execute the MapReduce job. Don't forget the `-Cluster` parameter to choose which HDInsight cluster to execute this job on, in case you have more than one. Then, within the same code, you use the `Wait-AzureHDInsightJob` cmdlet to wait for the job completion or failure. Finally, you retrieve the log output of the job using the `Get-AzureHDInsightJobOutPut` cmdlet (see Figure 12-3).

```
$wordCountJob | Start-AzureHDInsightJob -Cluster pshdclstr | Wait-AzureHDInsightJob
-WaitTimeoutInSeconds 3600 | %{Get-AzureHDInsightJobOutput -Cluster pshdclstr -JobId
$_.JobId -StandardError}
```

```
15/05/06 11:37:16 INFO impl.TimelineClientImpl: Timeline service address: http://headnodehost:8188/ws/v1/timeline
/
15/05/06 11:37:16 INFO client.RMProxy: Connecting to ResourceManager at headnodehost/100.112.184.67:9010
15/05/06 11:37:17 INFO client.AHSProxy: Connecting to Application History server at headnodehost/100.112.184.67:1
0200
15/05/06 11:37:18 INFO input.FileInputFormat: Total input paths to process : 1
15/05/06 11:37:18 INFO mapreduce.JobSubmitter: number of splits:1
15/05/06 11:37:19 INFO mapreduce.JobSubmitter: Submitting tokens for job: job_1430910538948_0002
15/05/06 11:37:19 INFO mapreduce.JobSubmitter: Kind: mapreduce.job, Service: job_1430910538948_0001, Ident: (org.
apache.hadoop.mapreduce.security.token.JobTokenIdentifier@6ace086b)
15/05/06 11:37:19 INFO mapreduce.JobSubmitter: Kind: RM_DELEGATION_TOKEN, Service: 100.112.184.67:9010, Ident: (o
wner=admin, renewer=mr token, realUser=hdp, issueDate=1430912203933, maxDate=1431517003933, sequenceNumber=1, mas
terKeyId=2)
15/05/06 11:37:19 INFO impl.YarnClientImpl: Submitted application application_1430910538948_0002
15/05/06 11:37:19 INFO mapreduce.Job: The url to track the job: http://headnodehost:9014/proxy/application_143091
0538948_0002/
15/05/06 11:37:19 INFO mapreduce.Job: Running job: job_1430910538948_0002
15/05/06 11:37:33 INFO mapreduce.Job: Job job_1430910538948_0002 running in uber mode : false
15/05/06 11:37:33 INFO mapreduce.Job:  map 0% reduce 0%
15/05/06 11:37:46 INFO mapreduce.Job:  map 100% reduce 0%
15/05/06 11:37:56 INFO mapreduce.Job:  map 100% reduce 100%
15/05/06 11:37:58 INFO mapreduce.Job: Job job_1430910538948_0002 completed successfully
15/05/06 11:37:58 INFO mapreduce.Job: Counters: 49
```

***Figure 12-3.** MapReduce Job output*

The preceding output shows the map-and-reduce process in the running code. The rest of the output is the 49 counters of the job, listed here:

```
File System Counters
                FILE: Number of bytes read=364953
                FILE: Number of bytes written=929898
                FILE: Number of read operations=0
                FILE: Number of large read operations=0
                FILE: Number of write operations=0
                WASB: Number of bytes read=1573207
                WASB: Number of bytes written=527522
                WASB: Number of read operations=0
```

```
                WASB: Number of large read operations=0
                WASB: Number of write operations=0
        Job Counters
                Launched map tasks=1
                Launched reduce tasks=1
                Rack-local map tasks=1
                Total time spent by all maps in occupied slots (ms)=8391
                Total time spent by all reduces in occupied slots (ms)=15500
                Total time spent by all map tasks (ms)=8391
                Total time spent by all reduce tasks (ms)=7750
                Total vcore-seconds taken by all map tasks=8391
                Total vcore-seconds taken by all reduce tasks=7750
                Total megabyte-seconds taken by all map tasks=6444288
                Total megabyte-seconds taken by all reduce tasks=11904000
        Map-Reduce Framework
                Map input records=33055
                Map output records=267975
                Map output bytes=2601773
                Map output materialized bytes=364958
                Input split bytes=164
                Combine input records=267975
                Combine output records=50091
                Reduce input groups=50091
                Reduce shuffle bytes=364958
                Reduce input records=50091
                Reduce output records=50091
                Spilled Records=100182
                Shuffled Maps =1
                Failed Shuffles=0
                Merged Map outputs=1
                GC time elapsed (ms)=67
                CPU time spent (ms)=8562
                Physical memory (bytes) snapshot=528752640
                Virtual memory (bytes) snapshot=829153280
                Total committed heap usage (bytes)=584056832
        Shuffle Errors
                BAD_ID=0
                CONNECTION=0
                IO_ERROR=0
                WRONG_LENGTH=0
                WRONG_MAP=0
                WRONG_REDUCE=0
        File Input Format Counters
                Bytes Read=1573043
        File Output Format Counters
                Bytes Written=527522
```

The counters give full diagnostics information of the job run. This helps a lot in realizing and optimizing the time consumed and the size of the bytes read in the process. However, in this example, you do not see the results of the function that run, because you export the results to a file named WordCountOutPut2 in the job definition command.

The following code generates a URI for the output file so that you can get it and read the results inside.

```
Get-AzureStorageBlobContent -Container storageforcluster -Blob "example/data/
WordCountOutput2/part-r-00000" -Context $storageContext -Force
```

Then, you search for how many times a word, **book**, is mentioned (see Figure 12-4).

```
Get-Content "./example/data/WordCountOutput2/part-r-00000" | findstr "book"
```

```
Name                             BlobType   Length
----                             --------   ------
example/data/WordCountOutput...  BlockBlob  527522
Handbook     1
bankbook     1
book    53
book,   10
book.   13
book:   1
book?   1
bookcart.    1
bookcase     1
booked  1
booked, 1
bookhunt     1
bookies 2
bookies,     1
booking 1
bookkeeper   1
```

Figure 12-4. *The results outputHive file in HDInsight*

Hive is one of the most useful platforms on Hadoop; it utilizes the MapReduce framework to submit SQL-like queries to the data and return the results. Some people consider it the data warehouse of big data.

Hive creates tables in the data files or file folder in the Hadoop system; In HDInsight, it can be a container or a blob in Azure storage. Queries to this table like normal SQL queries get translated into a MapReduce job executed on the cluster; the results are returned to the user.

Let's look at an example of working with airline data logs on Hive and see how PowerShell helps in the process.

For this example, you will use the airline and airport information from the US Bureau of Transportation Statistics, available at `www.rita.dot.gov/bts/sites/rita.dot.gov.bts/files/subject_areas/airline_information/index.html`. You will use it to generate air carrier summary data to analyze with Hive.

First, using the `Set-AzureStorageBlobContent` cmdlet, you need to upload the file to a container on Azure storage to create a table accessing this data.

```
Set-AzureStorageBlobContent -File "c:\airlinesdata.csv" -Container "storageforcluster"
-Blob "/example/data/airlinesdata.csv" -context $storageContext
```

You use the same context you created earlier to access the same storage. Also, you created a container named `data` to upload all the files to. A file named `airlinedata.csv` has been uploaded to the storage. Now, you are ready to create a table over this file, but first connect to the cluster using the `Use-AzureHDInsightCluster` cmdlet.

```
Use-AzureHDInsightCluster -ClusterName pshdclstr
```

You will receive a message that you are successfully connected to the pshdclstr cluster. Here, you can invoke queries on Hive and receive the results. Let's create the queries first.

```
$q= "CREATE EXTERNAL TABLE airlines(QUARTER string,UNIQUE_CARRIER string,UNIQUE_CARRIER_
NAME string,CARRIER_NAME string,ORIGIN_AIRPORT_ID int,ORIGIN string,ORIGIN_CITY_NAME
string,SERVICE_CLASS string,REV_PAX_ENP_110 float) ROW FORMAT DELIMITED FIELDS TERMINATED
BY ',' STORED AS TEXTFILE LOCATION 'wasb://data@pshdclstrstorage.blob.core.windows.net/
storageforcluster/example/';"
```

Assign a variable named `$q` with the table that you named `airlines`. This table contains nine columns, as mentioned in the create statement. You can see that it's similar to normal SQL, to an extent.

Hive doesn't handle quoted text so we use `"ROW FORMAT DELIMITED FIELDS TERMINATED BY ','"` to process the data and define its format in the the `.csv` file; the rows are normally formatted; the delimiter of columns is the `','`. The final part is `"STORED AS TEXTFILE LOCATION 'wasb://data@pshdclstrstorage.blob.core.windows.net/ ';"`, which tells HDInsight that the source file is located in a blob storage named `pshdclstrstorage` and in a blob named `data`.

Notice the `"wasb://"`, which is used to locate the files stored on the default HDInsight storage container, called `storageforcluster` in this case, to be accessed by the cluster data or code files.

■ **Note** You used the external table type, not the normal (internal) tables. When internal tables are created, it moves the file containing the data inside the cluster in `/data/warehouse/`. However, when you use external, files aren't moved, so the table is connected to the original file—in this case, all the data under the blob. So, adding more files of the same format to the blob will change the query results every time, without the need to rebuild the table.

Now, execute the query using the `Invoke-Hive` cmdlet. The `Invoke-Hive` cmdlet executes the query to the Hive framework on the cluster and returns the results with the `job_id`, or errors, if they occurred (see Figure 12-5).

```
Invoke-Hive -Query $q
```

```
Submitting Hive query..
Started Hive query with jobDetails Id : job_1430910538948_0026
Hive query completed Successfully
```

Figure 12-5. *The results of creating the Hive table*

To make sure of the creation of the report, you can list all the tables in the Hive metastore by using the following command:

```
Invoke-Hive -Query "show tables;"
```

PowerShell executes and returns two tables: `Hivesampletable`, which is a demo table created by default, and the `airlines` table, as shown in Figure 12-6.

```
Submitting Hive query..
Started Hive query with jobDetails Id : job_1430910538948_0027
Hive query completed Successfully


airlines
hivesampletable
```

Figure 12-6. *Hive query results*

You want to query the total number of flights flown in 2014 according to the downloaded report. Thus, you create another query and submit it to Hive.

```
$q2 = "select count(1) from airlines"

Invoke-Hive -Query $q2
```

For Hive to calculate the total number of records, it needs to submit a MapReduce job and return the results to the screen, as shown in Figure 12-7.

```
Submitting Hive query..
Started Hive query with jobDetails Id : job_1430910538948_0032
Hive query completed Successfully

21127
```

Figure 12-7. *The count query results*

To get more information on the job execution, such as status or the time the job executed in, use the Get-AzureHDInsightJob cmdlet along with the -JobId parameter. An example output is shown in Figure 12-8.

```
Get-AzureHDInsightJob -Cluster pshdclstr -JobId "job_1421053567758_0019"
```

```
Cluster         : pshdclstr
ExitCode        : 0
Name            : Hive: fbb4d286f5f94d8492f1
PercentComplete : map 100% reduce 100%
Query           :
State           : Completed
StatusDirectory : 6615b040-54c3-424d-bfa1-dddcb91fd781
SubmissionTime  : 5/6/2015 1:26:25 PM
JobId           : job_1430910538948_0032
```

Figure 12-8. *The job query output*

Some queries do not need to use MapReduce, such as retrieving the whole data set using the `Select *` command as Hive dumps back the whole file. Of course, showing 13,000 records is not something you want to read on a PowerShell console screen, but you can try to select the top five records by using the following command:

```
Invoke-Hive -Query "select * from airlines LIMIT 5;"
```

PowerShell returns the results back to shell. Five records can be human readable to confirm the correct creation of the table.

So, you have created a Hive table, but what about updating it? Can you update the data in the Hive table? Let's try to update all the values in the Quarter column from 1 to Q1 and see the results (see Figure 12-9).

```
Invoke-Hive -Query "update airlines set QUARTER=Q1 where QUARTER=1;"
```

```
    at sun.reflect.NativeMethodAccessorImpl.invoke0(Native Method)
    at sun.reflect.NativeMethodAccessorImpl.invoke(NativeMethodAccessorImpl.java:57)
    at sun.reflect.DelegatingMethodAccessorImpl.invoke(DelegatingMethodAccessorImpl.java:43)
    at java.lang.reflect.Method.invoke(Method.java:606)
    at org.apache.hadoop.util.RunJar.main(RunJar.java:212)
FAILED: ParseException line 1:0 cannot recognize input near 'update' 'airlines' 'set'
```

Figure 12-9. *An error submitting the update query*

You receive an error that the word *update* cannot be recognized. This is because the current version of Hive does not allow insert, update, and delete operations. Hive is for data warehousing; it is not a transactional data store, so it is very important to define the workload required to use Hive. Hive's edge is in using it for heavy scan-centric queries.

Another method for submitting a Hive query is to use the Hive job definition in the PowerShell library. Submitting the same query for the count can be done using the `New-AzureHDInsightHiveJobDefinition` cmdlet along with the query syntax. This cmdlet returns a job id that is used as an input for the `Start-AzureHDInsightJob` cmdlet.

```
#Define Hive Job
$hiveJobDef = New-AzureHDInsightHiveJobDefinition -Query "select count(1) from airlines;"

#Star Hive Job
$hiveJob = Start-AzureHDInsightJob -Cluster pshdclstr -JobDefinition $hiveJobDef
```

The job is submitted, but unlike the `Invoke-Hive` cmdlet, you don't see the results of the progress on the PowerShell; so you use the `Wait-AzureHDInsightJob` cmdlet to show the progress.

```
Wait-AzureHDInsightJob -Job $hiveJob -WaitTimeoutInSeconds 3600
```

PowerShell brings up the progress bar at the upper side of the console, as shown in Figure 12-10.

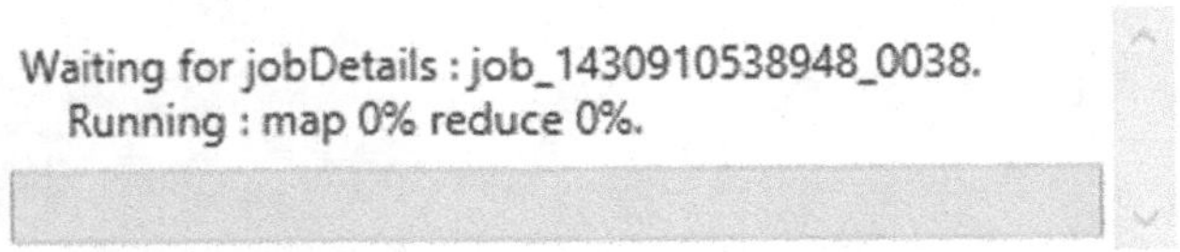
Waiting for jobDetails : job_1430910538948_0038.
Running : map 0% reduce 0%.

Figure 12-10. *Job status details*

Although, you didn't receive the result of the query, the brief results appear on the console. This is where the Get-AzureHDInsightJob cmdlet becomes handy, as follows, to show the results on the console.

```
Get-AzureHDInsightJobOutput -Cluster pshdclstr -JobId $hiveJob.JobId
```

You still can submit Hive queries on the HDInsight web interface when logging into the cluster page. The URL is on the dashboard screen when you click the cluster on the Azure management portal, as shown in Figure 12-11.

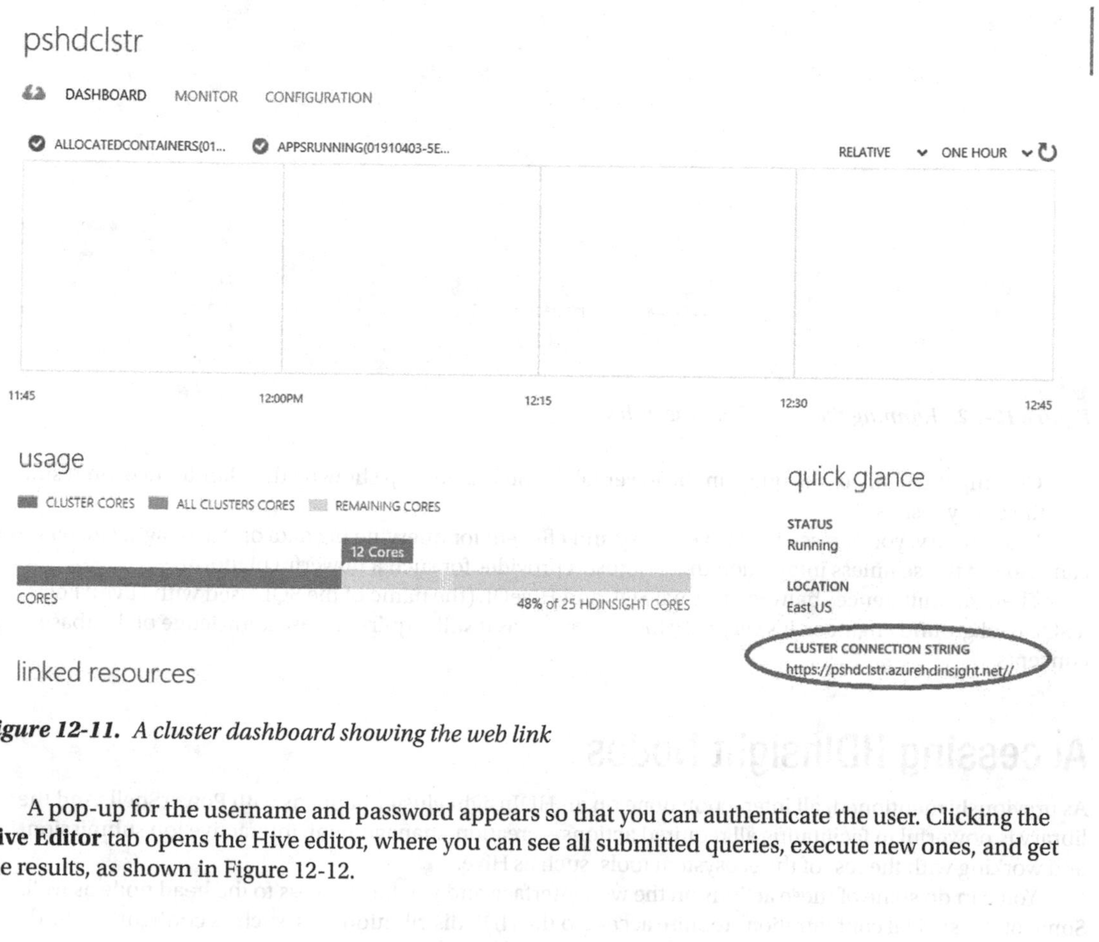

***Figure 12-11.** A cluster dashboard showing the web link*

A pop-up for the username and password appears so that you can authenticate the user. Clicking the **Hive Editor** tab opens the Hive editor, where you can see all submitted queries, execute new ones, and get the results, as shown in Figure 12-12.

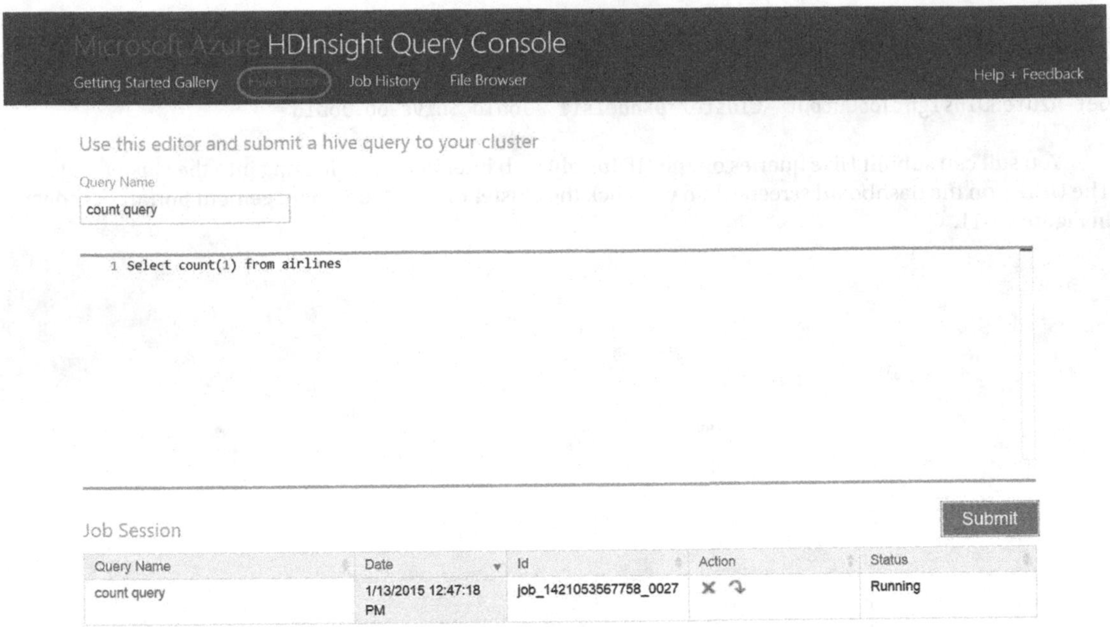

Figure 12-12. *Running the count from the web screen*

Clicking the name of the query in the lower table opens a pop-up showing the MapReduce job results and the query results.

In summary, you can see how Hive is easy and efficient for querying big data on HDInsight clusters. You can also see the seamless integration that Microsoft provides for such a powerful platform.

There are differences between normal SQL and HiveQL (the name of the SQL used with Hive). For a SQL background engineer, it's very easy to get around, as it still requires a base knowledge of database concepts.

Accessing HDInsight Nodes

As previously mentioned, all interaction done on an HDInsight cluster happens with PowerShell. And the library is powerful in facilitating all required actions—creation, management, interactive job submission, and working with the rest of the ecosystem tools, such as Hive.

You can do some of these actions on the web interface and you have access to the head node as well. Some of the special configurations require access to the HDP distribution files, such as configuring third-party tools. An example is the AVRO serialization configuration that requires access to the configuration file on Hive. For this purpose, you can use the `Add-AzureHDInsightConfigValues` cmdlet, or request remote access to the head node from the configuration tab on the Azure management portal section of the cluster.

When you open the configuration tab on the management portal, you see an **Enable remote** icon in the lower strip. Clicking it opens a window asking for a new username, password, and expiration date to specify when access to the head node will be revoked. The expiration should be within seven days of the creation day, as shown in Figure 12-13.

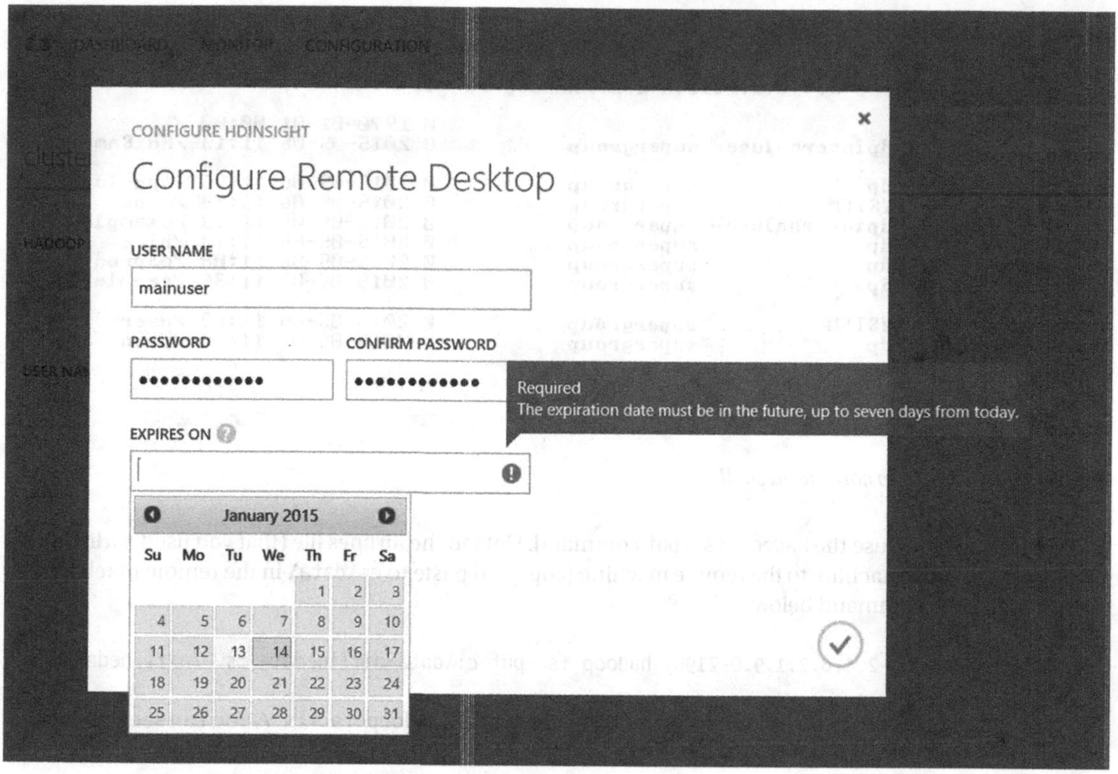

Figure 12-13. Head node remote desktop configuration

A few minutes are required for the configuration to complete, and a new **connect** icon appears. Clicking it opens a remote desktop configuration file that can be used to access the head node machine.

Entering the correct username and password lets you access the head node and begin interacting with the virtual machine. On the desktop, you find four shortcuts:

- **Hadoop Command Line**: This is a shortcut to the command line that uses the Hadoop shell, Hive shell, or the Grunt shell (Pig). You can use this command line to put files in internal HDFs and work with them.
- **Hadoop Name Node Status**: A web page showing the current status of node storage and connectivity.
- **Hadoop Service Availability**: A web page showing the all available services statuses.
- **Hadoop YARN Status**: This shows the currently running MapReduce jobs and the logs of the jobs on the YARN platform.

Let's use the Hadoop command line to interact with HDP. First, you can query the currently available files. As you can see, the command opens on the Hadoop exe location that resides under the `apps\dist\hadoop<version>` directory, where the version is being changed according to the distribution used in the creation. The following command lists the Hadoop system files (also see Figure 12-14).

```
C:\apps\dist\hadoop-2.4.0.2.1.9.0-2196> hadoop fs -ls /
```

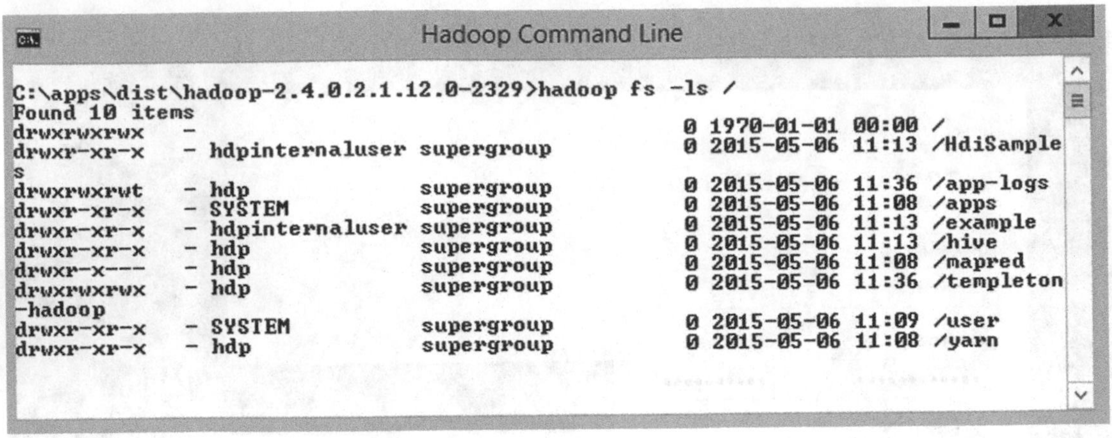

Hadoop Command Line
C:\apps\dist\hadoop-2.4.0.2.1.12.0-2329>hadoop fs -ls /
Found 10 items
drwxrwxrwx - 0 1970-01-01 00:00 /
drwxr-xr-x - hdpinternaluser supergroup 0 2015-05-06 11:13 /HdiSample
s
drwxrwxrwt - hdp supergroup 0 2015-05-06 11:36 /app-logs
drwxr-xr-x - SYSTEM supergroup 0 2015-05-06 11:08 /apps
drwxr-xr-x - hdpinternaluser supergroup 0 2015-05-06 11:13 /example
drwxr-xr-x - hdp supergroup 0 2015-05-06 11:13 /hive
drwxr-x--- - hdp supergroup 0 2015-05-06 11:08 /mapred
drwxrwxrwx - hdp supergroup 0 2015-05-06 11:36 /templeton
-hadoop
drwxr-xr-x - SYSTEM supergroup 0 2015-05-06 11:09 /user
drwxr-xr-x - hdp supergroup 0 2015-05-06 11:08 /yarn

Figure 12-14. *Hadoop command shell*

To add new files, use the `Hadoop fs -put` command. Upload the airlines file (that you used earlier in Hive) from the local machine to the remote machine (copy and paste to `c:\data\` in the remote machine). Then, you use the command below

```
C:\apps\dist\hadoop-2.4.0.2.1.9.0-2196> hadoop fs -put c:\data\airlinedata.csv /airlinedata.csv
```

This uploads the file to the Hadoop system. If you do another `hadoop fs -ls /`, you can see that the file is shown and you can tail this file to read it.

```
C:\apps\dist\hadoop-2.4.0.2.1.9.0-2196> hadoop fs -tail /airlinedata.csv
```

The last few records appear on the shell. Now you can create submit MapReduce jobs on this file and create Hive table accessing it. But remember that once the cluster is deallocated, all virtual machines associated will be deleted and the file will be lost. So, that's why it is always preferable to use Azure blob storage to keep the data persistent.

Opening the **Hadoop Name Node Status** shortcut accesses the status of the cluster, first showing a quick overview on the cluster. Also, all information regarding the data nodes are available in another tab. Snapshots, startup progress, and some utilities are available as well. Figure 12-15 shows the overview information available.

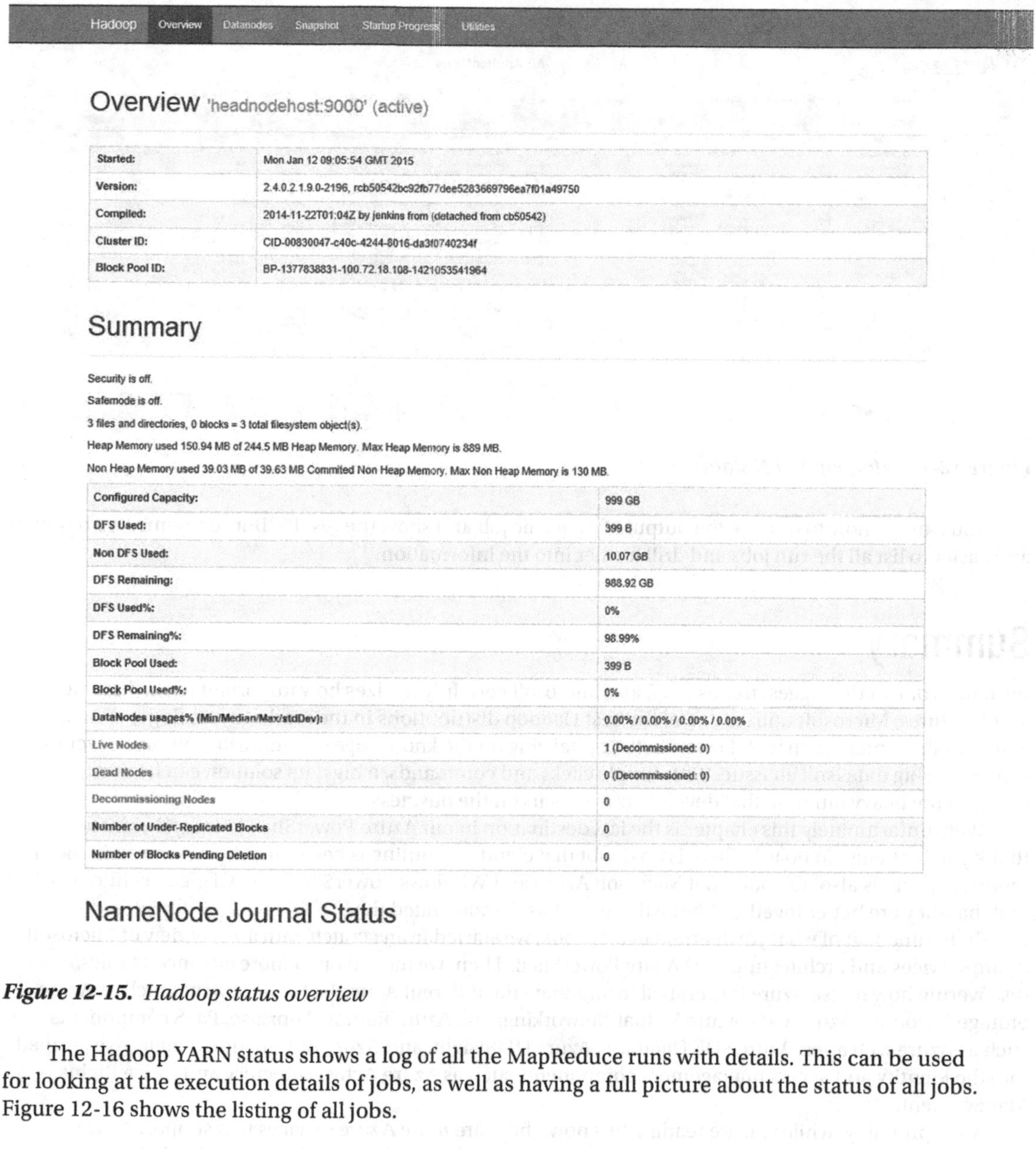

Figure 12-15. *Hadoop status overview*

The Hadoop YARN status shows a log of all the MapReduce runs with details. This can be used for looking at the execution details of jobs, as well as having a full picture about the status of all jobs. Figure 12-16 shows the listing of all jobs.

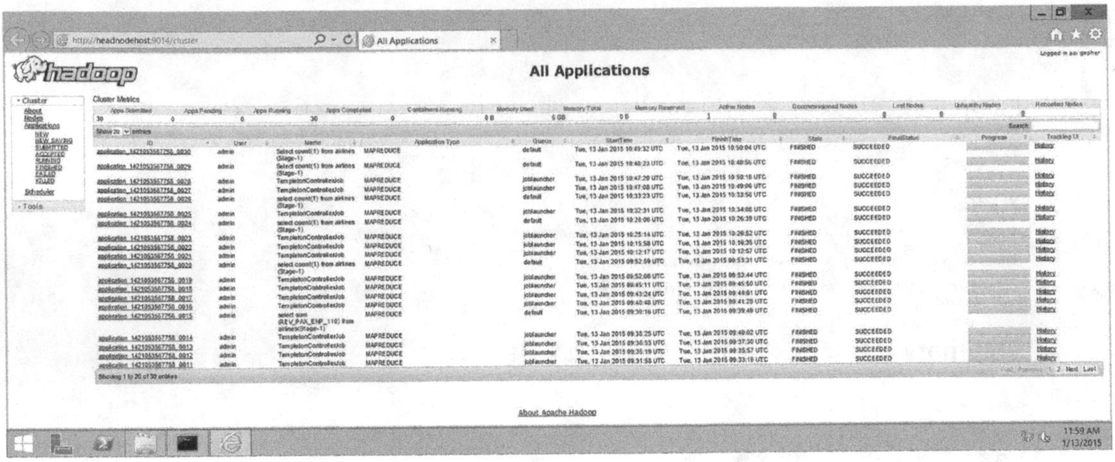

Figure 12-16. *Hadoop YARN status*

You can see how to retrieve the output of a specific job and show the results. But sometimes it's required and easier to list all the run jobs and drill further into the information.

Summary

Big data is one of the biggest trends in IT, and Microsoft certainly realizes how important it is. With a rich set of features, Microsoft utilizes one of the best Hadoop distributions in the market by adding it to Azure with seamless integration with PowerShell. Capitalizing on the knowledge of administrators and developers, processing big data isn't an issue. With simple clicks and commands, a big data solution can be created—doing all the heavy lifting so that developers can focus on the business.

Well, unfortunately this chapter is the last destination in our Azure PowerShell journey! I want to thank you for being on board. There is no doubt that cloud computing is becoming the new norm in the IT industry. There is also no doubt that Microsoft Azure and Windows PowerShell are two great technologies, and that they are better together. I hope this book has demonstrated that.

To remind you of what you learned in this book, we started from scratch with an overview of Microsoft Azure services and architecture, and Azure PowerShell. Then, we moved on to more advanced topics, discovering how to use Azure PowerShell to automate the different Azure IaaS components such as Azure Storage Accounts, Azure VMs, Azure Virtual Networking, and Azure RemoteApp; also, PaaS components such as Azure web apps, Azure SQL Database, Azure HDInsight, and Azure Automation. Finally, we jumped into the identity and access management components such as Azure Active Directory and Azure Rights Management.

Most probably, while you are reading this now, there are more Azure services that support Azure PowerShell, and even more updates to the existing services than at the time I wrote this book. However, as long as you understand how the service works, I guarantee you that the knowledge you gained here is enough to let you catch onto and adopt those changes and updates smoothly with minimal guidance.

Well, it seems that I can't stop writing! I hope that you enjoyed reading the book as much as I enjoyed writing it.

Stay Safe. I'll miss you. Good Luck!

Index

A

B

C

D

E

F

G

H

Printed in the United States
By Bookmasters